T0197198

WITHIN EACH OF US

KAREN DEKLEVA

BALBOA.PRESS
A DIVISION OF HAY HOUSE

Balboa Press books may be ordered through booksellers or by contacting:

Balboa Press
A Division of Hay House
1663 Liberty Drive
Bloomington, IN 47403
www.balboapress.com
844-682-1282

Holy Bible, New International Version®, NIV® Copyright ©1973, 1978, 1984,
2011 by Biblica, Inc.® Used by permission. All rights reserved worldwide.

Print information available on the last page.

ISBN: 979-8-7652-3712-0 (sc)
ISBN: 979-8-7652-3713-7 (hc)
ISBN: 979-8-7652-3714-4 (e)

Library of Congress Control Number: 2023914966

Balboa Press rev. date: 12/27/2023

I want to thank my editor for her patient and unfailing work in helping me to write this book for you, the reader. I also thank my husband and children for their support.

This book is dedicated to my son Chris.

CONTENTS

Section 4
Spiritual Tools for Core Self Connection

Section 5
The Blessings

PREFACE

We each desire a joy-filled life, to be capable of handling life problems with minimal conflict and have fulfilling employment and lasting personal relationships. Yet in our fast-paced, spiritually limited, complex world, it's all too easy to feel unfulfilled, question one's life's purpose, and resolve past harms or current stresses. Sometimes we don't know how to keep a focus on maintaining a happy life or simply desire to live with joy and contentment but do not know how. Within each of us taps the inner ability we have to access a limitless loving energy source to create a meaningful and joy-filled life. And, this source lives within you. It is one's authentic, loving, eternal identity, that provides an internal compass to assist you in creating a meaningful life as you expand your awareness of who you are as a spiritual creator. You will find greater clarity and greater love of self—and others—as you journey through life.

I was given the way to create such a life when I was three years old. Through the power of love, I escaped a sexual assault, as I called for God's help that day. Trembling with fear, I asked to be taken out of the ongoing experience. In my out-of-body conscious state, a figure appeared, whom I now identify as Jesus Christ. And I consciously experienced his profound love for me even though I was bad and had left my parents property. Being bad did not matter. Christ talked to me within this spiritually expanded conscious state I was experiencing. Christ told me that I could not stay with him and that I had to return to the human event. Because of the profound love I felt from him and for him, I desired to do whatever he asked. And so, filled with love, I consciously returned to the human event. Intuitively, in the same manner as Christ spoke to me, without words, I spoke to my captors and extended love to my captors. And the event ended. I learned many spiritual lessons that day, which I desire to share with you. Most importantly I learned to connect with my inner god self, the loving force within me, referred to as my "I am" core.

Fortunately connecting with my loving core self has allowed me to recognize unhealthy conditioning rules attempting to build me into a person who changes oneself to receive love from others. Of course, I falter along my path, but my personal goal is to live within a positive emotional state and have the freedom from conditioned learnings that attempt to limit my unlimited creative capacity. I find I can create the life I desire, overcome the financial, political, psychological, social, and cultural pressures of today, and wash off attempted negative self-feelings and beliefs. I ask for assistance and receive from my core, in connection with the creative energies that created each of us, to assist me in creating my life. Today, connection with my core continues to promote fundamental well-being and a stable sense of who I am. And helps me to live with inner peace, contentment, and freedom from emotional turmoil as a joy being. "I am" aware "I am" whole and complete just as "I am".

In my adult years I became a psychologist and trauma specialist on my journey of helping others to know who they truly are and to assist others in creating a blessed life. Over my forty-plus years of practicing spiritually informed psychology, I have taught relatives, friends and clients of all age groups to turn within to their spiritual core for empowerment and divine guidance. This approach has helped them to overcome even the most serious issues and live with joy. Because I have personally witnessed the power of inner-focused spiritual enlightenment in overcoming harmful habits and sparking amazing life transformations, I know the process works.

As I approached my retirement years, I want to share the blessings of spiritual self-empowerment. I want to reach out to as many people as I could to share my life learnings and help others reimagine themselves in their true spiritual form, to be freed from conditioning constraints and actively choose their life walk, building their personal identity freely. Answering my desire, through my "I am" core, I intuited this self-help book about how to awaken to the divinity we carry within. I share the processes, tools, and lessons learned from my spiritual experiences, studies, and clients' amazing personal journeys—and so, *Within Each of Us* came to be.

As you read their process of awakening hopefully, it will inspire you to undertake this awakening journey with me. Yes, true self-empowerment comes from *within*, from the spark of divine love that burns brightly within each of us. It is a path paved with love. As you stop, look within, and listen to your inner core, you learn to truly see and unconditionally love the real you. And your love will automatically extend to others. You will notice, with gratitude, blessings throughout your daily life.

Today, we urgently need to become more aware of who we are and spiritually awaken, considering society's many problems. The path humans have chosen is to follow is limited to conditioned concerns for *I, me, mine,* without sufficient consideration of the other person, which spreads from the individual to national and global communities. With narcissistic self-consuming concerns as the focus of consciousness, such as being consumed with building financial wealth, power, material success while individuals struggle with emotional stability, and a clear self-identity. At the same time exist worldwide poverty, food and clean drinking water shortages, and global warming destroying our habitat. Safety and security are lacking with divisiveness; racial unrest; terroristic religious and cultural hate crimes perpetrated in virtually any gathering place, including churches and schools; and drug addiction leading to the death of our children. We have abandoned each other and our spiritual identity. Notably, we remain primitive people.

Through repeating what works in "guaranteeing" survival, we developed conditioning beliefs, habits, and rules to live by. The reptilian brain structure called the ego is purposed to enforce this conditioning. The way ego "guarantees" survival is through its conditioned, narcissistic, self-focus goals. The age-old ego does not allow spiritual thoughts as one being a powerful, loving cocreator. Allegiance to the brain structure of ego is the culprit underpinning what is being created today, in direct opposition to the energetic love current of creation, which is oneness driven. The potential net result is self-focused imprisonment of consciousness, failure to become aware of our true spiritual-core identity, and potentially the onset of destruction of human life. As St. Pope John Paul II warned, we live in a culture of death. Our integrity and our future reside in the palms of our own hands. It's time to have faith in humankind and make the changes needed to become a human and divine person living in a land in which love rules.

From interior connection with your core, in communion with the creative force(s) that created you and the universe, you can reach beyond even the most limiting self-beliefs, material pursuits, and emotional turbulence to the calm waters of loving self-awareness. As you recognize this transformative self-awakening process at work in the client journeys presented on the following pages, you will gain insight into your own ability to break through the unhealthy patterns of thinking, feeling, and acting that block connection with *your* inherent superpower.

When the false veneer of conditioning is rubbed away, the fine-grained deep structure of unified consciousness, where loved-based intuitive knowledge and wisdom and a loving guided path for you resides shine through. You will discover how unbounded love can guide your life. Living within a loving reality, your vision will crystalize your own true core. And you increase the potential for experiencing a life-empowering miracle at every turn to meet your self-vision. Yes, *miracle* is a powerful word. And yet, miracles are what I have witnessed in my life, and in the lives of my clients and many others who are aware of their eternal and integral place within God's universe and lovingly create their future. And I want this for everyone. As you read about others' progression to spiritual awakening, I hope you are inspired to take faith-filled steps to change your life.

I seek to help others by sharing the processes, tools, and lessons learned from these personal journeys through the self-help book. This book is a journey and it will take time to reflect on new ideas and beliefs regarding your identity, and to utilize the tools and springboards. Don't be afraid to ask and receive confirmations on what is written.

INTRODUCTION

Awakening to Your "I Am" Core Self

> Within the inner self lay a divine, spiritual force, which, if rightly understood, provides you a new vision of yourself. As you increase your awareness of this side of yourself, you safeguard your future no longer burdened with life but having a destiny.
> —William James, father of psychology

WE ARE SENSORY creatures. And so, it is difficult to consider that we do not see, hear, feel, or touch in some way all that exists. We swim to the depths of the seas and fly to the moon and beyond as we strive to master the universe by placing the information we collect in our metaphorical sensory hands. Yet the known universe of earth is one dimension of consciousness. Within each of us, another reality is potent: your core consisting of a guiding soul and love-energized spirit, a metaphorical place that can help you uncover a new vision of yourself with direct awareness of your capacity to create your miracle life path and awareness of your eternal place in eternity. As we come to know and rely on this portion of self, one's internal compass, we each are assisted in walking an enlightened path and designing a meaningful, joy-filled life.

As eternal beings we are part of God, the infinite ground of all existence. As God said to Moses, "I am who I am" (Exodus 3:14) Throughout this book one's inner guide is referred to as the "I am" core self. The use of "I am" is to remind the reader that each of us is gifted a portion of "I AM" and integrated within the force field of consciousness, within your loving and wise "I am" core self. Awareness of your existence within the powerful force field of consciousness and using your creative and unique spiritual and human nature, is the thrust of this book. As well, the words, "I am" may remind you of the Israelites who were led out of Egypt, out of the land of slavery. Awareness of your enslavement to conditioning, which blocks out knowing your true essence and spiritual identity describes your present existence. The words "I am" hopefully will remind you to identify your unhealthy conditioning as we each benefit from breaking through the iron chains of conditioning. You have the ability to overcome the pressures of today and build a joyful life based in your unique identity. Ask for assistance and receive from your core.

And what price do you pay for such blessings? The price you pay is to own your primary identity as an "I am" core self or godly essence as your true identity, own your ability to create your life through your powerful "I am" creative potentials, use your intentional powers to create a joyful life, and abolish the unhealthy ways your ego controls your consciousness. Rather than this destructive way of being, such as limited self-esteem, addictions to things, people, drugs, materialism, suffering from states of sadness, depression, anxiety and worry. Instead, you take control and consciously choose your thoughts, feelings and actions according to your soul identity, human skills, and highest values and ideals. You own your true self. Likely this includes ways to help others spreading care on humanity. You follow the lead of your core and ripen the fruits of love within your spirit using the creative energies that created each of us.

Access to your soul self-identity grows with ever expanding beliefs in who you are at your core and through using your creative abilities. The end result is creating a miracle life path based within your loving self and without unhealthy conditioning limits. View yourself as a loving creator within loving unified consciousness. Through the words "I am" and core identifies oneself as a source of creation, eternal, unbounded by space and time, loving as desired, and having unfettered access to your godly soul and the unifying loving spirit. Soul and spirit are spiritual ingredients of who you are as an "I am" core self. And, your soul, gifted by God, carries the wisdom needed to help you choose a life path. And spirit is the gifted loving energy available to each of us as well. Yes, from the basis of being a member of universal, unified consciousness you are a powerhouse, creating your life at this moment, with awareness or without conscious choice. If you do not view yourself in these ways, conditioning has had its way with you and you are not free.

Within each of us, regardless of our station in life, our accomplishments, or our failures, exists this loving core foundation or "internal compass," your core "I am" self, complete with a guiding soul and force-filled spirit. This core is the real, eternal self. Your core inhabits your mind and body and tames the self-consumed nature of the human self to become unconditionally loving in thoughts, feelings, and actions, your true nature. Unconditional forms of love open the door to your core. When we are conscious, aware, awake beings at our core, we define ourselves as eternal and as important, truth-filled, justice-filled, loving creators of consciousness. We only need to so believe.

Often, believing in your core aspect of self does not fit into our everyday logical ways of knowing our human self and our world. We each cannot see the core or understand and know its movements completely, yet as the wisdom teachers have preached, each of us is an energy being with superhuman intentional capacities capable of creating a fulfilled life of meaning, wonder, and awe. We each have the capacity to design such a miracle life path. This miracle path includes healing ourselves from mental, emotional, and physical issues, such as cancers; attaining enough material goods to meet survival needs; and breaking free of spirit-blocking fear, anxiety, guilt, depression, or unhealthy protective anger; and thwarting desires for power over others or needing material possessions to feel safe and secure. All our harmful, learned habits are viewed as unhealthy, electronic ("e"), mental ("M"), affective ("A"), and physical ("P") conditioning programs or habitual patterns of being that constrain and dictate one's processing of and response to everyday life events. For understanding of your conditioning, eMAPs is the acronym used for identifying electronic, conditioned, ego mind control over your choices, "M" to identify conditioned mental beliefs and thoughts maintained by ego control over your choices rather than true free will. You will uncover how emotions support and trigger conditioned program, the "A" of eMAPs, and you will learn how the physical self in visceral and behavioral ways, "P," expresses these conditioned programs in harmony with mental and affective programs. You will likely uncover how you learned to create your present life down to the details honoring societal, social, and familial expectations. This book challenges human conditioning as enforced by the ego.

The problem today is conditioning blinds us from awareness of self as unconditionally loving and capable of designing an enriched, harmonious life for self and the world. The conditioned self is chained to the demands of the ego which has been forged by outside forces and lifestyle choices. And so, conditioning is designed to limit your awareness of yourself as a creative powerhouse. Learned beliefs rooting how you know yourself have been programmed into your human self, which is reinforced by the self-interest focused ego. Ego is a basic, old part of the human brain that controls much of your daily life, is driven to focus awareness solely on everyday survival and comfort concerns, and self enhancement. Unfortunately, in our secular world of today loyalty to the ego is unquestioned and leads to each of us thinking only of our loved one's, oneself and one's interests. Ego designs your self-concept, and this identity becomes primary. Ego has you seeking approval from others, being caught in defining one's self according to personal successes and failures, being addicted to pain and pleasure cycling, greed, materialism, limiting judgments, or personal fears and obsessions. The ego further develops rules regarding relationships with others, such as who to trust, who thinks and believes like I do, dictates rules to follow to love self, under what conditions to give love to others, and follows allegiance to a power-oriented, stratified social order. A need to belong and be loved reinforces the conditioned concerns or beliefs of the ego. These beliefs provide the interior walls of your self-made prison blocking out your core. You follow the conditioned instructions for choosing your thoughts, feelings, and actions, determining your self-concept. Religion may reinforce these conditioned beliefs believing God will love you if you follow the rules. And, if bad events happen conditioning further teaches that God is unknowable, relationally untouchable, and perhaps requiring you suffer. However, you have the present of free will to use in the present and you decide the rules governing your life through your higher will. If you desire to be a loving spiritual being inhabiting a human body, this is your higher will. As the reader reaps the benefits of self-knowledge gifted by the spiritual core, he or she begins to think, feel, act, and live in contentment as a "joy beings. "So, believe in your godly essence, know your true identity, "I am" a source of creation, eternal, unbounded by time and space, with intentional powers to create. I have been gifted these abilities, which resides in my wise soul and my spirit. "I am" designed to live a joyful life. Understand your relationship with God. God is within each of us. Belief in the "I am", the indwelling of God within each of us. To experience oneness with God encompasses our true identity and reason for being in human form. This is the foundation. "I am the way, the truth and the life", John 14:6. "I am" is the loving presence within you.

Three goals guide your journey to unbind conditioning chains and open your human self to your core. You will gain human inner authority over ego and conditioning, the first goal, and uncover the power of your intentions, the second goal. To assist, a self-designed meditation practice, learning to watch yourself go by through conscious, mindful self-observation, understanding the power of beliefs, and overall exploration of the power of your intentions in determining your actions, thoughts, perceptions, and emotions creating your personal reality are shared. The eMAPs controlling your life are identified. If you choose, you will work with unhealthy thoughts, difficult emotions, and physical issues with courage, patience, a humbled dispositions and reap the benefits of self-knowledge gifted by the spiritual core. Self-knowledge includes how thoughts and feelings become physical expression. Love and its power to heal the physical self is revealed through the personal journeys of clients. Their spiritual journeys are inspiring and illustrate the principles discussed.

Loving unconditionally is the third key and begins within you. Choosing to know yourself as primarily a loving, spiritual being will automatically occur as you remove the thinking and emotional blocks to self-awareness and open to the desire to be a loving creator. Choosing to know yourself as a *loving* creator is the third key. As you own your identity, it is natural to open floodgates to unconditional loving. Unconditional love is strengthened with guided imageries and springboards. Intuition uncovers your core through observing the moving of earth reality for you by your core, as well as identifying core communication. Neural road maps complement your journey for holding onto the real you will be offered. To think, feel, and act with love is our true self and fertile ground for creating your miracle life path as you desire. Yes, you, an ordinary person like me, have extraordinary potentials. In fact, we each are a Jesus in the making. He showed us the way.

If we choose this sacred path, it can link each of us to wider realms of living, where learned, unhealthy, conditioned beliefs have no control. Joy abounds in this inner place of harmony and loving abundance, instead of consuming concerns. You witness a loving life surrounding you with gratitude. Could it be a false assumption that you must strive for joy through human pursuits when the true joy of conscious empowerment is readily available? If you desire inner harmony in mind, body, heart, soul, and ever-growing awareness of self, follow the lead of your core self. When you are willing to do so, you become aware that you are one with creation, one with all that exists and all exists within consciousness. Can you allow yourself to connect with and create through your loving core self? The natural god self within each of us is living, thinking, feeling, and acting with love toward yourself and others.

You have already connected with your core self when experiencing spirit-lifting events. Certainly, this occurs during peak experiences of joy, such as weddings and after the birth of one's child. However, awe-filled moments and feelings of being within the flow of life occur in everyday life as well, such as when exercising, meditating, walking while noticing the beauty of the day, or listening to favorite music. Being in the flow is learning too just *be*. You are totally present to the present moment, aware, and conscious. At these times, while being less aware of your personal self, ego survival concerns for personal safety and security, cultural pushes for achievement or social position, or worries are not upfront in your mind. Rather, you are simply aware of yourself within the moment. Being in the flow is an awakening experience in which one's consciousness shifts and, with awareness, you feel more real, more present, more awake, and more alive. On closer inspection, if you mindfully observe and witness yourself, aware of self-awareness, a sense of wholeness reverberates within you. If you stay aware of awareness in that moment an underlying felt sense of profound love occurs. Free from mental chatter, you have connected with your deeper "I am" core self, becoming spiritually conscious. At these times, your consciousness can wondrously expand, and as your vision opens, you recognize your intentional capacity to create your life. Through grateful loving awareness of your place within consciousness, you have produced a loving and honest flow for yourself, others, and the powerful, creative force that governs the entire universe. This is not magic but the groundwork for living as a joy being. When the human self and your core agree, you experience joy.

Within this internal natural human and divine state of being, openness, receptivity, wholeness, unbounded love, and unity reside. It is where one notices that the loving creative forces within consciousness support and sustain each of us. With flexibility, openness, and receptivity in mind and heart, you can choose to circle around your inner "still point," your "I am" core self, and receive intuitive knowledge, guidance, and wisdom. Your walk on earth is revealed and becomes much easier and joy filled. The ego and its focus on *I, me, mine* is no longer in charge.

You may ask, "How do I know these spiritual happenings as truths?" When I was a young child, I put myself in a dangerous situation and had a spiritual encounter with Christ. My human self was too young and not conditioned to block out awareness of my true identity. In the encounter with Christ, I experienced profound love, and his love integrated me. My core self, spirit and soul, and my human self, mind, heart, and body, became one under the desire only to love as he loved me. I spread love to my captors and love stopped the event. Experiencing Christ's love within this spiritually consciousness state transformed and empowered me with the knowledge of my intentional capacities to create through the power of loving. I also experienced my spiritually unbounded nature of not being limited to earthly time and space and being of an eternal nature. Christ said, now is not the time to come with me, implying there will be a time we are together in all ways. And, I recognized there is no difference between my higher will to be loved and loving and Christ's love for me and each of us.

The "I am" core self is the way to clear our vision from conditioning. Looking through soul-filled, loving eyes, you view life happenings clearly. Consciously aware, you are illuminated by the radiant light of an immense, unified, loving consciousness, God, within you, instead of shrouded in the mists of conflicting human emotions and achievement and relationship needs. You can learn to loosen the grip of conditioning habits by focusing core awareness on the internal self. If your awareness cycles in any other direction, such as believing that you are only the sum of what you have been conditionally taught to think and feel about yourself and the world you live in, you are asleep at the wheel of consciousness. Thoughts are only thoughts, and feelings are only feelings, residing within the conditioned self. They are not the sum total of who you are. Step away from limiting beliefs of who you are. This reality is fragmentary, designed by human conditioning, which blinds you to the authentic, luminous, spiritual-soul nature that is your inheritance. Make your life walk more fulfilling. Step out of preconceived notions and beliefs, traumas, hurtful habits, and the isms such as racism which limits thinking. When you metaphorically step into your core self, you are in spiritual territory, in a higher personal-consciousness state of mind. The time pressure of an everyday balancing act loses its foothold. Your core self easily melds within your human frame, and your awareness lifts into the natural rhythms of life and your core self. You look at life according to the blessings it provides you and follow the lead of your wiser self.

Knowing who you are as a unique and necessary builder of consciousness, with a unique soul and an available loving spirit, empowers you. Become aware of your place, position, and power within consciousness, expand your self-concept, and own and act within your loving identity. Own your creator status with full love and trust; unite the human you with the creator you for wholeness in mind, body, emotions, spirit, and soul. Know that the real answer to one's identity lies within. Just as early in life a child comes to know personal identity through his or her parents' eyes, each of us can discover our true identity through conscious core connection. Just as we remain personally connected to our parents throughout life. So too we are forever an integral essence within God's unified, loving consciousness.

However, this is not to say that conditioning itself is bad. We have evolved societies based on cause-and-effect reasoning, providing organized structure with limits, boundaries, and rules that make life predictable and feel safe. We assumed roles that enhanced social rules. We each depend on habits for structured daily functioning, such as eating, exercising, sleeping, brushing teeth, and paying bills. And these are some of the blessings of culture and conditioning. However, love needs not to be conditioned. It is freely given by "I AM" and your unique "I am" portion, your core self. And, forms of love needs to be freely received and returned. This kind of unconditional love provides security in these ever-changing times.

When you steadily gaze at your own inner loving light, which is knowing yourself as loving being, you intentionally control the pulls and pushes of conditioning that negatively influence your life choices, you mold your life experiences based on inner spiritual connection. You consciously create according to higher minded values in which forms of love rule, such as self-worth, humility, nondefensively relating, right action, accountability, patience, forgiveness, nonjudgment, loving acceptance, gratitude, and a desire to be of service to others knowing we are all one in consciousness. Suffering and inner conflict and turmoil are without a home as you unchain from the joy-robbing habits of human conditioning. Yes, you will experience pain, a necessary challenge to be lovingly accepted on the road to joy and awe. Resources to meet the challenge are provided. Your core self has guided you back to yourself and holds a sacred space of dignity within you. The authentic core shines forth as one returns home to oneself. Joy and gratitude are the natural result.

Take the evolving step of handling daily life decisions by believing and following your authentic identity as an eternal, loving member of consciousness. Knowing and acting on who you truly are, a unique, gifted spiritual and human being. Doing so will automatically spiritually awaken you, lifting your awareness into higher realms. Align your human self with your core self and know yourself as a powerful, intentional being who has broken free from unhealthy conditioned patterns that have kept you from being a "joy being." Experience personal and spiritual autonomy as your human nature assists in leading your life and the ego bows to your core self. As a loving, awakened being, your human and core natures integrate; you feel whole and complete. Wholeness in consciousness with mind, emotion, body, spirit in the flow of a human and divine life. Honor the holistic self and live within the earthly and spiritual reality in which blessings shape our life's journey.

And now, I invite you to discover, experience, and expand awareness of your identity and connect with your loving self and creator capacities to build a spiritually conscious life of well-being and joy. Doing so is the goal of *Within Each of Us*. Enjoy the journey.

Notes

_____

_____

_____

_____

_____

_____

_____

SECTION 1

Who Am I?

You are not a drop in the ocean.
You are an entire ocean,
in a drop.
—Rumi

CHAPTER 1

Unchanging, Universal Core Self Qualities

If we could see ourselves in spirit, we would be truly in awe of self with just a glimpse.

—Edgar Cayce

*O*N THIS JOURNEY *to connecting at a deeper level with your core self towards becoming a more conscious cocreator, I ask that for two months you accept as truth the listed core self qualities and identified beliefs. Change to a more joy filled life requires enlarging our beliefs to align with higher values existing within one's true identity. If you do not become more awakened to your true spiritual nature you can always return to you past beliefs.*

Universal/Unified Consciousness

Consciousness can be described in three words: everything, always, and everywhere. (Deepak Chopra)

Let's begin where everything begins, within a universal consciousness. Consciousness is comprehensive including all that is, has been, or will be. Past is written into consciousness and is available to each of us for knowing. Present is present while the "will-be' future is fluid. The ingredients forming the future is occurring in unique ways and subject to change due to each "soul and human being" having spiritual energy and 'free' will to create their future. Yet, all is part of universal consciousness and all is one. This is your first new belief we are all one within a unified existence. Yes, you are a portion of unified consciousness.

The next belief is to recognize that universal consciousness is the infinite and unified ground of all existence that we each exist upon and create. Yes, each of us resides and creates within unified consciousness, belief number two. Free will is given by the God powers. You create your life, conscious or not. Perhaps view consciousness as surrounding you and within you.

Each of us is unconditionally loved at all times a third belief. We each are loved without judgment. To be unconditionally loved includes being loved without judging according to what is morally right or wrong, which can be viewed as another form of love. As universal consciousness is nonjudgmental amoral and unethical requests are answered as well. This can explain why Hitler existed and nations go to war. Creation is in our human hands.

A fourth belief, universal consciousness desires to answer requests, which is a form of love. Requests are answered based on all of you, including soul, desiring the request, reflecting the strength of the desire. Oftentimes we are not aware of our true desires as the ego mind is always working at controlling our thoughts and feelings. Fortunately, core connection strengthens a request as it is the energy of love being added to the request. Requests based in truth, living love, and justice lead to designing a miracle path.

Personal Consciousness

Although there is one unified consciousness, conditioning has taught each of us to view ourselves as separate(divided) peoples. So, to understand consciousness we can view consciousness from a personal angle. This is strictly a mental division. On this journey to knowing yourself as a spiritual being, we begin with awareness of self, which includes all your thoughts, feelings, deeds, and experiences. This is referred to as one's personal consciousness.

As you are a portion of consciousness, consciousness is always within ear shot. You are consciousness in the making and as such are an important cog in the ongoing creation wheel of consciousness, part of the machinery that creates the universe. You are so important that everything you have ever thought, felt, done, said or experienced are eternal, and held within unified consciousness, aware or not. You as an important component of consciousness is belief number five.

The idea that we each are creating consciousness may be a new thought. Yet you and I are creating consciousness right now. Yes, you have created the human and spiritual life you are residing in right now even when the life you have conditionally created is not reflecting all of your true desires, values, hopes and ambitions. This is due to conditioning in which you build your personal consciousness based in who you have been taught to believe you are as reflected in your conditioned emotions, thoughts, habits, and actions. You are a conditioned identity, belief number six. Who you create yourself to be, your public face, is influenced by culture, significant others, education, experiences, all of which design your personal consciousness. Consider what this means. You have been conditioned. Perhaps we can view personal consciousness at this level of awareness as the protective and limited mask of the human self. Hopefully your soul's inner movement also influences your life choices and becomes more important than the limited and conditioned public face throughout your life.

The question on your true identity as a member of consciousness, with the power of free will to create what you desire, are you truly free or has your will been conditioned by living within a particular culture, cared for by parents with certain beliefs and goals for your life, and particular, social ways of interacting? For example, is it part of your culture and upbringing to view yourself as an unlimited creator? Generally speaking, one's awareness of being an integral and important creator within consciousness is outside your personal awareness, bounded by learned limitations. As a general rule, you are not aware of anything beyond what your conditioning allows. Conditioning limits contribute to creating a life based on others' expectations limiting your creative potentials and access to your true identity, belief number seven.

Yet you are more than a human being with earthly issues living in a limited body. You are a divine creator, sourced within consciousness, and therefore, your nature embodies unbounded creative power. Yes, you have unbounded creator potentials, which is limited only by conditioning. To empty consciousness of thoughts reflecting external reality's magical claim of your soul, to empty emotions that knot your spirit, and release conditions of the body that crystallize the possession of your soul, is living within core connection. As primarily a soul, your soul monitors, processes, and suggests responses to the personal information carried and collected within consciousness on your soul journey to awakening to your true identity. As your awareness expands into this reality you enter an *expanded consciousness state* in which you know yourself as having the ability to create, understanding the power of your intentions through empowering a desire with strong belief. At this stage you are mostly creating through individual intentions that require strong motivation.

Unified, Loving Consciousness

Because the "I AM" is all, and you and I area manifestation of the "I AM", we are all capable of choosing to be unconditionally loving at our core. What does this mean to you? I take it to mean that I like you, being within our truest nature are loving and need to love oneself, belief number eight. As a manifestation of a loving "I AM" your core easily center around a universal loving oneness for all existence. If you choose to create by striving to be a loving person in thought, word, emotions, and actions you enter a higher, *loving conscious state*. This is the stepping-stone to living a life filled with love, inner peace, and joy. You are in communion with your true identity as an "I am" core self, a unique loving soul and spiritual essence. You love yourself with all your human flaws and express kindness and care to all others. The greater your awareness of your true identity, the more your desires fit within the framework of being a loving person, the greater your freedom to create your life. As you strengthen love on the material plane, core connection, you can access higher planes of consciousness for knowledge and wisdom to assist your life walk. As you ask, you receive. The natural laws of consequence, such as reaping what has been sown, works in your favor. You reap more love, kindness, care, miracle building materials. Perhaps, herein lies the answer for all existence. What shape would our world be in if everyone was caring, respectful, helpful, loving in their unique human way?

Consciousness

Takeaways

We are each a portion of unified consciousness, belief number one.

You are a portion of unified consciousness with a capacity to create your life from this ground of being, belief number two.

As a portion of universal consciousness, we are part of oneness and always loved. We each are unconditionally loved as is all that exists, belief number three.

Consciousness is always in ear shot desiring to answer our conflict free requests, belief number four. Loving requests are answered quickly.

Each of us is an important and unique portion of consciousness, belief number five.

You are a conditioned identity in thoughts, feelings and actions, belief number six.

Conditioning limits contribute to creating a life based on others' expectations limiting your creative potentials and access to your true identity, belief number seven. Living within a conditioned identity limits knowing self as a creator

Conditioning has each of us more concerned with pleasing others and meeting significant others expectations, which become ingrained as part of the conditioned personality and more important than one's true desires.

To be loving is your natural state, belief number eight.

In an expanded consciousness state, you are aware that the power of creation is within you and each of us.

In a loving consciousness state, you choose to set a personal ideal of being a loving person in thought, word, and deed. Your intentions manifest at warp speed

In an ascended consciousness state, you exist within a higher plane of consciousness with wisdom ad knowledge and capacity to communicate directly with the "I AM".

Springboard: Activities for Core Self Connection

- Spend some time thinking about you being part of a unified consciousness that desires to meet your requests.
- Try this guided image. Think of living in everyday personal consciousness as living in a valley with large cliffs surrounding you. The cliffs prevent you from seeing what lies beyond. When you expand consciousness, your awareness, you travel to the top of the cliffs and the cliffs no longer constrain your view. You realize that you exist beyond the boundaries of everyday living. You travel above the cliffs through acts of kindness, generosity, humility, and patience, to name a few. With loving acts as an energizing force, your intentions create in an ascended consciousness state—create at warp speed.

Notes

_____

_____

_____

_____

_____

_____

_____

_____

Creation Is in My Hands

> God supports and sustains the universe in every movement in an ongoing act of creation. (Bernard Haisch, astrophysicist)

As each of us is an integral portion of the initiating consciousness, the substrata of creation, you are creation. This means you are the underlying, invisible, invigorating, loving powerhouse that continuously creates within consciousness. Think of what that means. You are consciousness in the making; you are the energetic, vibrating force of consciousness creating according to your choices. Be aware of your eternal existence and cocreator status.

Within the "I am" core self is access to soul guidance and spiritual energies for creating. We are vibrating energy. You are the energetic, vibrating force of consciousness, with the power of free will to create what you desire. In the scriptures and spiritual practices, spiritual energy has many names, such as Holy Spirit, chi, and Shakti. This energy provides your life and is a component of who you are. Spiritual energy exists throughout the earth, the whole of the universe and consciousness, and resides within you while also never leaving the heavens. The vibrating love energy bridges heaven and earth. When you desire to be loving soul responds with a plan to help and spirit is activated. You have all that you need for a meaningful, fulfilling life. Through conscious awareness of your loving creator status within a unified, loving consciousness, you truly are the light of this world. You are a divine being energetically powering this world. Also, be a light unto yourself.

Awareness of your creative capacities adds a spiritual dimension to your self-concept. As your awareness of your spiritual soul makeup continues to deepen and expand, as you use your creative skills to create a purpose driven life, your sense of self will also broaden.

Your creation superpowers do not stop on the earth. The entire universe, on all realms of existence, seen and unseen, is your home. This includes earth, heaven, and realms presently unknown to us. Your ability to create is limitless. Creating is your natural state as you harness and direct creation.

Love unifies personal and universal consciousness, and you cocreate within the divine intelligence that guides all things. Your core self is the transcendent factor within guiding you to love, with human self and core self in alignment, your identity blossoms. You uncover the natural wholeness, integration, and unity. You have ignited your miracle path. Who you choose to be is created. Recognizing yourself as having the "I am" powers of creation within you is the foundation for a miracle life. You will limit yourself only by not identifying with your cocreator status.

Through forms of love, such as patience, peace, humility, kindness, emotional control, goodness, joy, mercy, forgiveness, and other acts of kindness you extend your love to others.

Creation

Takeaways

As a creator you are a powerhouse. You are designed to create.

You exist as a vibrating, energetic force, with free will to create your life.

The entire universe, on all realms of existence, is your home.

Be aware of your creative unbounded capabilities. You are the seat of abundance.

Through the loving creative power within your core self and with your human self in alignment, you harness and direct creation and can build a miracle life.

Springboards

- Think of your core self, spirit, and soul as your primary identity with love as your guide.
- Your core self is like a lighthouse whose love beacon illuminates the inner horizon—the guiding light of your "I am" core self within you.

The supreme Self, the eternal Lord, enters into the entire cosmos and supports it from within. (The Hindu Bhagavad Gita)

Breathwork Springboard

Tuned to the source are those who live by breathing Unity: Their "I can" is included in God's. (Beatitude 7, interpreted from Aramaic by Neil Douglas Klotz)

To get in touch with your creator potentials one can begin with the breath. Our first breath begins the human journey. "Now the LORD God formed a man from the dust of the ground, and breathed into his nostrils the breath of life; and the man became a living being" (Genesis 2:7). One's first breath activates the inner physical self with biological life, unites the human self and core self, while providing a life-giving ingredient to the physical self. The Bhagavad Gita translated by Swami Prabhavananda and Christopher Isherwood describes a beautiful companionship between breath and connection to God. "An eternal part of me enters into the world ... With a drop of my energy, I enter the earth and support all creatures. I enter breathing creatures and dwell within as life-giving breath ... entering every heart I give the power to remember and understand."

Conscious breathing is a continuously moving, receiving, and giving cycle moving your energetic currents. When you focus your attention on breathing, you are centering your powerful attentional and intentional creator abilities on your energetic force field. Creative potentials and heighten inner perception occurs with deep diaphragm breathing. Through breathwork, you learn what yogis and the spiritual healers of today know: breathwork activates your energy field, grounds the body to the earth, energetically binds the "I am" core self to the body, attuning the body and mind to behold the inner self. Through this binding connection, breath can be used to bring about inner unity in mind, body, emotions, and one's "I am" core self, belief number nine. The degree of belief you place in this idea is not important. What is important is recognizing that breath can help you. In this book are several breathing exercises to assist you attaining peace and spiritual awakening.

Because breath can activate your psychic life force, it can also conjure up previously dormant, powerful currents of psychic energy that will guide you to spiritual unfoldment, inspiration, and bliss. And as you experience bliss, you assimilate spiritual power known in classic yogi traditions.

Through intentional breathwork you can direct your consciousness to the spiritual plane of infinite possibilities. For example, not only does breathwork energetically bind the human self to your core self, but it also can assist in your own healing. Through opening any of the body's energy centers, known as chakras. Through intentional breathing into these power centers, you can heal the physical component associated with the chakra. For example, by opening the base or first chakra, you will feel more connected to the earth. Physical body parts of leg and feet, which connect you to the earth, assimilate energy which assist in healing the related body parts of a chakra when energized. Another example, I am on a journey to express more love and work on opening my fourth chakra, my heart chakra. I breathe imagining it opening like a rose. When you open your sixth, or third-eye, chakra, your intuitive skills increase. Opening the crown, or the seventh chakra, will increase your connection to God, if you so intend.

Breathwork

Takeaways

Breath connects you to your inner spiritual life force as it binds your core self and the human self, belief number nine.

By breathing deep into the diaphragm, you energize your body, and you heighten inner perception and your creative potential.

Breathing into areas of bodily discomfort can aid the healing process.

What you consciously intend and activate through breathwork is created.

Springboard

Read up on chakras.

When feeling anxious, take and hold deep breaths to a count of 4-5-or 6, whichever is comfortable. Breathe out slowly, wait a second on empty breath, and breathe in again. Repeat until anxiety passes.

Notes

_____

_____

_____

_____

_____

_____

_____

_____

Unconditionally Loving, Your Highest Ideal

> Love is the only sane and satisfactory answer to the problem of human existence. (Erich Fromm)

This may seem like an impossible goal, to unconditionally love in our secular, fear based world. It's not a romantic love, it's not sharing your life as you do with a friend or lover. Perhaps it's being so filled with gratitude that you want to spread thankfulness, care and compassion to others. It is viewing all life with care, and genuine respect recognizing godliness lives within each of us, that everyone has a core self, and everyone can be a source of love. It is what we desire to feel towards ourselves and represents the kind of world we desire to live within. You and I are energized by tapping into the natural reservoir of love.

Your core self is unconditional loving, which is a path to joy living.

And you cannot connect with your core until you unconditionally love yourself. Unconditional love is a transforming energy that resides within a unified consciousness and within each of us. Fortunately for each of us *the energy of* Love is continuous and abundant, existing on an infinite continuum. Loving is spiritual intimacy which is *loving care for self and others.* Unconditional love cannot be corralled and belongs to no one person or soul. Unconditional love is unifying and extends from an intelligent source within consciousness. This source is commonly known by your name for God. As unconditional love *is one with your core*; it never dies. It is the true place within which safety, security, joy, and eternity are known. At the very core of our existence, we are loving beings creating consciousness. We are Christ in the making. Never be afraid to reach within the depths of self to open the floodgates of your core self. Unconditionally accept and own a spiritual self-definition. You do not need to be perfect, nor do you have any requirements for emotional health or physical health. No matter who you are and no matter what you do, or have done, you have access to unconditional love within your core.

The desire to love oneself and love others without conditions does not easily exist in our American repertoire. It is the desire to love and be loved that fuels conditioning. We desire to be loved by significant others and follow their rules to attain love. One's conditioned identity, public face, is formed through this desire. Character is formed and personality modified according to rules of loved ones and social forces. Conditioning excludes one's true spiritual identity. The fact is that all of us are inherently loving beings and inherently unconditionally loved within God's universe. If one could accept this fact, many of the self-esteem and mental health problems witnessed today would be nonexistent. We strive to be loved, yet it is inherently our nature and automatically given by God.

So how do we relearn the ways of love? To unconditionally love includes, but is not limited to, self-acceptance; nondefense relating with a desire for openness, companionship, and attunement with others as they are; tolerance and practicing humility; warm, compassionate, and empathetic communication; loving-kindness; mercy; practicing self-control; and awareness of self as a cocreator within the loving universe of God, other acts of spiritual intimacy including *loving care for self and others*. These are ways of being that may feel unsafe, particularly toward strangers. Yet unconditional loving is transformative and gives meaningful shape to spirituality and is an aspect of your true identity, who you are. You have nothing to fear.

This unconditional loving begins with yourself. Within your being, unconditional love ignites a mystical union with loving attachment between the human self and core self. You only need to open your heart with sincerity; believe in your Christlike core self-identity and being awake at the wheel of creation with vitality; and expressing many loving thoughts, feelings, and actions to all others. To unconditionally love oneself you own your holy, pure, loving, worthy, and guiltless spiritual core nature. And expressing forms of love freely to others without cost is being unconditionally loving. This is what unconditional love is all about. This means no matter the human mistakes and pitfalls that have occurred.

When you unconditionally love you are aligning soul and spirit with your human self. You are on the path Christ has shown us. You know love and are loving. In a holistic way you travel the inner river of peace, contentment, and joy. You are free of inner conflict and are personally and spiritually integrated in mind, body and spirit. The more you choose to allow love to guide you, the more harmony and health you experience. Your awareness is not magnetically determined by external life encounters. You have authority over your life. No matter what is happening in the external world your life is fully alive and joy filled. You exist within Christ's identity and know yourself as an integrated component of God's unified, loving consciousness. You have in your hands the keys of creation.

It is unconditional love that can guide each of us to release oneself from personal issues, emotional problems, and physical discomforts as you experience the integrative and transformative power of unconditional love. Healing occurs from the position of intimately knowing yourself as a human and divine being, with your identity structured on higher values of love and inherent self-worth. Through stopping to notice, looking within for communication, and listening to the intuitions, insights, the messages and signs from your core, unconditional love guides you as love expands within.

Unconditional love not only unites the internal self but also produces loving attachment between you and another. We have all heard a rendition of "Love your neighbor as yourself," and perhaps have wondered why we are supposed to do so. It's hard enough sometimes to love yourself when major mistakes have been made, to love your neighbor when his political views differ, or when the neighbor has directly harmed you. Yet doing so releases inner joy. Have you noticed when you do a charitable action you feel good, your spirit lifts? Imagine living in that vortex. Imagine walking around looking for ways to express kindness and care to another, to be the smiling face lifting another's spirit? It is not a surprise that unconditional acts of service are a pathway to joy. Unconditional love is a transforming energy, a vibrational field lifting your awareness into a higher level of being, lifting the human self into spiritual realms specifically when you express a form of love to another, belief number ten.

Love penetrates feelings of separateness and isolation, providing a union and a knowing of another, which feeds back into knowing more of oneself. Accountability for wrong-doing remains; -it too is a form of love. However, one is never defined by mistakes, faults, poor decisions. As you give love you receive love, sometimes sevenfold. You will experience loving happenings in your life as a unified, loving consciousness and core self are interacting in your life. You may find that your feelings of unconditional love extend automatically to all that exists. And you may experience the feeling of oneness with all that lives.

When we talk about being spiritual, nothing is more spiritual than love. In a harmonious way, we share the universal destiny to use our own forceful, spiritually empowered ability to create an unconditional loving state within self, spreading to a loving relational world. An earthly spiritual goal to express the many forms of love available, intentionally and authentically, in our interactions with one another, which will provide a safe and secure new earth. When we love unconditionally, we create a loving world, a new earth formed through global unity. Loving is the path for personal upliftment, soul evolvement, and social and global survival and unification. Now as a loving being the light cast by your flame filters to the conscious level of reality. It is no wonder that within each of us comes the directive of the "I am" core, which champions us to unconditionally love.

Allow oneself to give love and care unconditionally and freely, that is, at no expectation from the giver and with no cost of the receiver. Always do so while preserving your integrity and autonomy. Intentional willingness to change present ways of being that block the knowing of one's spiritual core is needed.Overcomer the feelings of separateness and isolation, and do not believe others automatically mean to harm you as ego may suggest. In fact, studies have been conducted that put light on others' motivation and has found others are trustable and generally do not desire to harm.

Loving will eventually be the energy that guides each of us to our eternal home. The emotion of love not only provides the path to your eternal home, but you also consciously and intuitively can travel the eternal path and place yourself on the river of love to speak with deceased loved ones, or God, if intended. Your creator capacities are unlimited. Live beyond personal or societal limitations of the moment toward unconditional love or care. Open your eyes, mind, and heart, and become more conscious of who you are. When you stop imposing conditions for loving self and loving others, you live wholly within your nature.

View yourself as a loving being and own your spiritual identity. Create a loving reality by acknowledging your spiritual birthright position and by using your human will to express unconditional care and love through its many forms. And allow yourself to receive it. Unconditional love is the way that "Ask, and you shall receive" works best. As you cycle in unconditional love, love cycles back. You create a meaningful life. It's time to awaken and discover that unconditional love is not just in your midst; it is a living, breathing part of you. Just as love lives in you, so to in all others. When you follow the guidance of your "I am" core self, you own your identity as a creator and create through the spiritual power of love. Your human and spiritual natures become integrated and respond as one. You receive the blessings of integrated wholeness in body and spirit. And love ignites abounding joy and your personal miracle path. So, *intend* to feel unconditional love for yourself and others, and *trust* in unconditional love illuminating your life path and eternal path home. And you will discover and assume your true place and position in God's eternal landscape.

Unconditional Love

Takeaways

Your core self is unconditionally loving. It is your essence. Live wholly within your true identity.

Ironically, your desire to love and be loved is the tool the ego uses to form the conditioned self.

Aligning with your capacity to unconditionally love requires being conscious of self and consciously thinking, feeling, and acting in loving ways as identified as fruits of the spirit. Don't just portray love; work on radiating love.

Loving others as you love yourself provides joy and lifts you into an awakened spiritual realm, belief number ten.

Unconditional loving leads to blessings, such as intuitive knowing, guidance, and wisdom. Your journey through life is fully alive and joy filled.

Unconditional love is the emotion that binds the "I am" core self to the human self and to the intelligent force that creates all things.

Your very essence and true identity are to unconditionally love. This is your miracle path to joy.

Accountability for wrong actions is a loving response.

Springboards

- Imagine the unconditional love within you is like the air you breathe. Like air fills the earth, feeling love fills you, every organ in your body. Now imagine unconditional love is like the air surrounding each of us that fills every crevice of earth, just as breath fills the human self.
- Live in a state of gratitude. From the moment you wake up, begin your day with thanks and end your day in the same way.

- Practice being loving rather than being loved.
- Within Judaism lies the mystical Kabbalah teachings. The Kabbalist Rav Berg expounds on the Kabbalah concept of giving until it hurts to "be God." This is an idea to consider!
- The Dalai Lama prescribes compassion for happiness. "If you want others to be happy, practice compassion. If you want to be happy, practice compassion."
- Practice In lak'ech. The Mayan practice, translated as "You are my other self," which does not recognize spatial boundaries between self and others. This means how I treat you is how I treat myself. If we are all one, to inflict pain is to harm self; to love others is to love self.
- Find and repeat your favorite love-related Bible verse such as Psalm 139:13. "For you created my inmost being; you knit me together in my mother's womb."
- Identify the rules you follow to receive love or give love.
- Look for ways to express kindness to others everyday.

Where there is no love, put in love and you will harvest love. (St. John of the Cross)

Without Love, humanity could not exist for a day. (Erich Fromm)

If you love everything, you will perceive the Divine mystery in things. Once you perceive it, you will begin to comprehend it better every day. And you will come at last to love the whole world with an all-embracing love. (Fyodor Dostoyevsky)

Keep your face toward the light and the shadows will fall behind. (Edgar Cayce 310)

I am universal Love (Deepak Chopra)

Notes

_____

_____

_____

_____

_____

_____

_____

I Am" Unbounded by Space and Time

> Time is not absolute. The underlying reality of all things
> is eternal, and what we call time is really quantified
> eternity. (Deepak Chopra)

In order to reach beyond the conditioned limitations of ordinary life
and to know yourself as a loving spiritual being living within a human
body, a willingness to view yourself in a different way is necessary. A
deeper, richer level of self-awareness is needed. Within each of us lies
the truth that one's core self extends beyond space and time boundaries
on earth, and is infinite and eternal. As one's core self, having a soul and
spiritual energies, we each are unbounded by space and time and as such
we have unbounded creator capacities. I learned the truth of this fact
in my awe filled spiritual encounter with Christ. Besides learning the
power of love, with awareness I traveled unbounded through time and
space to meet my benefactor. Have you ever lost track of time because
you were in a creating process? My encounter was similar. Neither space
or time defined my limits. To believe so is likely a new belief for you,
number eleven.

As human beings, we perceive and work within the physical

limitations of our encasement in space and time. We feel much more comfortable viewing ourselves as contained within and bounded by the physical body. However, as an aspect of consciousness, we are unbounded. For example, our thoughts travel without body limits. Thoughts travel through a loving connection, within consciousness, towards another. Recall we are all part of one unified consciousness. If you so choose, through consciousness, your thoughts travel as you connect with other loved ones through limitless time and space. I recall a time when my young son called out to me because his bus made a doughnut in the snow and he was scared. He was ten miles away in earth distance. I called the school to find out what happened and was given this information. My son only knew he wished I was there. I also recall a professional woman entering the throes of clinical depression as her mother entered her death cycle. I'll call her *I need a mother*. To help herself handle the loss of her own mother, *I need a mother* desired the help of another "good mom." The name assigned in a client's journey represents their creator challenge. She and I, with sincere care and loving connection between us, simply admitted that finding a second mother would be helpful. This intention energized an event that could not be explained by our "logical" minds. A long-lost aunt, with whom *I need a mother* had not had contact for twenty years, called *I need a mother* "out of nowhere." The aunt had previously been a loving maternal source for *I need a mother* but was lost to her when her mother cut off their relationship connection. And *I need a mother* was in awe of this perfectly timed happening. She felt she had been blessed by a miracle, although likely she helped create the miracle through her strong intention to feel cared for by a mother figure, which her core self, residing within consciousness, heard. Loving intentions/thoughts do create at warp speed. And no thoughts are unheard.

Is it possible thoughts travel like unseen radio waves? This is how you know when a loved one needs you and how intuitive readers "read" your mind. This is the energetic power of a loving heart-to-heart thought connection within consciousness. And picking up another's thoughts without space or time constraints is not limited to intuitive readers. Like Christ we can connect with another without space or time limits using our superpowers, just as we use the internet to connect with others.

Yes, it may be difficult to imagine that we each are connected, one to another, in an all-encompassing yet boundless force field of energy known as consciousness. Yet any one of us can connect in a millisecond with another because of our shared consciousness. You can send a caring thought to another person, and don't be surprised when that person calls you saying, "I was just thinking about you."

You are a spiritual energy being without time and space constraints. Recall that Einstein clarified that physical time and space, like matter, are transformable as energy. We transform our energy into creative thought, into movement, and create, such as converting energy into the movement of brushing your teeth or building a thirty-story high-rise. So, we too, as energy beings, transform energy when we leave our material bodies and our life cycle completes. We return to higher consciousness, maintaining our energy essence without spatial boundaries or temporal limits. We do so as we are infinite and eternal within our true form, a soul with spiritual energy within unified consciousness. And perhaps you as a core return to earth carrying new information to heal wounds from past incarnations and with a new set of circumstances for experiencing who you are. To help understand that you exist beyond spatial or temporal boundaries, take the faith step of believing that your consciousness is not contained by the physical boundaries of your body.

And you may ask how is it that most of us is unaware of one's limited time and space superpowers? Yes, Conditioning has blocked out awareness as it places each of us in a time-driven causal world. Our day is powered by clocks, watches, and other time keeping gadgets. Managing time and having enough time are concepts that seem to be a source of stress in today's society. We too often believe we do not have enough time to finish our to-do-lists. We multitask, attempting to optimize the use of time, even though doing so is health depleting. And we have been taught to believe our existence is determined by a biological clock. Yet time and space limitations are conditioned beliefs that represent only the human conditioned you. These beliefs do not consider your spiritual nature. What if the scientists and prophets from the past are correct and past, present and future exist in a oneness dynamic? What if underlying Earth reality is eternity and time is a quantification tool to assist our understanding of oneself? As well, what if time is simply a conditioned concept that block out your eternal nature? It is probable that the ego wants to be the one who provides your survival.

But we do not need to give up our concept of earth time, although spiritual matters are not time conditioned. We do rely on earth time for soul evolvement as your spirit flows between heaven and earth. And at times soul progression depends on time orientation, as each of us spiritually evolves within a time frame of earthly living, probably through living many lifetimes.

Be Quiet within Time and Space

It is rather amazing how being in touch with the inner self places you at the right place and the right time as you cocreate your miracle path. Do you remember when you were at the right place at the right time? Likely you were listening to your core self in a quest to manifest an intention, a desire. As you give yourself quiet time and allow yourself to "just be," with intention you will receive intuitive-interior hunches or external signals as to what to do next on your life path. Expect this on your travels. You will be guided.

Also, we can use time for personal healing that occurs when one nurtures, protects, and emotionally bonds with one's core self in the present moment. As Christ reminded us, healing comes from within. The result is wholeness in mind, heart, body, and soul.

If you choose, you can also spiritually connect with deceased loved ones by traveling the spiritual river of unconditional love within consciousness. And never think these loved ones are limited by space, time, or human death. They can see you today as clearly as your neighbor can see you in the present. We each exist not only within human consciousness but within unified consciousness. How often I have heard persons talk about a deceased loved one communicating their presence through the sense of smell, such as a father's favorite brand of cigar or cologne, and others report feeling a loved one's presence. And loved ones in the nonbody conscious other realm can see potential future events in the earth realm. You also can peer into the future, if you so intend.

Spiritual Time-And-Space

Takeaways

Within our spiritual nature, we are unbounded by time and space, belief number eleven.

Recognize you are whole and complete without time and spatial boundaries.

Our thoughts on earth travel unseen like radio waves, within the human community denoting spiritual oneness.

Each of us is gifted the capacity to time travel to past lifetimes and to visit the future for a heads-up on happenings and knowledge of one's identity.

Learn to manage time, and do not allow time to manage you through giving yourself quiet time.

Give yourself quiet time, and being quiet within earthly space leads to interior core self connection. Life guidance follows.

Springboards

- Hold onto a loving intention throughout earth time until your request is answered.
- Imagine that your essence extends beyond your bodily framework of skin and bones, while your human capacities are fully intact, and you are very conscious-very present. Next, imagine your consciousness leaving the confines of the human body, powered by your intentions, and immediately traveling, unseen, through time and space. Send a thought to a person you love. Energize the thought with strong belief in your spiritual capacities. With awareness of your intention, you are stepping into consciousness.
- You can track your life in time by journaling time events, your actions, and atypical thoughts and feelings to become aware of your spiritual path.

- How do you manage time, or does time manage you?
- Time is important. To spiritually awaken you need to give yourself core self evolving "being time." It's time to control time by not allowing time to run or limit you. Learn too just be.
- Awakening is awareness of awareness, and awareness requires time for you to become aware of your own presence beyond the limiting constraints of human conditioning. Give yourself an hour or three of "being time" every day. Does that sound appealing? By doing so, you are extending your life span as "being time" promotes stress reduction, which promotes longevity.
- Save your eyesight, and follow the sun, getting up with the sun and reducing activities, including eye strain, by "going down" when the sun goes down. Summer is for activity, and winter is for moving inward and resting.
- Recall a time when you connected with another, alive or past on, just when you were thinking about that person.

Notes

_____

_____

_____

_____

_____

_____

_____

_____

"I Am" Eternal and One with All Creation

> We are travelers on a cosmic journey, stardust, swirling
> and dancing in the eddies and whirlpools of infinity.
> Life is eternal. We have stopped for a moment to
> encounter each other, to meet, to love, to share. This is
> a precious moment. It is a little parenthesis in eternity.
> (Paulo Coelho)

Like all life-forms we are energy, and we are a part of the energy system
forming consciousness. Indeed, we are consciousness, charged with
using our powerful creative force to build a loving earth. This creation
energy exists within each of us, keeps us alive, and manifests within
consciousness, which exists forever, although the human container
perishes. When you pass from this lifetime you will uncover that all that
is left is conscious awareness of who you are within one's "I am" center.

Eternity

Springboard

* Create your world through loving thoughts, words, and deeds, to
  begin to experience immortality. Once you align your human beliefs
  and thoughts with this core knowledge, you accept your place and
  position in eternal reality.

  > Death is simply a shedding of the physical body like
  > the butterfly shedding its cocoon. It is a transition to
  > a higher state of consciousness where you continue to
  > perceive, to understand, to laugh and to be able to grow.
  > (Elizabeth Kubler Ross)

CHAPTER 2

Listen: Your Soul Is Calling

> What lies behind you and in front of you, pales in comparison to what lies inside of you.
>
> Ralph Waldo Emerson

WHAT DO YOU think when you hear the word *soul?* What does it mean when someone says his music has soul? Is it possible that within each of us lies your identity as an individuated soul? When your thoughts, feelings, actions like music, art, literature appear to come from somewhere else, that creativity is you in alignment with your soul. Soul is not your human personality, although soul influences your personality. Your soul, with access to creation energies from a loving spiritual essence, is who you are. And soul is who you remain when you pass from this earthly world.

Soul is the intermediary between earth and the higher realm of higher souls or heaven. And you, as a soul, are purposed to design a life that works with the talents within your human self, your human personality, and the loving strengths evolved and carried within your soul identity. Part of one's soul is interconnected with your unique spiritual gifts or fruits, like the mix of a fine wine. Another part of your soul, often referred to as psyche, is very much in the world working on aligning human wants and needs with your eternal self. Soul guides each of us to create opportunities for positive experiences if intended.

You, as a soul, have chosen the circumstances of your life, including your parents, where you were born, your body type, the key elements of your life, including the vocation you choose, the children you bear, the persons with whom you interact. You as a soul choose the best set of circumstances to meet your human and core self desires.

Your soul is not a mentally or emotionally controlled mechanism of the human mind or physical body. Your soul knows your uniqueness, such as physical needs, your human talents, and aspirations. Your soul knows who you are, who you have always been, and who you desire to be before human conditioning set in and established your human self-concept devoid of a spiritual identity. Its knowledge is not limited to your present lifetime. Your soul can be viewed as having an eye into consciousness as your soul knows your present, past, and potential future. This also means you, as a soul, have access to eternity. It carries spiritual progression and human experiences that have harmed, as well as evolved your soul. However, soul mostly is concerned with the present day and helping you to live a joy filled and meaningful, loving life.

Your soul knows better than your conditioned self what you truly need to be happy and healthy. And so, your soul will continually push and pull you to meet your spiritual and human life desires based within your true intentions. Soul, knowing you intimately, desires to mediate your human choices toward guiding you to become a force for love in the world releasing the wholistic self. Doing so helps you to live in inner harmony among the physical, emotional, mental, and spiritual self. This is integration, wholeness. Soul's highest goal is to guide your human life to unconditional love creating. Identify yourself as primarily a loving, spiritual being.

Although we each have the capacity to create a miracle life as a loving being, unfortunately, many of us have either been asleep at the wheel of consciousness or desire unloving experiences such as power over others. The conditioned human self, with its ego mind gatekeeper, can rule your life, keeping your awareness in subconscious realms. The ego is strong. If you choose to follow the ego, it does not reside within a unified, nonjudgmental consciousness, which desires to meet ego's requests. At these times, you are unknowingly or knowingly choose to walk a more difficult life path than you would walk by following loving guidance. Who is in control of your will; you choose.

If the path you have ego chosen is not aligned with your innermost true desires, your soul can expose these false self-beliefs and needs that have blocked out core self-connection due to the selfish life focus. If stardom, wealth or power is part of your fate or chosen destiny, soul can provide and does so without harming others while you feel blessed. However, if these are ego alone desires, at these times you may need learning situations to assist you in taking the next step on your awakening path. Trusting in your core self, which you cannot see, can be difficult at first, until you notice soul movement and awaken to your creator capacities.

Your soul is creative, resourceful, persistent, and relational. If you decide to break through conditioning barriers, your soul will energize you and guide you to people, situations, and experiences for spiritual awakening. It may speak through persons in your personal world, such as spiritual directors, therapists, friends, spouses, and even the neighbor next door. And, as soul will use any avenue to communicate, it will provide you perceptions, dreams with symbols and images, or intuitions to assist meeting your true intentions.

Awakening to the Good in the Bad

Soul, using anything and everything to communicate and fulfill its purpose of aiding you in designing a fulfilling life sometimes design bad events. Usually these are to awaken you to being off the path you truly desire. At other times we create these bad events. For example, negative thoughts fuel negative feelings and physical issues as we cycle in negativity. Considering an undesired event as an opportunity for self-awakening goes against the rational mind.

Some may say it is naïve to not think God is dead or never existed or doesn't care when noting the problems, we face today. And if God is not around then a core self does not exist. Yet many of the journeys described in this book begin with persons experiencing bad events that fortunately lead to well-being. For example, I recall a woman who described herself as having a protective wall made of brick that kept people emotionally distant. She knew it developed from the verbal and physical beatings from her father. I tend to think she chose this dad in the hopes that her amazing capacity to love and forgive would change his heart. It didn't. Soul relationship contracts are made, and sometimes they are successful and sometimes not. Remember you as a soul chose your parents and the circumstances of your life knowing the potentials for growth and failure. But the beatings awakened her to her loving nature not wanting to be like Dad, and also built a foundation of determination and resilience within her, which catapulted her to financial success. Then soul movement led her to a man who helped her drop her protective wall. Their relationship helped her to heal her emotional wounds with her dad.

We can grow so much in one lifetime and perceived negative events can in part produce growth opportunities. Doing so does not minimize pain and the difficulty of living with pain or in negative environments. Let's not remove human responsibility for bad events, and do not forget that we each have individually made mistakes on our spiritual journey that can cause bad events. There is much more going on beneath the surface of ordinary life. The reason for living on earth really has more to do with soul growth than with living one's imagined perfect life.

Turning to the ego to cope with misfortunes only leads to more misfortunes as ego's job is always to find the problem or enemy. And, the ego is not in control of earth's happenings, although it believes it is. Remember the ego does not know your soul's passageway and cannot interpret happenings according to your deeper, core base. It is true no one wants to experience "bad" events. Yet, within undesired events, some good exists. The ego cannot so interpret; it sees only danger. For example, although COVID-19 has put all of us on alert to danger, anxious about becoming sick, angry that others don't wear masks, and angry and sad that loved ones have died. At the same time, good has happened. We have witnessed the astounding capability of the international scientific communities in developing vaccines in record time and treatments to help patients. We have applauded the selflessness of health care workers who risked their lives daily to care for the sick. And telehealth technology has evolved, enabling doctors to evaluate and treat patients who are unable to visit medical facilities. Families have grown closer together. And we have awakened to the fact that we are all in this pandemic together, as one people, a global family. Now we face a new crisis: a global war being fought with arms, finances, cyberattacks, and social networking blocks, building walls to keep humanity separated and unsafe. Can you find the good in any of these events birthed by humans? Perhaps horrific events are part of the world's transformation process, out of which will be born a unified humanity.

Despite our limited human vision, we each seek to discern what our experiences, including perceived undesired events, tell us about our life choices. You can rise above human problems and find a way to assist the human self in spiritually handling life events, accepting all that life presents with courage, humility, and patience. *Always* the underlying evolving spiritual intention is to honor all of self and the other.

However, just as soul can move forward in spiritual progression it can fall from the spiritual plateau based on your choices.

Soul

Takeaways

Within each of us resides our true identity, an authentic and unique soul with the capacity to create a unique destiny when all of you is in agreement.

Soul yearns to be the organizing principle of your life and to free you from conflict.

Your soul is creative, resourceful, and persistent, and it will use any avenue to communicate, such as unplanned spontaneous thoughts, perceptions, dreams, images, symbols, life events, and persons within your personal world.

Soul is timeless; it exists in the past, present, and potential future while focus on the now moment.

Own that you are meant to be here on Earth; your purpose evolves as you evolve.

Following the nature of spiritual existence your soul's path is always perfectly harmonized for the individual and within the unified universal levels.

Springboard

Humanity in its former state, or natural state, or permanent consciousness, is soul. (Edgar Cayce, record 262–89)

There is a spark within us that knows God-an inner light beyond every kind of knowing and feeling. This is the spark that is one with God, and when we let ourselves be alive to this light, we come into a still desert where all is one is God... is me. (Meister Eckhart, Book of the Heart)

Notes

_____

_____

_____

_____

_____

_____

_____

_____

_____

"I Am" Intuitive

> Intuition does not denote something contrary to reason,
> but something outside of the province of reason. (Carl
> Jung)

Within each of us are naturally gifted intuitive abilities giving us the ability to know beyond the boundaries of words and reason. Intuitions are unplanned spontaneous knowing, answers to questions, and requests originating from a quiet mind and core self connection offering guidance. From this place truth speaks. Expressions of wisdom, unconditional Love and power emanates from intuitive soul guidance. Using your intuitive abilities may feel foreign to you as we live in an externally oriented world and may not spend much time in contemplation, meditation, or inner reflection, which opens intuitive channels. Sometimes we each need to stop, look within and listen. When you need advice, no matter how large or small the issue, spend a moment in inner quiet and ask for advice. Relax and listen for intuitive advice. This is setting an intention for intuitive connection that will improve your intuitive reach. Pay attention to thoughts and feelings moving within you, particularly if they step out of usual thinking and feeling patterns. As you follow the intuition from the soul within, you will have a deeper, broader understanding of who you are. No one knows better than you as a soul the way to health and happiness.

Sometimes you intuitively receive a spontaneous feeling or thought that resonates as truth but is not a feeling or thought you want. Likely, the something you think you don't want is opposite of a habitual thinking and feeling program that promotes safety but not change and growth. The something you believe you don't want is your soul communicating a progressive step for your life path. It may be time to approach a new situation even though you are afraid. Notice how you feel when you undertake these new activities. Listening to your intuitions means giving up the ego deciding what is right and what is wrong.

Honor your intuitions and set your intention to believe there must be a good reason that you received something perceived as unwanted. For example, years ago, I kept intuitively receiving a feeling that led to thoughts that I should open a private practice. I did not consciously-ego involved-want this, as I liked having guaranteed medical insurance, and I had three children to support. But, honoring the knowledge that my deeper spiritual self, my wise soul was intuitively advising, I accepted the challenge. I followed the guidance, and it turned out to be a good idea. From the perspective of rational thinking, it was a big financial risk. And yet opening my own practice turned out to be a very good happening in my life. *Always*, and I do not use that word lightly, following your soul intuitive communications leads to a happier life and stronger and stronger intuitions.

A striking example of a person trusting her intuition is the journey of *I Just Know*. The name I give to a client represents the human and divine conflict that needs resolved within the conditioned self-identity. In some cases, I include a post-therapy name that reflects the client's enlightened state. The journeys related in this book are intended to help you have faith, hope, and trust in your core self and to help you understand that we each are on a spiritual journey. Well, *I Just Know* is a woman in touch with her core self. This client taught me the lesson of listening to my soul. I met her early in my career as a professional therapist. She was seeking counseling at the advice of her medical doctor because she refused to believe she did not have breast cancer. It was the early eighties, and *I Just Know* had completed a mammogram that did not detect any cancerous growths, nor did her self-examinations. Yet she remained convinced she had breast cancer, stating, "I just know it." Under the advice of my supervisor at the time, I was to begin a program of helping her to change her belief system. I knew she did not have a psychosomatic nature or beliefs in having the latest deadly diseases. I was at a loss as to why she held so strongly to her belief. However, I mistakenly followed my supervisors' recommendations. I felt very uneasy following this protocol. Therapy went nowhere; we were stuck. She discontinued therapy. A few months later, *I Just Know* returned for one session to advise me she had discovered cancer on her breastbone, an area the mammogram had missed. From that day forward, I vowed to honor the belief that the inner guide communicates and to view the voice within as the voice that heals. When one's spiritual core speaks, it's best to listen!

Intuition

Takeaways

- As a soul you are gifted intuition. Intuition assists you on your life path sometimes providing a heads-up on upcoming events, deeper understanding of oneself and overall closer connection to core self.
- Intuition can expose false self-beliefs, which has led to psychophysical disease, relationship problems, feelings of unhappiness, or loss of a sense of purpose.

Springboard

As for intuitive advice. Spend some time in the quiet and listen to any feelings or thoughts that step out of the usual pattern.

Notes

The Art of Meditation

Be still and know that I AM God. (Psalm 46:10)

Within each of us lies the most powerful tool for awakening, meditation. This ability to meditate exists within each of us and leads to the inner space of the level ground of the unified consciousness where all things are created. As previously mentioned, for you to have a happier and healthier life, it is time to empty consciousness of consuming thoughts, limiting beliefs, fears, and other emotions that knot your spirit and block your soul connection. In effect meditation is a key that leads to inner peace and a happier and healthier life. Meditation reaches an inner state of self-awareness and can provide intuitive insights and wisdom as you attune to the flow of consciousness within your inner core. The goal is to center your being on 'no thoughts, no emotions, no movement'. Meditation is learning to be in the control seat rather than the ego mind.

Meditation also can be viewed as a mental training exercise in which you gain control over your thoughts, rather than your thoughts controlling you. Yes, it may take time to control your mind to the point of being quiet, but it is worth the work. Whatever chaos and superficial issues the ego bombards your mind to maintain control over you during meditation is dissipated, replaced by a shift to relaxation, inner peace, and centeredness. Technically through meditation the ego and conditioned self step to the mental background. They are at rest allowing an opportunity to recenter and quiet thoughts, feelings, and visceral self. On a basic level you gain control over your thought processes, related feelings, and visceral expressions. This fact is observed in studies highlighting an inner shift to the relaxation system of the body displayed by such variables as decreased metabolic rates and slower respiration. Setting aside time to meditate also increases the energy flowing into your body from the higher planes, which increases your healing capacity. And it is believed that meditation builds circuitry for executive functioning along with an increase in intuitive insights from the higher level of spiritual processing you have entered.

It takes time to quiet the mind and the amount of time is on a large continuum. A friend of mine started a meditation practice in her thirty-first year and before turning thirty-two was actively talking to God, her intention. I, however, have been meditating since I was young and only recently have connected directly to God. As a young child I had difficulty falling asleep. I would hear a train whistle in the distance and imagine I was riding on the train, imagining I was seeing the beauty of natural landscapes. The train whistle conditioned me to use my imagination and to turn within, which gave me a feeling of peace. I would fall asleep and very likely have wonderful dreams. If you have difficulty falling asleep, use your imagination and imagine a wonderful journey as a step into a meditation practice. Over the years, I learned I didn't need to use my imagination anymore to help myself sleep; I just needed to quiet my mind.

There are many avenues for meditation. Any activity that quiets the mind and lifts your spirit is a meditation practice. Riding a bike, jogging, and yoga are some examples of physical activities that lead to a quiet mind. Take advantage of the quiet mind and sit afterward for twenty minutes soaking in the quieted mind and listen for inner guidance to pop in to your mind.

There is also the classic way for meditating. Start in the morning, before you are scheduled to get out of bed. The time just before sunrise is believed to be the best time for meditate. The energy on the earth is quiet. Set aside ten to twenty minutes before your mind starts its day, and be quiet and attentive, focusing on your inner self. You can begin by focusing on your breath. Then focus on your entire body noticing and releasing any physical discomforts. Or repeat a centering phrase periodically reflecting your spiritual reason for meditating, such as finding peace, feeling love, or being happy. Your phrase works best if reflecting a form of love within your spiritual ideal. Repeat the centering spiritual phrase to dislodge unwanted thoughts and return to the quiet state.

Thoughts of the day's events may pass through your mind, which is the normal clearing out of mental clutter. Let them pass by and refocus on your breath or centering phrase. The chores and activities you have planned for the day may enter your consciousness. Let them go. The ego may remind you of all your fears and faults, for example, by evoking memories of your poor choices and bad decisions, igniting worries about what others think of you or fueling guilt feelings that you are not being productive when meditating. It is easy to become caught in a cycle of experiencing negative thoughts and feelings when quieting your mind. You can try to push them away by ignoring them, but they will return. Instead, acknowledge them, and let them pass by. Do not invest any energy into negative or positive thoughts when meditating. And keep to your intention of reaching for your inner quiet state. The ego is trying to regain control by these strategies to make sure you are desiring quiet time. The ego is not familiar with quiet. But remember while the ego may be the master controller, *you are the programmer and boss*. You are on a learning journey, so any poor choices or bad decisions you make are impermanent aspects of your earthly path. And what we pay attention to defines our personal consciousness, as attention and awareness direct the flow of energy. So set your goal to meditate and work toward quiet time. You are the boss. And before meditating ask for an answer to a dilemma or for an insight in to your life experiences. Answers are provided at some other time in your day usually.

Even if you haven't immediately quieted your mind during meditation, or do not feel more relaxed and centered, do not worry about it or think you have failed. Allow meditation to work for you by allowing meditation time to work. The mind is following its habitual path and needs time to learn to refocus. You will experience benefits simply through intention setting, as meditation awakens the spiritual capacity *within each of us*. I have been meditating for years, yet on some days, I can meditate for two hours and still experience mental chatter. But I also notice that as those days progress, I have benefited in some way, by developing more patience, by becoming more appreciative of the moment, or my mind is sharpened. Success is about desire and determination. As you take control over your mental chatter, you will declutter your brain and experience a state of inner calmness. This calm state is a doorway to the guidance and wisdom from within your core self.

Meditation is not a way to escape from the world. Instead, it is a way to quiet the conditioned ego, which gives you back mental and emotional control while placing you in the interior quiet moment of awareness, uncensored. If I have had a stressful day, I will also meditate at night. And I may fall asleep before I've reached inner peace. But at such times I experience quality sleep. So please stay with the practice.

Deepening the Meditation Practice

Over time, as you continue meditating your inner consciousness deepens, the feeling of oneness and unity with all that exists becomes constant and evolves into your way of perceiving life. You experience the presence of love surrounding you, you know this love *is you,* you are now aware of your eternal nature, and you know yourself as an integral part of a loving consciousness or God rather than a human personality with worries, worldly strivings, and a conditioned, illusionary identity.

Desiring to be quiet and meditate can subconsciously increase the energy flowing into your body from the higher planes, which increases your healing capacity or contact with deceased loved ones. Notably, 70 percent of Americans today are reporting contact with loved ones from the other side often through dreams, smells, and the feeling of the loved one being present. Usually this occurs immediately after a loved one has passed on, but the experience is not limited to this event.

Speaking of contacting the realm beyond, I remember a time when I had an after-death communication. My then recently deceased dad visited me during meditation. He was crying. He was not a crier, but every time I entered meditation over a two-week period, he was there, crying. Thinking he was concerned about family members I would ask questions, such as "Is Mom dying?" or "Is something going to happen to my siblings or my children?" But I received no answer. In my core self, I knew there was a vital reason for this event. In my ego self I was feeling discouraged as I was losing my center of inner peace and joy as I was being prevented from meditating. I called my sister to see if she had a suggestion. She was very close to our dad. My sister did not have a suggestion, but the next day her buff husband fell in the shower. She called me to tell me he fell in the shower, saying I spooked her. I immediately went into meditation. And my dad appeared yet again, but he was *not* crying. I then told my sister to rush her husband to the hospital, and doing so ended up saving his life. The emergency room doctor immediately inserted a pacemaker. And the doctor explained that my brother-in-law had a heart virus. He also said if my sister had waited only thirty minutes later to get my brother-in-law to the hospital, he would have died. Never let contact from the other side scare you; the loved one is expressing their love.

I have learned firsthand that many things become possible with an open heart, willingness to follow the spiritual call, and an empty mind. One such experience began when I received a phone call from my quick meditator spiritual friend. She told me that as she was meditating that morning, God had instructed her to call me and ask me to meditate and come to him. Although I often ask for assistance, as I began to ponder the idea, I immediately heard my conditioned ego scream, "No! You're not worthy of talking directly to God!" And so, a feeling of shame and unworthiness overcame me. I told her that because I was booked all day and hardly ever have cancellations, doing as God had instructed was just not possible. However, after talking with her, I listened to my phone messages, and as the wiser "I am" had arranged the meeting as God would have it, I had *two* cancellations. At that point, even though I still had some belief I was not worthy to speak directly with any image of God, I acknowledged that I felt I needed to feel worthy of writing this book and likely my wiser soul knew I needed a God connection to continue on this journey. I was wanting a connection. I thought that it just *might* be possible, considering all that had just taken place! And so, I went into meditation. I sensed that I physically passed through Jesus, the guardian of earth, according to my beliefs, and with amazing speed I found myself in front of a man who stood chiseling at a large, white mountain, a task that seemed almost as daunting to me as my efforts to write this book. Knowing my God as formless and shapeless, and a shapeshifter, I assumed the man was my image of God, though He appeared to be a common laborer. God simply wasn't the all-powerful looking being I expected. He looked to be in his late sixties. Yet in hindsight I realize he was the perfect God image for me, as my beloved dad died in his sixties.

I walked closer until I was in conversational distance and asked, "Why are we meeting?" He looked at me, probably wondering if I had forgotten asking for help, and I immediately felt shame, which he simply dismissed, brushing it away from me as one brushes off a bug. It worked. He seemed intent on chiseling at the white mountain. I sensed him telling me that he needed help. The mountain was large, and the task was monumental. And he wanted me to chisel away as well. I felt perhaps he was telling me that through this book, I was to chisel away and help others chisel away at the rock-hard conditioned self to reveal the inherently perfect, spiritual identity *within each of us* and use this part of self to create one's world. This experience guided my writing about shame, self-worth, self-concept, and persistence.

The whole event reminded me of Michelangelo's self-described role as simply releasing the already created, physically perfect form of David from a block of granite, a work of art I had seen a year earlier. Within my soul and God's consciousness we knew this image was resonating in my mind. And he used it to communicate to me, on my level, his desire that I write this book, and to reaffirm my desire to write it, letting me know the book is in me and I just need to release it. God shape-shifted into an image appropriate for the task to motivate me to work through any feelings of inferiority and finish this book. This was my highest desire. God presents himself as needed to help mold each of us into awakened beings upon being asked. Sainthood in not required.

My God image then opened his coat and displayed a universe of stars and waxing crescent moons against the black sky. He intuitively said, "This is for you," which I interpreted as the "I AM" has created the universe for all of us. And, I do like looking at the universe of stars. It reminds me of God and how small I am yet loved. I also knew *he* was metaphorically communicating on more than a concrete level. But I was not picking up the symbolic or metaphoric meanings. To this day, I am not sure of all the meanings within this image, but I have come up with a few ideas. I know that through my training as a psychologist, darkness and the moon represent human emotions. At night we process emotions, while during the day the conditioned ego controls us. I also read a crescent moon spiritually symbolizes fertility, perhaps new beginnings. Maybe the crescent moons represent each of us on a new journey, hopefully owning our cocreator status as the light of our universe. Back to the images of moons, I also read a waxing crescent moon symbolically encourages positivity and faith. I think that he was letting me know that as I seek to help, others become fertile grounds for a spiritual awakening. I must have faith and keep my thoughts positive to help others do the same. Perhaps he is also reinforcing my belief in the power of thoughts as fertile ground for change. And I too needed to change some of my unloving ways. For example, he had to brush off shame from me so that it would not stand in the way of our communication. And my thoughts need healed as I can be negative and have unhealthy angry thoughts regarding the political nonsensical happenings and lack of respect and consideration in our political culture being expressed.

Yes, he was reminding me that I am writing about emotions and particularly positive emotions which too often lie hidden in the dark recesses of one's person. Perhaps he was also pointing out what Luke of the Bible said about the ending days of the world. "There will be signs in the sun, moon, and stars. On the earth, nations will be in anguish." Perhaps my God connection was giving me a heads-up on the surfacing of worldly human evils to be faced and cleansed, such as the Ukrainian war.

While writing this section, I attended a workshop on mystical Islam religion and the Kabbalah. Notably, I haven't seen another workshop on this issue since, an example of perfect timing. The Sufi instructor said that the dark matter of the universe allows the light matter to be seen; that is, the dark gives definition to the light. As we now scientifically know, much is happening in the dark matter of our universe and new stars and galaxies are being discovered. The Kabbalist instructor further clarified the universe concept as a spiritual faith walk in which one is striving to go beyond the limits of this world and meet God as known through the limitless, always expanding universe.

Meditation

Takeaways

Meditation requires quieting one's thoughts and feelings.
Know you cannot fail. Taking the time reaps benefits.

When you stop mental chatter, you enhance mental clarity and become aware of subtler spiritual movement in daily life achieving connection with the flow of life.

Meditation, along with maintaining an open heart and being willing to act according to spiritual values, guides one to spiritual awakening.

Meditation fosters awareness of the unity in all of life.

Springboards

- If you are having difficulty quieting your mind, start your practice with music, a walk in the park, exercise, or reading. Do an activity that relaxes you. Then sit down, and be quiet for ten to twenty minutes.
- If you are having a problem with thoughts, beliefs, feelings, past experiences, or personal relationships, you can bring the issue to mind and ask for assistance at the beginning or end of your meditation. This is a conversation between the human you and your always available "I am" core self, which is inherently in communion with a divinely intelligent force. Pay attention, and note any answers you may receive as you go through your day.

> "By more constant meditation, and putting into action day by day a little more patience, a little more love, a little more forgiving, a little more prayer. These develop the mental of the subconscious to that point of spiritual activity." (Edgar Cayce 538–30)

Notes

_____

_____

_____

_____

_____

_____

_____

_____

Your Unique Soul and Spiritual Energy Patterns

> You were born to achieve, to release your inner power,
> to fulfill your uniqueness.
>
> Eric Butterworth

Each of us, within one's "I am" core self, has unfettered access to universal loving qualities for expressing unity in the world. As mentioned, there are universal loving strengths within spirit and include, but are not limited to, loving-kindness, love, joy, peace, patience, goodness, faithfulness, humility, mercy, and self-control. These universal strengths, exemplified by Christ, and in union with your core self, are available to each of us. When one thinks, feels, or acts in loving ways, one activates one's core self within oneself. Likely you may feel the spiritual lift. As the spiritual strength becomes a habit for you, soul carries the strength through lifetimes and the strength becomes an aspect of your identity.

Each of us has walked a path that has developed these spiritual gifts to varying degrees. Some of us give until it hurts; others are known for kindness and generosity for example. Your path today in part reflects your unique spiritual strengths. And your path can be designed by you to evolve remaining spiritual strengths. One's life purpose evolves as the human self spiritually evolves, following a path that is always perfectly harmonized for soul evolvement at the individual level as well as the global level.

The design of who you are and what you are here to do is carried by your soul. Your soul carries past harms to be resolved, strengths acquired within other lifetimes, and your present purpose for incarnating. Just as a plumber has a set of tools designed for his job and his tools differ from those of a computer analyst, you also have specific blend of spiritual energy, within your unique core self, as well as within your human makeup. You know your unique blend by discerning what makes you feel good and what you have a passion for doing. Your unique strengths are not merely reflected in your specific chosen career, such as a nurse, but most importantly in *how* you do your job.

Your unique mix of spiritual strengths, or fruits of spirit, melds within your unique soul that steps beyond heredity and societal forces. In total it is the way you feel to be you, it is your "I am" core self. When we are expressing our spiritual strengths and meld them within the destiny of your soul, the essential-real you is felt. As you choose your primary identity as a divine-being, the blocks to owning your spiritual inheritance are removed, you move forward on your soul path. The feeling of being lost, or the reduction of self to the sum total of your thoughts and feelings, dissipates as the authentic you is brought to the surface of your awareness. As you honor your soul's calling, you awaken to the authentic, unique, fully human, and fully spiritual person you are, a person with a purpose and a destiny. As James Hillman, a Jungian psychologist, suggests in his book, *A Soul's Code*, we each come into this world with a unique desire for self-expression. And like so many visionaries suggest, the world wants you to be here. It makes sense that the more you know yourself, the more you will know your personal calling and your unique place and position in consciousness.

If you choose spiritual awakening, listening to your inner voice and following desires which step out of conditioning you will awaken to your spiritual calling. However, your purpose for being here in this lifetime can be avoided due to your allegiance to ego conditioning. If so, your soul will carry its purpose to your next lifetime. Gains in core self evolvement also carry through lifetimes.

At the basic molecular level, we are energy. Edgar Cayce, a luminary spiritual healer and teacher known as The Sleeping Prophet, postulated in the mid-1940s, six basic, energy patterns of your soul's: artist, philosopher, builder, teacher, nurturer, and healer. Within each of us is a mix of these patterns, which correlate to knowing one's purpose for incarnating. The builder energy pattern we see in architects, who express building-related energies by designing buildings. But, computer programmers for example are also builders, building networks. Managers are builders, building groups of people to design or sell a product. And generally speaking, each of us creates or builds our life. An artist can be an interior designer, poet, or journalist for example. Teachers teach and mothers nurture yet we all are called to nurture others, mother and dad's also teach.

The fourteenth Dalai Lama, Tenzin Gyatso, is known for his spiritual strength of compassion, through which he builds a more compassionate world and ignites healing in others. I'm sure he has many other spiritual strengths that he has activated within his spirit, which has led to receiving spiritual gifts, such as intuitive knowledge and wisdom. Another example is my father who was a one-line joker. Through humor, he nurtured others. He loved to tell jokes. His eyes would twinkle as he told a joke laughing out loud. My experiencing him was usually at the dinner table. He was also a humble man who took his faith seriously. His way of self-expression was to befriend persons who came in to his shop. He would nurture others with his joke telling, lifting the spirit of persons who were strapped financially, sad, or subjected to racism. In this way he was using healing energies. He was a patient man with good self-control as well as kind and empathetic, nurturing spiritual energies. Through activating his spiritual energy pattern, he was a happy man with a harmonious relationship with his god.

Spiritually based "I am" core self authentic, autonomous, and individuated signatures are evident in spiritual and political leaders from the past, such as John the Baptist, known for his persistent evangelization towards building a Christian community, as well as in the heroes of our times, the bright lights who, like sunlight, touch so many people. Two such heroes are Dr. Martin Luther King Jr., a builder, philosopher, and healer, and Pope John Paul XXIII, who brought religious nations together for global healing. He was a builder of religious community, a teacher, healer and perhaps a prophet. Others include Mother Angelica, who sent messages of comfort via her radio broadcasts while building a network of faithful Christians, and Mother Teresa, who nurtured the less fortunate at basic physical levels while building an army of helpers. Each of these persons had their own unique energy blend. These six soul energy patterns can have a mix as numerous as the stars.

Your Unique Spiritual and Soul Energy Patterns

Takeaways

Each of us has walked a path that has developed spiritual energy patterns to varying degrees.

We each have a specific and unique blend of energy patterns which likely has been collected through many lifetimes.

Your unique spiritual blend of energy entails six energy patterns: artist, philosopher, builder, teacher, nurturer, and healer.

Your unique blend correlates with your particular human skills, spiritual mix, and culminates in a life purpose, your reason for incarnating.

As spiritual energy patterns are activated, one feels inner harmony and peace

You can know your unique blend by discerning what makes you feel good and what you have a passion for doing.

Springboards

- Identify your spiritual energy pattern.
- Identifying your passions. Notice what you think about, feel, say, or do that lifts your spirit.
- Ask a friend to describe you.
- Spend time appreciating your individuality, your uniqueness. No one has ever existed or will exist that is like you.
- Clearly define your spiritual and human life ideals and goals. Write down for future reference your global.
- Read *Your Soul's Code* by James Hillman
- Think of what you enjoyed doing in your playtime, whose life stories you read, heard about, or watched on television, which resonated within you. These are your hero's and heroine's. Compare what you enjoy doing today with the childhood activity. Can you recognize similarities? These answers reflect your basic energy pattern and human skills.

Out of the depths we find the union of soul and spirit.
(Oscar Wilde)

Who can tell a rose to be beautiful? You know within
yourself your ideal. Be as near to that ideal as possible.
(Edgar Cayce)

SECTION 2
Earthly Living

CHAPTER 3

The Real You versus the False, Conditioned You

> Every judgment, perception, thought, and feeling are conditioned into your awareness and manifests as a set style known as your character making all that you call self, relative.
>
> —Carl Jung

WITHIN EACH OF us lies the desire to create a life that is enjoyable and meaningful; safe and secure; and meets our needs for fulfilling personal relationships. To truly be joyful, the chains of conditioning that shackle our "free" conditioned will to the habitual patterns of thinking, feeling, and acting that block awareness of self as capable of creating one's desired life need broken. Yes, it is difficult to imagine that the conditioned you, the person gazing back at you every day in the mirror, is blinded from your creator potentials. When you choose to turn inward, you can make conscious what is unconscious, your individuated, authentic, core self-identity. And you can choose a primary self-definition as a loving spiritual entity, living within a human frame. If you now want to grab hold of your human conditioning and change the thoughts, feelings, and actions keeping you from having the life you desire, eMAPs, electronic like mental, affective and physical habits, let's first understand how you developed your present life.

Conditioning begins as your life begins. The inborn need to be cared for initiates the conditioning process as an infant, dependent of caretakers for nurturance and comfort, learns what works to gain caretakers' attentions to be fed, cuddled, and overall cared for. During the early formative years, the child's brain is in a highly suggestible *hypnotic* state. It's like a sponge sponging up parents attitudes and behaviors, without thought. Before the age of reasoning, which is approximately six years of age, your human identity and self-concept is rooted to follow the beliefs, values, attitudes, norms, expectations, family traditions, and opinions of your parents. I think of this phenomenon as being similar to imprinting in newborn animals. I recall reading how a brood of ducklings followed a dog around and learned to "bark" like the dog, whom the ducklings perceived as their mother. Through the same type of process, the toddler learns what works to meet needs for nurturance, comfort, connection, and security. Can you recognize how some of your life choices and ways of being reflect your parents' ways of being? The toddler internalizes parents personal truths that become your personal truths. Notably, these truths are not based on objective reasoning. Whatever has been programmed into a person as truth is believed to be the truth, thanks to the power of conditioning. As Ken Wilbur, author, philosopher, and spiritual teacher, observes in his book *Integral Spirituality*, we live by "the myth of the given." That is, we unknowingly perceive and believe our subjective feelings and thoughts are objective truth-objective reality. This means what you have been raised to believe how you have been conditioned to feel, think and act is the real you.

The close relationships in the family are the model developing one's self concept, which is the conditioned self or concept of the person you believe you are. Think of what this means. Consider the hypnotic power of conditioning as it forms your beliefs that morph into learning how to earn love and give love and even how to withhold love, attain acceptance, self-esteem, and self-worth. All early beliefs are structured on parents beliefs, opinions, and attitudes, and later by large cultural patterns and attitudes. You internalize beliefs, attitudes, etc. and this becomes your conditioned self, your "public" face. The product of the way you have been conditioned to view and identify yourself. This is your conditioned-conceptual self. But the conceptual self you believe yourself to be is not the real you; it is the person you have been conditioned to believe yourself to be! This process holds sway throughout one's life span. As a child grows the need to be approved of, valued, and loved is defined by what pleases one's parents and later other significant others, such as teachers, peers, relatives, friends, spouses, and bosses. We each rely on these social networks to stabilize one's sense of self, who I believe I am.

Although parental influence is largely a subconscious process, parents remain the giants influencing your identity. Unresolved emotional issues in the family are also integrated within your self-concept subconsciously and often repeat in one's own life. This conditioning process extends to how we relate to others and decides the interpretations of events in the world at large. Each of us will screen the environment to corroborate interpretations, blind to any information that is not in agreement with your conditioning. And this process is metabolized by neural networks formed in the brain, patterns of thoughts, feelings, and related behaviors. The powerful, all-pervasive conditioning process explains the insane actions of individuals and societies. Terrorists teach their subordinates to hate Americans and they hate Americans for example. Or, one has been taught that black Americans are inferior to white Americans. One's "free" will has been turned over to conditioning.

The personal beliefs, which have been conditioned into your being blocks awareness and connection to one's internal guidance system of soul and spirit, the "I am" core self. Conditioning keeps you *unaware* of your place and power within creation. When this occurs, the knowing of self as an integral component of creation, unlimited and unbounded remains unknown. Conditioning itself is not bad. However, you are more than your conditioned thoughts, feelings, habits, and limited perceptions based on external standards. Society needs conditioning to develop rules that evolve society with its members being of a spiritual nature. Our spiritual nature needs to move into the foreground of life.

In the spiritual realm, is it probable that one's soul chooses one's parents, considering all the circumstances into which one will be born. This would imply that your particular brand of conditioning is meant to be on your soul's awakening path. Prior to birth, your soul may also consider the spiritual strengths, human talents, genetics, proclivities, personality style, race, socioeconomic status, religious affiliations, societal forces, and potential for spiritual growth in choosing your family and circumstances. I have even heard it said that a particular sperm is programmed to unite with a particular woman's ovum to create the seed that is you. That's a new idea. I also attended workshops promoting the idea that we are conscious beings when in utero. Because we are conscious beings, unbounded by space and time, and possess the ability to focus our attention and awareness, I decided to travel to my in-utero period right before my birth. I felt chills periodically during this travel and wanted to know why. I asked my mother what foods she craved when pregnant with me and she said, "It was August and I ate ice cubes to cool off." Although I was receptive to the idea of being conscious in utero, it was this experience that gives me pause to consider these ideas as true. I am still amazed at finding out I felt my mom eating ice cubes. We do not come into the world with a blank slate.

Often the parent-child match works well even though sometimes the human you is left with problems to resolve reflected in the parent-child relationship. Blame is not appropriate or really helpful in understanding the roots of the relationship difficulties. Soul never blames; only the ego blames. The more intimately you know yourself, human and spiritual portions, the easier it is to walk a meaningful life path. With love and insight, you forgive yourself and your parents for "mistakes" along the joint life path through understanding.

We are all on a soul's journey with an innate desire to give and receive love, to belong and have life comforts. Human conditioning uses our need for love and belongingness to mold each of us into a conditioned self. It's time to open the interior doors and spend some time analyzing your beliefs for awareness of negative and separatist thoughts, which keeps you separated from your spiritual identity. To choose expressions of love in feelings and actions will assist in opening the interior door to knowing yourself from an expanded spiritual perspective. If you lack spirituality in shaping and defining what you think and feel, it is time to allow a loving you to be in charge.

The question is "What are the beliefs of your tribe of significant others that you identify with and emulate?" Does nationality, race, religion, needs for approval, or financial success determine your actions? If so, who is really in control? Or would you prefer to view yourself as a powerful, intentional, loving human being residing within your core self and feeling and extending peace and care for all life at all times? Are you ready to believe that within self, in your core, you can choose to be a loving person, and you can trust in your core's unconditional love for you? Can you believe that no matter what is occurring in your life, underneath the surface of the event, you are a significant component of consciousness, which desires to meet your requests? Can you believe that you create your life moment to moment?

Fortunately, the "I am" core self is always ready to intervene in the disingenuous conditioning process. It is the desire to love and be loved that guides your life now. Ironically, as mentioned the desire to express love and be loved forms the conditioned self-concept defining the human you. We mold ourselves to obtain the love and approval we desire from our caretakers and to fit into desired peer groups. We are faced with an evolvement dilemma: to know love in human relationships, one must meet conditioning-imposed requirements, some of which are necessary for society to evolve, and some of which oppose the knowing of self as a loving creator. Have you ever been told you create your life?

Conditioning

Takeaways

To truly be joyful, we must first break the chains of conditioning that shackle us to habitual patterns of thinking, feeling, and acting, *eMAPs*, which block awareness of who we are as a spiritual entity.

Before a child is capable of reasoning, the brain absorbs parents' attitudes with *hypnotic* strength, and the child mirrors his or her parents' behavior.

The inborn need to be cared for initiates the conditioning process. The feeling of being approved of, valued, and loved is defined by what pleases the parents, and later, additional significant others, such as teachers, peers, relatives, friends, spouses, and bosses.

Each of us has conditioned identity or concept of the person you believe you are. Your conditioned self is your "public" face and the product of the way you have been conditioned to view yourself.

The illusionary conditioned self represents one's conditioned thoughts and feelings.

Our creative power of "free" will has been turned over to a conditioning process that blocks the internal guidance system of soul and spirit, the "I am" core self. We have lost our way.

We each can automatically accept the spiritual truth that we are loved and are loving eternal beings with inherent self-esteem.

Escape the mentally conditioned state controlled by survival concerns and fears, and freely design your life. As you break free of fears, worries, the creation of false faces, and the pursuit of false gods, such as addictions to things, people, work, or drugs, the events of the ever-changing external world no longer grab hold of or define you.

Springboards

- Notice what you are thinking, wishing, perceiving, believing, and feeling. Start a journal. Take an inward journey to your childhood and note if your thinking etc. reflects your parents values.
- Establish personal and spiritual goals to be your unique face of love in the world.
- Briefly describe the message about who you are from your parents. Add a spiritual description that fits in with your parents' concept of you. Compare your description with your personal goals and spiritual ideals.
- Make a statement of who you are ideally. Be your ideal self in all situations.

> Our own corrupted Entity is reborn on a higher level each moment that we take another step toward our own emancipation. (Lao Tzu interpreted by Ralph Alan Dale)

Notes

_____

_____

_____

_____

_____

_____

_____

_____

Meet the Ego of eMAP Programs

Throughout your reading the ego has been mentioned many times. Our eMAPs for living, rooted in beliefs, are enforced by the ego. When we hear the word *ego,* most of us think of a person who is very prideful or centric. And we commonly refer to such a person as having a "big ego." However, when I talk about the "ego" in this book, I am referring to a mental structure in the brain that is a conditioning guru, responsible for identifying and negotiating reality to provide physical safety, emotional security, and self-enhancement. As the master controller, gatekeeper to your perceptions, and center of attention it prefers a self-involved *I-me-mine* focus. The ego controls your life through the eMAPs learned in childhood and modified throughout your life. These are your conditioned habits that form the conditioned self in character structure, personality, and self-concept. These habits comprise an electronic mental ("M"), affective ("A"), and physical action ("P") conditioning program referred to in this book as an eMAP. What we repeatedly think and feel becomes our conditioned identity or what we believe about ourselves. And we each design a life that reflects these conditioned beliefs. This becomes the face, or conditioned self-concept, that we show to the world. One believes this is truly who one is and ego is there to back up the belief.

The ego is part of the initial layer of the brain referred to as the reptilian brain. In its more primitive functioning, it evaluates danger, plans attacks, and determines how to obtain food and shelter for survival. In its evolved functioning, it becomes consumed with self-interests, such as how to meet the desire for power over others, self-importance, material wealth and comforts. Recognize that choices based on power to attain authority over others, and other narcissistic pursuits, you are functioning guided by your reptilian brain. As well ego believes by keeping your life predictable and viewing change as physically threatening it is providing safety and security. Unfortunately, we hold allegiance to the ego as it is familiar, and perhaps we believe it has kept us alive. We feel secure within our eMAPs, our own particular way to repetitively think and feel as survival strategies. Do you recognize that building a life on learned limitations enforced by the ego is acting like a reptilian caveman?

Survival is important. However, in pursuit of survival, we have lost sight of spiritual considerations. For example, in America we reside within a stratified, competitive society. Ego uses the inborn need to be loved, have good self-esteem, and receive approval from significant others to keep each of us loyal to the ego. Self-worth comes into question as due to conditioning we learn to be happy and feel good about ourselves only based on success in the external world. When we do not meet important others' cultural expectations of success, one is susceptible to thinking poorly about self. We employ competitive strategies to materially succeed that often overrides caring for others. How else could the crash of 2008 have occurred? The mortgage and stock brokers had to not care they were selling faulty merchandise. And research identifying the addictive effects of OxyContin were known without a change in marketing it as a nonnarcotic. Parents also feed the narcissistic, competitive ego by planting the seeds to achieve in their children by providing them with technologically sophisticated gaming devices that promote competition in playtime. Oftentimes, video game competition is escalated to an alarming level. In some versions of video games, after "killing" the enemy's soldiers and winning the battle, a player concludes the game by killing his or her own soldiers. And, we transform subjective reality as seen on television news stations as objective reality. Television has become the definer of the truth. This is conditioning at work and conditioning creates and controls one's sense of self and one's worldview as it blocks out knowing the "I am" core self.

When you are not connected with your core, conditioned fears regarding maintaining love and feeling good about oneself, perhaps at times feeling alone, deprived, and perhaps helpless and hopeless are your attentional focus. Ironically, we do not accept the spiritual truth that we are loved and are loving eternal beings with inherent self-esteem. Instead, we limit our knowledge of oneself based on external factors—others' feedback or life happenings, limiting your capacity to create a meaningful life. Belief in the possibility of being unconditionally loved is discarded and inner conflict erupts. Conflict signals a lack of harmony between your core self and your human self. Feeling unloved is a powerful feeling and belief that stunts personal growth and autonomy. I recall the journey of a woman who designed a very unhappy life because she invested in conditioned beliefs that she was not lovable. I identify her as *Why Me?* which represents her major life belief that blocked self-awareness and the issue for which this client sought therapy. The name assigned represents the eMAP issue to be resolved. And "Why me?" became *Why Me?* as she had spent her forty years wrestling with feelings of being unlovable. She regularly attended church, felt she worked hard doing good deeds, and believed she was a generally a good and faithful person. However, she had recently gone through a relationship breakup that, felt to her like the last straw, her last hope for having a companion. She believed that her prayers for a male companion going unanswered were proof that she was unlovable, which was how she felt throughout her childhood years. And now *Why Me?* found herself in another undesired spot, sitting in front of a therapist and asking, "Why do these undesired things happen to me? Am I unlovable?" As we discussed her feelings and beliefs, it was clear she felt poor about herself and would need to reroot her self-esteem in something other than negative self-beliefs acquired in childhood, unchaining and reworking conditioned habits. Clearly doing so was part of her agenda to awakening to her true identity as a loving being. And, an aspect of our unbounded, eternal nature can be to carry over conflicts and harms from past lifetimes into the present. Perhaps in this lifetime your soul has the agenda to heal itself from past experiences.

We each have eMAPs we live by. In the case of *Why Me?* the "M" or mental aspect represented her thoughts that she was not lovable. The "A" or affective component was her feeling of sadness and anger over the thought that she was not lovable. And the "P" or physical component involved external and internal elements; specifically, her subconscious acting in ways that expressed her strong belief in being unlovable. And as the body viscerally expresses our eMAPs, likely she was building toxicity within her body due to living in the stressful states of sadness, anger, and victimization beliefs. She was not ready to hear her God loves her. I recommended semiweekly appointments, and *Why Me?* felt even more defeated and victimized. We agreed to meet twice a month if she would correct her negative thought pattern ("M") by repeating, "God loves me," every time she thought otherwise, as her Lenten promise; read the book *The Shack,* and watch the movie *Dead Man Walking.*

Two weeks later, *Why Me?* returned, stating the tasks helped her to start believing that undesired events did not necessarily point to her God not loving her and instead occurred because she did not love herself. She had changed her ingrained, conditioned way of thinking, the eMAP she lived by, recognizing that she was blocking out self-love. She was not designing a meaningful, satisfying, contented life. Knowing thoughts, feelings, and actions go together in a harmonious way, changing her thought pattern in turn would change her self-feelings enough to open her interior door to her true identity and creator capacity to become self-loving and open her to receiving love from others. Often what we fear we manifest as unknowing we are following the natural law of what one thinks, one creates. To break through her negative thinking cycle, her next therapy task was to pray for whatever experience she needed to know deep in her heart that she is lovable.

Your core self, in alignment with its purpose, will never stop trying to connect with your human self and open your consciousness to awakening choices that provide a contented and joy-filled life. At our third session, *Why Me?* was a transformed person; an invisible hand was at work. She related that she was shocked when one day, while in prayer, she heard inner dialogue and knew, "I was not controlling it." She simply heard within herself, "I love you." *Why Me?* did her therapy task and chose to use her creative powers to pray, with belief, that her God would find a way to confirm their loving relationship. She was again on the lookout, but this time for a love-confirming event. And with strong belief, her intention manifested. She expected a personal miracle, and she was paying attention to events in her life to be certain she caught the miracle. Often, we are so used to our thinking habits that changing any thoughts or behavior requires lots of attending. Conformity to long held beliefs, particularly in viewing self as having limited creator capacities and feeling rejected, or victimized often rules the masses. Unhealthy conditioning limits lead to not knowing oneself and one's ability to create a meaningful life as the ego will lock out your capacity to create a desired life.

Why Me? received a second confirming miracle she defined as her God's love for her when her mechanic, through the gift of connection we each have residing in our consciousness, told her he was instructed in prayer to talk to her about his God. Her mechanic stepped out of the comfort of rational thinking, and following his core self, he told her how he prays every night to God and was told in his prayer to talk to her. At the end of their conversation he said, "God must really like you." Her once powerful belief changed. Without a doubt, she believed that their God loved her and likely she continues to do so. In her transcended state I now call her *God Loves Me*. The decision of *Why Me?* to confront her negative self-beliefs opened the door for her soul to talk directly with her. Can you believe this? She has healed her human self, and her soul has met one of its agendas of undoing negative self-belief. We each are creators and an integral part of consciousness. We each need to uncover the conditioned eMAP ways we negate our true self and cocreator status. We can choose to be loving as we create a loving world and love ourselves and others as part of the underlying, universal consciousness that creates our world.

Her belief of not being loved is not unique. When you are not connected with your core, conditioned fears regarding maintaining love and feeling good about oneself, perhaps at times feeling alone, deprived, and perhaps helpless and hopeless are your subconscious, conditioned, attentional focus. Ego always seems to manage to consume your time and energy, becoming the false god in your life. Ironically, we do not accept the spiritual truth that we are loved and are loving eternal beings with inherent self-esteem. Instead, we limit our knowledge of oneself based on external factors—others' feedback or life happenings, limiting one's capacity to create a meaningful life. It seems that self-doubt and questioning whether one is loved, smart enough, or good enough are common examples of human conditioning controlling self-perceptions and defining self-concept. And, at the base of our issues lies fear. Ego is energized by the feeling of fear. It is a fear mechanism. In particular ego fears change and fears love as it does not understand this feeling. The ego energizes itself through fear although you may interpret it as desires to overcome or achieve something for self-enhancement. Underneath achievement can be the desire for security lacking a sense of security from your spiritual essence.

For you to have a happier and healthier life, it is time to release conditions of the mind, heart, and body caused by conditioned conformity pursuits and freely design your life. While this may sound simple, you may find it difficult as it requires a drastic change in perspective. Specifically, you need to identify and break free of societal, cultural, and at times familial influences that determine your identity and control your thinking, feeling, and actions. You will need to recognize that your life designed by the conditioned self, which you may believe is the real you, is in fact a false face you have developed through conditioning. Autonomy occurs when you undo the false wrappings of conditioning and choose to resonate within your spiritual nature and, at the same time, express a deep appreciation of humanity in general. This is how we grow and mature. False faces are shed for spiritual awakening in favor of truth and honesty. Any fears you may have of owning your spiritual self and breaking free of unhealthy eMAPs, which are part of your social face, need to be short-circuited through not responding to ego interpretations. When you break free from all the ways ego has installed fears through the addictive pursuit of the false god of greed, addictions to things, people, drugs, or obsessive thoughts, the events of the ever-changing external world will no longer grab hold of you or define you. Think of what this means for you. Certainly, releasing these conscious consuming ways of being will afford you time for self-reflection and going within for core connection to know who you truly are and create your true desires.

Being human we each are subjected to the magnetic pull of the ego. Relying on and being loyal to the ego's narcissistic ways to enhance self-survival fuels our many addictions, obsessions, and life problems. Ego keeps each of us in a repetitive cycle in which, ironically, the ego merely continues its search for threats, pointing out you are not safe and secure, or it keeps you addictively cycling in ego-produced mental states which can produce chronic physical issues, anger, anxiety, clinical depression, self-doubt, guilt, worry, or its opposite, entitlement and arrogance, or personal isolation on your quest to feel good enough and loved. And, the thoughts and feelings that exist with these emotional states are our false gods as they consume our attention and intentions, including control over your beliefs, thoughts, and feelings. Think of what this means to you. How is ego controlling you? Ego reinforces your public face to maintain its conditioned definitions of who you are.

Although our technological advancements connect us with everyone throughout the world, they also rob us of our sense of belonging. Ironically, we rely on the ego to keep us safe and feeling self-worth yet the ego is incapable of solving problems; it only perceives problems. Only the higher thinking and feeling mind can solve problems. Yet when the ego is in charge, it blocks the higher mind and moves your spiritual essence to the background of consciousness. Spiritual actions, such as acting with care and respect at all times toward others and clearly knowing who you are as a cocreator within consciousness, are not considered by the ego. When the life focus is on *I-me-mine*, we have lost our guidance system, the capacity for spiritual awareness and integration within the human self. Connection with one's core self is blocked.

The ego also fears spirituality as it cannot control it, the ego works at controlling your beliefs regarding spirituality and it will suggest God does not exist or does not love you. The ego must be quieted for awareness of oneself as a creator. If the question is "How can I overcome the dissonance that vibrates through my life," it's time to gain authority over the ego and give your allegiance to your authentic "I am" core self-identity. We can become more conscious and choose how we want to feel, think and respond. We can choose fear as the creation tool, creating inner and outer conflict as the ego desires as seen in wars, or inner peace and love for self and others as the creation tool.

Ego and Change

To reach a state of empowered intentional creating that provides passage to a joy filled eternity requires giving up conditioning which focuses on *I-me-mine* narcissistic pursuits, and all the ways the conditioned reptilian ego has conditioned you to respond to life. Be prepared for ego knows you well. In its attempts to control you, it will skillfully adjust the existing eMAP program to keep control over your attention and to meet its overall goal of avoiding change while pursuing selfish opportunities. Ego will use all of its knowledge of what works to keep you bound to your eMAP habits.

Today the ego wants to keep the external world stable and predictable for your safety and security. This is not a rational response as the external world is not stable and change is always occurring. And, security truthfully comes from your spiritual core. Yet, as it is fueled by fear, it is continually in operation finding something to fear, looking around every corner for the enemy, looking for signs, gestures, and sounds that signal danger. So don't be surprised if you have anxiety or panic and fear change.

The ego will even turn against you when it deems necessary. If the ego is left to its own mechanisms, it will eventually label your actions toward change as threats and produce an inner voice to stop you. As a conditioning guru and fear-seeking mechanism, it exerts its power as a way to stay in control, keep you safe from illusionary harm which it easily perceives, and maintain its self-importance.

Yet, your core self, in alignment with its purpose, will never stop trying to connect with your human self and open your consciousness to awakening choices that provide a contented and joy-filled life. She trusted in her creator- intentional abilities, changed her thoughts as she did not listen to her fearful ego mind and its" not lovable eMAP comments and found herself.

Allow yourself to believe in your spiritual identity, which is the new "M" of eMAP, and build your life.

Evolvement of eMAPs

The ego controls your life by the eMAPs learned in childhood and modified throughout your life. These are your conditioned habits that form the conditioned self in character structure, personality, and self-concept. These habits comprise an electronic mental ("M"), affective ("A"), and physical action ("P") conditioning program referred to in this book as an eMAP. The goal of an eMAP is to repeat learned life patterns as a way to simplify life experiences and maintain the rules and values that you have conditionally learned. The ego, along with its eMAP programs, possesses compelling power. As your executive commander, the ego is the gatekeeper determining what you will think about, become aware of, and believe about yourself.

With its eMAPs, ego accomplishes the amazing feat of harmonizing the internal and external events of your world. And your brain harmonizes by developing neural pathways, wiring the eMAPs. The repetitive nature of the ego simplifies your life and you think the same thoughts, feel the same feelings, act in repetitive ways, and develop well-worn neural roads. Of course, there are times when you have a creative thought, a sign of core self connection, and do create. Although your everyday life is conditioned, the ego can evolve as you apply firm authority and think, feel, and act cultivating kindness, empathy, and other forms of love in mind and heart.

In contrast, if you allow the ego to continue to be your life coach, you will be unable to discern spiritual reality and know your authentic spiritual identity. And as a result, you will be unable to experience the flow of creation within you. You will not know how to consistently live beyond emotional turbulence or feel *unconditional* love for self or others, much less feel a firm and consistent sense of unified belonging within our global world. In this way, bound by the ego, we individually and collectively fall from the spiritual plateau where we are all one.

It's time to break through conditioning. It's time to stop cycling in learned eMAP habits of emotion and thought. It's time to become spiritually aware of the unconditional love that surrounds you, is you, and provides you the transformative power to create a joy-filled life. Honor the fact that no matter what is occurring, your "I am" core self is the real you, powerful and creative. And your core is always ready to assist you in your life walk if you desire to be awakened.

Evolution of Separateness and Selfishness

When the ego is not in agreement with your core self, and you desire to be a source of love and care in the world but are not listening to core advice, you experience emotional turmoil. This is a sign you are off your spiritual path. The ego may also step in to quiet the inner turmoil through using isolation strategies, repression and denial of the inner conflict, which produce inner separation. You separate into human parts internally: the conceptual self that ego controls and the blocked-out conflicted self, as well as; the spiritual core self is blocked-out. Your awareness is absorbed by the illusion that the ego is protecting you through the separation process. As the ego is an *I-me-mine* functioning structure you can become a self-indulgent, narcissistic person, blocked out from your loving core self. As well, you can become an anxious or depressed person living in an isolated world without trusting relationships. This process exists on a continuum.

In fact, these separation strategies build a dual world in which we judge self and others in hurtful ways. And separatist beliefs incorrectly feel right due to conditioned loyalty to the ego. The effects of separatist strategies are easily witnessed in many of today's societies. Americans have been conditioned by the American culture to be motivated to compete rather than cooperate. And the ego separation strategies can be witnessed as it separates out the human race according to culture, race, religion, ethnic origin, the have and the have-nots and subject and object. We become trapped and constrained within the separatist conceptual framework rather than enjoying the freedom of natural wisdom. These separation strategies are weighted judgments and can lead to racial unrest, ethnic cleansing and genocide, terrorism, and wars.

If you are unsuccessful in achieving your desired social position, you can join subculture groups that are readily accessible on the internet. Some of these are hate groups with rigid identity boundaries based on exclusion and whose goals are to cause harm to those who are different.

Although the higher-evolved brain recognizes the need for global unity, our ego remains in charge. Our spiritual strengths, which support unity, are not being fully employed to discern one's true individuality or to achieve the goal of global unification.

Because you have your own ability to create, you can raise your consciousness, which is awareness of your soul essence and spiritual connections. Alternatively, you can intend only to follow the ego and its narcissistic desires and addictive clinical states and remain separate, encased in your physical form. Doing so will keep you in the cycle of striving for safety, security, selfish pursuits, and possibly without consideration of others. And as long as you allow the conditioned ego to impose boundaries for knowing love, joy, and your inherent spiritual nature, you will continue cycling on a conflicted path without knowing your authentic purpose or destination. Steeped in this type of physical reality is a loveless path.

You choose, think, feel, and act in ways that enhance one's spiritual strengths and human talents or allow your conditioned self and its ego gatekeeper to decide how to give and receive love and make the decisions in your life. Know that when the ego and your soul work together, you can access the larger, loving realms where wisdom and the ability to create your miracle path reside.

Defining Selfishness

Most Christian teachings suggest the need to care for others without defining the initial need to fill your own cup with self-care first in order to freely, without conditions give to others such as expectations. For some of us caring for self is believed to be a selfish act. However, healthy selfishness is a necessary first step before you can truly be of help to others. You cannot give genuine care to others, which is a form of love, until you love yourself. When your cup is full of love and care, it overflows to others, if intended. Let each of us 'love others as we love ourselves.'

A Word on Perception

Perception brings things to life; it makes things appear real. Until we see something it does not exist. And, the ego, in charge of perception, is very selective in what it perceives. To see something, it has to fit into the eMAPs, the way you know reality to exist. For example, likely the Bahamians did not see Christopher Columbus and his Spanish ships on the horizon because it was not a reality they knew. However, as they came to shore on canoes, the Spaniards were likely seen. If the ego were not selective, the amount of information would be overwhelming and we each would live in ongoing chaos.

The ego selects according to its conditioning. These are the rules and constants we live by, the eMAPs. The eMAPs adjust according to our mood of the day, the amount of stress being experienced, and the day's events. At the same time, the amount of eMAP change is restricted as your eMAPs basically stay within a predictable range keeping life predictable. So how do we change to responding to all life events with a form of care? How do we manage the angry eMAPs, the materialistic and narcissistic pursuits, which are part of the American fabric? As James Hillman reminds us, "You can't create a new personal reality as the same personality." Change is difficult as the ego fights for sameness. Always you are the programmer and boss. As you change your behavior, thoughts, and feelings, perception will change. The journey will have struggles as the ego tries to maintain control, but it's worth the work to know and feel your underlying position as a divine creator within consciousness and your perception opens to the beauty and awe within self and within life.

Transcending Ego

Do not malign the ego, you need the ego. It tells your where to place your feet, orienting you to the here and now to aid survival. Ego also organizes your thoughts, feelings, and behaviors to keep you from being overwhelmed with information through its eMAPs for living. Not all eMAPs are unhealthy, only the focus on *I, me, mine.*

The ego is really not your enemy. It is not wise to split off from the ego and place it under the guise of repression and denial. Rather teach it to transcend. As the gatekeeper to awareness, the ego's desire to feel important through interpreting life situations. This skill can be employed to help the ego transcend. It has been designed by you, following the particular ways you think, feel, and act. Patterns of thinking encouraging "I am" core self connection contain the spiritual potentials of your life and are the pathway to becoming a joy being. Once you take authority and choose a loving path, be firm and loving toward the ego. Continue to step away from unhealthy conditional eMAP responses. The ego, unable to handle ambiguity softens, and awareness expands. This provides a spiritual focus. Now you are also using the higher evolved brain. This part of the brain has the capacity to create a state of inner coherence within the brain that is felt as inner peace. You begin to live at the base of the mountain of creation, carried along by the loving, abiding flow of spirit that springs from your core self. When in this peaceful flow decisions are based on loving self, and loving your neighbors. You accept all that happens, without worry, resting confidently in the protective arms of the timeless, boundaryless, unifying source of love. This internal peace is the groundwork for living as a joy being. And the ego can play a role as it transcends and maintains its power and position by informing you of spiritual happenings in your life. The transcended ego witnesses the intersecting of spiritual life and earthly life, according to your intentions.

Ego

Takeaways

The ego is a mental structure in the brain that is a conditioning guru responsible for identifying and negotiating reality to provide physical safety, emotional security, and self-enhancement.

The ego organizes your thoughts, feelings, and behaviors keeping you from being overwhelmed with information by developing eMAPs for living.

The ego, along with its eMAP programs, possesses compelling power. As your executive commander, it is the gatekeeper determining what you will think about, become aware of, and believe about yourself.

The conditioned ego, with its eMAPs, accomplishes the amazing feat of harmonizing the internal and external events of your world. And your brain harmonizes by developing neural pathways for the eMAPs. You think the same thoughts, feel the same feelings, and act in repetitive ways, as these are your well-worn neural roads.

The ego is energized by fear.

The ego has now evolved to be a narcissistic mechanism geared to enhance survival by fueling our many addictions, such as working incessantly, the desire for power, wealth, stardom, materialism, and emotional states, such as anger, anxiety, worry, and depression. These false gods consume your attention and intentions, while moving higher-mind spiritual values to the background of consciousness.

When the ego is in pursuit of selfish desires and you also desire a spiritual path, inner conflict is felt.

As part of its narcissistic pursuits, the ego employs the brain tool of separation. It separates the human race according to culture, race, religion, ethnic origin, and the haves and the have-nots.

When an opinion becomes a weighted value, you have a judgment. Judgments that separate self out from others, block connection with your authentic "I am" core self. And as you judge others, the judgments fall back onto you. Keep this in mind the next time you find yourself negatively judging.

As the ego separates, it perceives enemies. At a group level separatist actions leads to genocide, terrorism, and wars.

Ego can cause internal separation as it attempts to manage inner conflict with repression and denial, strong defense mechanisms.

Ego is needed in a transcended form to keep your reality oriented while it also informs you of spiritual happenings.

Springboard

- Do you give freely to others or are expectations involved such as the other will be appreciative, return the giving and you will receive?
- Identify common ways of thinking, I always_____,I think I am _____.
- What judgments to you live by?
- Identify your narcissistic desires, money, fame, drugs, sex …
- Identify your thoughts, feelings and actions which support I, me, mine.

> There has been in the experience of the individual the necessity of pruning much of their own ego, that the "I am" may find greater expression. (Edgar Cayce 657–3)

Notes

_____

_____

_____

_____

_____

_____

_____

Intentions Creating Our World

> In just the degree in which you realize your oneness with the Infinite Spirit, you will exchange disease for ease, inharmony for harmony, suffering and pain for abounding health and strength. To recognize our own divinity, and our intimate relation with the Universal, is to attach the belts of our machinery to the powerhouse of the Universe. One needs to remain in hell no longer than one chooses to; we can rise to any heaven we ourselves choose; and when we choose so to rise, all the powers of the Universe combine to help us heavenward. (William James in lectures at Harvard, 1900, as quoted by Ralph Waldo Trine)

We are powerful human and divine creators, which has been discussed. Within each of us the power to create using our free will is an unchanging universal law. We use our will to create an intention. We create through core connection or conditioned will controlled by learned beliefs designed and reinforced by one's ego. We each create what we intend. We all know that thinking about something sets into motion the doing or building of that something. We build on earth those things you intend, think about, resonate with, and believe in, and you apply your will to make them happen. Intentions have led to mastering climbs to the highest mountain peaks, flying on the winds, traveling to space, and swimming in the deepest parts of the ocean. When spiritual love is involved toward others, we do such things as feed the hungry, care for the sick, and educate our young.

As energy follows thought, what you think is what you intend to create. Recall something in your life that you consciously created. First, you felt the desire to create it, and you set the intention to do so. Then you did what was necessary to meet the intention. And throughout the whole process, you planned and evaluated until you met your goal. Perhaps the right persons came along to assist you in meeting your goal. Perhaps your personal goals reflect the achievement desires of your parents, along with your natural proclivities and genetic predispositions. And perhaps, through maturity, you have formulated autonomous goals as well.

When you dream a dream, choose a career, or imagine how you your life is going to go, you begin the process of setting an intention to create your desires in everyday reality. Today's dreams become tomorrow's outcomes. However, wanting is not as powerful a creation tool as believing. It is believing in an event happening to such an extent that you see it happening. The manifesting steps are; Intend a creation, see it, feel it, and act to make that something you desire happen.

There is a caveat, what you request has to be truly what *all of you* desires, including your soul. Most of us are not conscious enough to know our true desires, and most of what we create is subconsciously created. You have been programmed to think certain thoughts about yourself, others and the world at large; you feel certain ways, conditioning effects from life experiences. For example, if your caretakers and you believe you are unimportant, not really loved, and should not think highly of yourself, your intention is set to manifest these beliefs, even though consciously the self-beliefs have not been chosen by you. As well, if your parent is an anxious you have a higher likelihood of being an anxious person. We are hypnotically programmed in early years to reenact the experiences we encounter in our early years and we then internalize the conditioned beliefs and act within those set parameters. Even though you did not intend these thoughts and related feelings the process is automatic. Unfortunately, even though these intentions are subconscious, we each are held accountable in consciousness. We are also accountable for consciously chosen thoughts, including negative and fearful thoughts. It's not surprising that if you think bad happenings are coming your way, you are intending bad happenings. Don't be surprised when the bad happens.

If you desire to create your life consciously, you will need to stop creating your life based on learned conditioned beliefs and limited self-concept. As a client once remarked, "By my strongly wanting something and believing in receiving that something, I have created it." All of your intentions vibrate in consciousness and consciousness awaits your empowered requests that it fulfills without judgment. Again, empowerment means all of you are in agreement. To decrease the dissonance that vibrates through your life, impacting your choices, gain conscious control over your beliefs. Begin by identifying yourself as primarily a loving, spiritual, eternal, creator no matter life circumstances, and follow core guidance. Through using your creator powers for loving intention, you are guaranteed passage to core guidance. This leads to a life worth living.

When you send out a love request, synchronicities and miracles happen. The greater your awareness of this unfolding energetic dynamic in your life, the more insight you will receive, and the greater your control in designing the life you desire. When living in a spiritually conscious loving state of mind, you are peace filled, find meaning and purpose as you see through soul-filled eyes that penetrate the cycle of repetitive eMAP thoughts, beliefs, feelings, and actions.

Be Certain and Clear with Intentions

I once read that angels desire to answer our requests, but they have to know what the request is clearly before a request can be answered. The idea that angels are waiting to answer our requests is a comforting idea and being clear about a request makes sense. If you think you want ___ but you have doubts, the intention cannot be answered. So be certain and clear about the exact something. And see it happening in your mind's eye. Remember to see it, feel it and act upon it. I experience the unifying loving consciousness answering requests when I began to consider retirement. I knew exactly which state I will retire to; I will have palm trees out my window and a view of an ocean with small, quiet waves. I will be able to see stars at night and a Catholic church and grocery store within walking distance. It would be what I could afford. Can you imagine a home with a view of a beach, which is not flooded with street lights and stores and is reasonably priced? I was in search for about five years and throughout this time I was not strong in my belief that consciousness would be able to realistically grant my intention. I had doubts. One day a friend of mine found her dream vacation spot and I decided I could do the same. Now with full inner agreement and full belief, I "accidentally" came upon the exact place that met all my requirements. It took some time for me to believe with clear and firm intention. Once I did, my ideal place manifested quickly; the loving consciousness was waiting. One day I heard my soul, who usually does not speak in words say to me, "you really like this place." Soul reminded me that it was my human self in doubt not my soul.

The Power of Group Intentions in a Cause-and-Effect World

We live in a causal world in which human actions lead to consequences or results. An individual inherently has great power to manifest a desired intention. But when humans gather in a group, in person or remotely, and concentrate on an intention, their collective will carry even greater manifesting capacity. In joining together, the group accumulates group powers to bring about a happening. The transformative power of the whole is greater than the capabilities of its components.

Sometimes, in our world choices are made without consideration of the value to society leading to a fragmented world within consciousness. Global warming, food scarcity, wars, and genocide are examples of global fragmentation. We do not respond from the loving unifying base of consciousness. The fragmentation also extends to the universe, which is also part of our oneness. Notably, there are studies that correlate wars on earth with solar flares, which damage satellites and radio communications, perhaps reflecting the poor communication between the loving universe and human actions. At the moment solar flares are increasing as is hate, terror and wars. Perhaps we have lost the belief that we are intimately linked to animate and inanimate nature and can destroy our world. Loving actions also affect the universe and we can use social media and other technological advancements to build a healthier, more loving world.

Through our intentions, we think, perceive, organize, respond, search, and learn. And at times we destroy. We each choose our destiny and are always an energy force field on earth, creating what we intend in consciousness. The questions are these: How are you setting your intentions? Are you seeking to create a caring earthly world or create only to promote narrow self-interests?

Intention

Takeaways

Your capacity to create is an unchanging law. And we each create through the intentions we choose or through the subconscious ego.

What you believe, you intend and create. As an important portion of consciousness, possessing will power to design your life, you have the ability to choose how you desire your life to unfold.

Within each of us lies the creative, intentional ability to choose one's primary identity. Are you an eternal component of consciousness with unbounded creative potential, desiring to activate your spiritual nature and be a loving divine being within your human body? Or are you only a human being?

Take the evolutionary step of handling daily life decisions by believing in your authentic identity as an eternal cocreator. Knowing and acting on who you truly are will transform you through the power of unconditional love as you set the intention to align your human self with your core self. You are a powerful, intentional being with capacities to break free from unhealthy conditioned patterns that prevent you from transforming into a "joy being."

Follow this path with intention setting: Intend, see It, feel it, and do it.

Be clear with intentions. God is in the details.

Springboards

- When an opinion becomes a weighted value, you have a judgment. Judgments separate self out from others and block connection with your authentic "I am" core self.
- Life is cyclical and, as you judge others, the judgments fall back onto you. Keep this in mind the next time you find yourself judging.
- View yourself as a powerfully creative human being, using your intentional powers, and ask for and follow core guidance.

Notes

The Gift of Imagination

> Imagination connects us to the center of existence while
> distinguishing imagination from a fantasy that separates
> us from reality. (Kathryn Wood Madden)

To assist in Seeing an intention manifesting, use your gift of imagination. Within each of us lies the amazing capacity to shape personal reality, sometimes through the gift of imagination. When you clearly and repeatedly *visualize* within your mind what you want to create and strongly *believe* that it will occur to the extent that you *see it happening* in the present moment, you have the ingredients for making your dreams come true. This is a power of imagination within one's mind.

Imagination has served humans as a creative tool since ancient Egyptian times. Archaeologists have found hieroglyphics that depict airplanes on the inner chambers of tombs. During the Renaissance era, Leonardo da Vinci developed design concept drawings for diverse inventions, from a helicopter to a humanoid robot, many of which were ultimately built, although in modified form, hundreds of years later. Recall Walt Disney's mantra for children to "wish (or imagine) upon a star" to create their dreams. He created his dream of a wonderland for children. Our modern-day imagination has similarly "taken flight" with flights to the edge of space. And we can time travel to the future and walk-through faith-opened doors and make your dreams come true by using the gift of imagination. What you *believe* in, you can create. In all situations, imagination can assist in guiding our personal journey by providing the vision or the creative leap to design the life we desire. And imagining opens up new pathways in the brain, changing neural firing patterns to support the change you desire.

Imagination assists in deepening self-awareness, reaffirming yourself as a powerful spiritual presence and cocreator of your life. And imagination is not limited to what is happening in our present everyday reality. It helps to design our futures and enables us to time travel to the past to heal painful memories in the present, a wonderful present. This is therapeutically known as reparenting, inner child work, or trauma therapy.

Power of Images

> Images foster wonder rather than conclusions and make for people of wisdom rather than opinion. (Thomas Moore, PhD)

It is believed that each of us carries an image of God. Certainly, Renaissance frescoes, church icons, and statues give us images of holy figures and God. And it is easier for us to relate to holy figures and God when they are imaged in our likeness. Perhaps God is a shapeshifter taking an image that works best for each of us while he remains the "I AM"-nameless and formless. Within our personal image we carry our ideas on God's image and who we are meant to be, which is not affected by our conditioning. The image of the idealized self, which likely helps guide your psyche and soul in designing a truly individuated life, represents who you are meant to be. To know who you are note the qualities you are known for, which gives you a glimpse into the idealized self, such as kindness, cleverness, consideration of others, being a helpmate, a predictor of cultural movements, a champion for the underdog, etc. The more your present life fits the image that your soul carries of who you are, the less inner turmoil and more life satisfaction you experience. Images are an important aspect of our mental capacities.

Your soul, while its first preference is to communicate through your feelings, soul also communicates through an image rather than words as often words cannot adequately express all your soul wants to express to you. An image communicates meanings on many levels of understanding. An image communicated many meanings to a client I refer to as *I Am a Black Diamond*. He came for therapy because he did not feel self-worth. After inducing a light trance state, I asked him to visualize what he would feel like or look like if he were a person of value. He started visualizing, and his core created an image of a black diamond. At first, *I Am a Black Diamond* was somewhat shocked at seeing the diamond image. But he was also comforted and intrigued by its black appearance and believed the black diamond was the right "fit" for him. An art student at the time, he found black appealing for its stark contrast with other colors and felt it mirrored his choice of thinking, acting, and dressing differently from others who followed cultural norms, which he now felt was a personal strength. As well, he thought that black was more masculine and mysterious, additional qualities that he liked. Although natural black diamonds are rare, they can have imperfections and are less expensive than other diamonds. Nonetheless, it is a diamond and precious and valuable. He accepted the image and the objective information regarding black diamonds. And although he had always strived for perfection, he decided that like any possible imperfection in a black diamond and in himself was simply a sign of authenticity, a viewpoint that reflected his personal lifestyle goal. He came to own this mental image as his core telling him that his life was of unquestionable worth and imperfections make him who he is, unique self-esteem. When one seeks guidance from your core, the image that one receives, down to the details, is an important guiding symbol.

Through images we can also enter the path to healing ourselves and move forward on our spiritual path. I recall a time when my allergies were seriously affecting my breathing. I frequently prayed for an answer, and one day, coming out of mediation, I was given the word *rhizomes*. I discovered rhizomes are edible tuberous plant stems that are included in herbal allergy medications. I ate tubers, and my allergies dissipated. Another time I had underlying resentments I needed to address, as they were causing illness. I asked for a spiritual awakening, and in meditation I received the mental image of a holy card with a likeness of Christ's sacred heart. I interpreted the image as guiding me, "Keep your focus on my sacred heart, and open yourself up to love." Knowing this was a healing image, I held it mentally close. And I began the second phase of my healing spiritual journey. I reflected on how Jesus preached about creating a loving world. I also realized that when love was lost in a situation, he too became angry, which gave me the impetus to express my displeasure in such situations as well knowing resentments are often unexpressed anger. I hold the image close and rely on it daily, particularly with difficult personal relationships in which I recognize I close my heart and build resentment. And I continue to hold onto what Jesus taught. "Your faith has healed you" (Mark 10:52).

Imagination

Takeaways

Imagination assists in designing a desired life when strong belief is added to the desired image or request.

Imagination enables us to time travel to the past to heal painful memories and time travel to the future to increase the possibility of healthy desires and life goals becoming reality.

Images can assist in knowing your innermost image of God and your ideal self.

Within each of us is carried an image of God.

Springboards

Imagining Connection to Your Sacred Identity

- Imagine your authentic nature and spiritual essence is ethereal, sparkling, luminous, and beautiful, rich colors. You are pure consciousness-light through which no darkness can enter.
- Visualize yourself as spatially and temporally limitless, existing beyond the boundaries of your human body and having creative abilities.
- To further increase your psychic energy, imagine you are breathing in God's spirit. Imagine it is entering through the top of your head and landing in the midframe of your body, referred to energetically as the solar plexus area. This is an excellent meditation practice.
- Visualize being connected to every other human being through an unseen, loving, energy-filled cord, which extends from your heart to another's heart, and also to all others alive or on the other side if desired. This is the way to connect with deceased loved ones. If desired, imagine your cord reaches into the heart of Jesus.

- Imagine that you are like a diamond, the most precious mineral substance on earth-beautiful and brilliant. As a diamond, you have many facets, and as most diamonds, you also have flaws. Would you throw away a diamond because it is imperfect? Or would you still cherish the diamond for its unique, although flawed, beauty and inherent worth? You are, in fact, more precious than a diamond.
- Identify your ideal image. What motivates you? What do you have a passion for doing? How would you like your epitaph to read? How do you want to be remembered?
- When an image presents, ask, "Why did my soul produce this image? And what does it mean? What insight is my wise soul providing?" Identify the emotional and mental issue.

Notes

_____

_____

_____

_____

_____

_____

_____

_____

CHAPTER 4

The Cyclical Nature of Earthly Living

Life is about rotation. (Thomas Moore)

Perhaps you have noticed that you cycle. At times, we are spiritually centered and cycle in spiritual thinking, feeling, and acting with unconditional love. And at other times, we are solely earth focused. Cycling is a human way of being. Being of the earth we cycle like the earth on its axis within the Milky Way Galaxy, moving through the universe, and all the while, the seasons change. Winter brings the cold, followed by spring's gentle warmth. Plants germinate and grow, and the cycle completes with decay; new birth occurs the following year. We cycle in thinking, emoting, moving, and creating. The way in which each of us repetitively cycles in habits, the pursuit of our dreams, the desire to be cared for and feel a sense of belonging in relationships, and perhaps, to be successful in our spiritually driven human pursuits are examples of our cyclical nature. It is within these repetitive habits of thoughts and feelings we can uncover the changes needed to experience the contentment and joy we desire.

Change and growth are part of our spiritual and earthly cyclical nature. Our energetic force field is always in movement. As we explore, we cycle toward greater complexity and diversity. We do so until our life cycle completes, and we leave the human body and enter pure consciousness until soul returns with new information to heal the wounds soul carries from past incarnations and new skills for creating a loving self and safe, secure, and caring world for all. And very likely our cyclical nature stays with us as we pass to other realms. Change, growth, and desire for deeper unification continue after we transition.

One day, I was guided to recognize we never stop learning and experiencing, not on earth or in the spiritual realm. I was in my office getting ready for my next client. The room suddenly filled, almost to capacity, with human-looking spiritual souls. They were all standing perfectly still, attentive. I didn't know why they were there, but I went on with my day. As I counseled my clients, I noticed the spiritual souls were listening so attentively. I thought they were learning how to manage the difficult condition of clinical depression from my counseling depressed clients. I thought all these souls were spiritually evolving, perhaps cycling upward with the intentional desire to overcome depression for the transitioning to their next earthly journey. And so, we cycle in learning and evolving, prepare each of us to become authentic, individuated, unconditional loving being within the unified oneness of reality.

I desired to explain our cyclical nature with a concrete example of cyclical, earthly living promoting oneness between animate beings. I wanted the example to be about an out-of-the-ordinary experience, but something to which anyone could relate. My logical mind was at a loss. However, while keeping this request alive between my human and core self, I developed a desire to see eagles. In hindsight, I realize my soul was beginning to orchestrate an event to meet my request.

About a year later, I happened to be thinking about cycling and eagles while enjoying sailing. There was a warm breeze that day, and I spoke to my core self about the beauty of the moment, feeling grateful, as I watched two birds fly in a circle upward. I thought again about how life is circular, down to these two birds flying circularly upward. When I directed my husband to see this beauty, he said, "They are two eagles!" At that moment, I realized my cyclical experience was happening, an answer to an intentional request to see eagles I had made over the past year, and my other request to experience an out of the ordinary cycling. Periodically, cyclically, during the previous year, I visited places where eagles are seen just because I wanted to see one. I never did. But at that moment, when I least expected it, my intention was being answered. Think of all the synchronistic actions required for this event to occur! My husband and I had to choose to sail on that day, the wind had to be blowing in a certain direction for us to take the course that we chose, which happened to be where the eagles were flying that day, and we had to be there just at that particular time to witness the event. The experience reflects lots of planning by my core self within unified, loving consciousness. Yet I was not humanly consciously planning any aspect of the experience, as further evidenced by the fact that my husband chooses the course to sail. A few times since that day, I've sailed in the same direction at the same time, but I have not seen eagles again. However, I have the beautiful memory to fall back on when life becomes confusing. And several times as I was editing this section, I witnessed eagles flying in my neighborhood! I've lived in this neighborhood for thirty years and only while editing this section they appeared. I think to remind me to finish this book. I think to myself that I am always cycling, just like the eagles, hopefully moving upward on the wings of a loving unified consciousness.

The cyclical nature of human and spiritual life is historic. Without a doubt, these are tumultuous times. History suggests that humanity follows a cyclical pattern of experiencing times of turbulence followed by substantial personal and cultural growth. Today, we may benefit from reflecting on the time of John the Baptist and Jesus, when the Jewish nation was focused on the imbalance of power and wealth caused by the Roman occupation. The Jewish community was experiencing internal unrest and daily strife, with an ongoing fear of becoming a slave to the Romans, which was a real threat. Although a sense of desolation and despair existed, John the Baptist prepared the way for Jesus. He preached about the importance of focusing within one's self, on one's own thoughts, feelings, and actions, to break free of the consuming and paralyzing focus on the personal assault, political and financial war being waged by the Romans. Specifically, he suggested a change in consciousness by turning within to cleanse one's thoughts and feelings to loving thoughts and feelings to prepare for connection with Christ the savior. This approach constituted a turn of consciousness from focusing on external pressures and negativity, and fearful thoughts, feelings, and actions to focusing on living within a loving state of mind and heart. The human figure of Jesus embodied this approach. He was a man who possessed no worldly riches but miraculous internal riches. Integrated in mind, emotions, body, soul, and spirit, Jesus lived as the loving expression of integrated oneness, a unified human-and-divine man within a unified reality. He manifested a pathway to health, fulfillment, and inner joy. And through his life faith walk, Jesus became our example of how to think, feel, and act as a human being transforming Jesus into Christ, the revered holy figure emulated more than 2,000 years after his death. Today we need a turn in consciousness to be the loving, individuated human-and -divine being we each are.

Cyclical Nature

Takeaways

As human and divine beings, we are always cycling in habits, the pursuit of dreams, the desire to be cared for, and the need for belonging in caring relationships.

We each desire to be loved and experience contentment, joy, and follow a life purpose.

Change and growth are part of our spiritual and earthly cyclical nature.

Springboards

- Your eMAPs are cyclical programs. Note what behaviors, thoughts, and feelings you cycle in. Are you angry, happy, or sad most of the time? Do you complain every day? Do you express gratitude daily? How often do you think about building your personal material kingdom?
- Make a note of what thoughts, feelings, or behaviors are blocking you from your core self.

Notes

_____

_____

_____

_____

_____

_____

_____

_____

The Law of Attraction

We each cyclically live according to the natural law of attraction. We are energy beings and as such we attract and repel other energy beings. We draw toward ourselves people with similar thought or emotional patterns. Your powerful energetic capacity to create follows personal, intentional desires to be with people like you in thoughts, opinions, moods, and actions. As you move out into the world, you attract people who think as you do, feel as you do, and act as you do. In layperson's terms, "birds of a feather flock together."

Many of our initial desires develop in childhood. For example, if as a child you desire to rescue Mom who seems unhappy due to limited financial resources, don't be surprised that the man or woman you find attractive has a quality of needing rescued. This dynamic produces subconsciously the feeling of love for a man or woman. The ego likes familiarity and creates the familiar from past experiences developing eMAPs. In the example one needs rescued and one needs to rescue.

The law of attraction can work for you or against you in your life. If you think of yourself as depressed and feel depressed, you can attract others who feel and think as you do in a shared consciousness. If you find yourself residing in a vortex of fearful attitudes and beliefs, you can attract persons with similar fearful energy patterns. If you are happy, you pull toward yourself other happy people and live within a positive vortex.

Don't simply sit back, shake your head, and wonder why the universe appears unkind. Don't look outward; look inward! If you energize positive intentions, you will invoke in-kind positive experiences that uplift and fulfill you, meeting your positive intentions. If you energize negative intentions, you will invoke in-kind negative experiences and will attract persons experiencing the same eMAPs.

Although the reptilian ego brain is wired to always be on the lookout for threats to survival, and your conditioning can be traumatic, the good news is that intention produces change. The brain can be rewired to focus on positive thoughts and release unwanted attractions. In fact, on a daily basis, our intentions receive an in-kind response. This is the energetic capacity within you, fulfilling your intentions. However, the pull of a familiar attraction is strong, like that of a strong magnet, and you will need strong intentions to break free of the magnetic pull. To break the law of attraction's negative pull, change your disposition and find persons representing how you consciously *want* to think and feel.

In psychological terms, your capacity to make real what you believe is referred to as self-fulfilling prophecy, which points out the power of your intentional choices in creating your life. The fact that your prophecy comes true is due to the power of your intentions. If you feel blessed, you should not be surprised that blessings come your way. Your actions coincide with your beliefs, and you create your prophecy. Sometimes we are not aware of the power of our intentions and attend more to what we don't want. Attention is a creator tool. It is a mistake to focus attentions on what we do not want as attention empowers an intention. Do realize that what you are attending to materializes. I recall traveling with a coworker who strongly stated every time she drives on a particular road she is hit with a boulder from the hillside. I made the mistake of not realizing how she was setting her intention. And, the unusual occurred, we were hit with a boulder. As my daughter states, "we manifest what we desire". The nonjudgmental universe hears your thoughts, and meets your request, you can think about a thing and it comes your way. And this nonjudging consciousness does not understand no.

Desires for materiality also follows the natural law of attraction.

Within the energetic surroundings you attract materiality. Know that the stronger you set your will with belief, the more likely you manifest your intention. There's no magic involved. It is your creator capacity in which you move the external world to meet your needs whether it's people with the same intention or things. However, be careful not to build a selfish material world through listening to the ego mind.

Healing follows the same rules. If you believe you can heal yourself from maladies, so you can. It may take time, a change in diet, and certainly awareness and change of the attitudes and emotions that contributed to an illness. A strong desire and belief will set the law of attraction in motion for healing. The right doctors will come into your orbit, you will hear about medicines, herbal remedies.

The law of attraction points out that we are always cycling, pulling toward ourselves people, things, and experiences following the natural law of attraction. At times willingly, we follow the lead from our core self, even if it points us in a different direction. Let your soul pull you to people and places that meet your innermost desires. Alignment with your soul, is always preferred. The question is this: are we cycling upward or downward? When you are creating through your "I am" core self, your creation wheel spins upward, with gusto, creating your miracle path.

The Law of Attraction

Takeaways

The law of attraction is the concept that as an energetic creator, you answer your intentions by energetically pulling toward yourself situations, circumstances, and people that meet your conscious or subconscious intentions.

The law of attraction follows your attitudes, beliefs, feelings, thoughts, and actions, energetically pulling toward you like-minded people and experiences.

The law of attraction is in perpetual motion.

Your soul will work with you to break negative energetic pulls.

Springboard

- Which way is your creation wheel spinning? To spin upward-spiritually intentionally surround yourself with positive people.
- Identify your family dynamics to understand your energetic pulls.

> Surround yourself with people who are going to lift you higher. (Oprah Winfrey)

Notes

_____

_____

_____

_____

_____

_____

SECTION 3

Unplugging the Conditioned You from the eMAPs That Drive Your Life

CHAPTER 5

Your Mind Matters: The "M" or mental aspect of eMAP programs

Mind is the builder. (Edgar Cayce)

E of eMAPs

To understand our conditioning, we will analyze the mental, emotional, and visceral eMAP responses that create our habits, which influence our personality and identity. We develop an immediate response toward happenings in our personal environment. The quickness with which we develop these response habits is represented by the letter "e" of the abbreviation. The "e" represents the electronic way a thought, feeling, and behavior associated with the particular happening is triggered. For example, when the ego perceives a threat or an opportunity for self-advancement, it triggers a nerve impulse, an e, that activates a thought, emotion, and visceral body expression. The "e" has been triggered and the response is lightning fast. And the whole eMAP process occurs without conscious thought or choice.

The "e" further stands for ego as it is the ego who chooses the eMAP for a situation. So "e" is to remind each of us that ego is at work interpreting our lives for us. To control one's reactions and automatic conditioning responses, you will identify and stop the automatic "e" response.

"M" of eMAP: Mental as Life Builder

Within each of us, mind is the builder of life. Mind provides attention skills. What we think about we create in one's personal consciousness and in universal consciousness. Every thought, feeling, image, and action, initiated or experienced, is registered in consciousness. And what we create in thoughts follows our beliefs, often programmed in to each of us through a powerful conditioning process. We manifest what we believe, designing our lives to fit the conditioned beliefs. You are whom you have been taught to be. To refresh your memory, the "M" represents the eMAP mental habits based on *beliefs* that influence personality and form a conditioned self-concept. The "A" or affective state refers to emotions. And "P" refers to the physical actions or internal visceral responses experienced. The "e" refers to the lightning-fast way ego builds eMAPs responses. We habitually cycle in these conditioned mental, emotional, and physical ways.

Beliefs are the Mental Groundwork for eMAP Building

The most powerful aspect of conditioning is establishing beliefs. Beliefs are the mental groundwork for life building. Our beliefs are the basic building components, the conceptual bricks and mortar, which form how you perceive your world, as well as the interior, invisible wall system that gives structure to how you know yourself. Beliefs are the groundwork for responding to external and internal events, building the concept of who you believe you are and designs your life down to the details.

As mentioned, a toddler's mind is like a sponge learning and internalizing caretaker's beliefs, values, and opinions. The toddler takes in this information producing a hypnotic effect in which early family experiences establishes beliefs regarding whom to trust, how the world works and who you are. We each live under this hypnotic state which is an automatic and rigid process of building a conditioned identity. Beliefs formed and internalized before the age of reasoning are the strongest beliefs we possess. This means that many of your beliefs about who you are, which encase your identity, do so without your conscious choice! For example, I recall asking a child who was repeatedly burned with lit cigarette by his dad what he thought. He repeated the words of his dad. "My behavior was bad." In asking dad why he burned his son he stated, "my dad disciplined me this way and I turned out ok." This is an internalization process in which this child has internalized as his own his dad's beliefs. And, the belief travels through the generations. This is an extreme example, but your beliefs can be as strong.

As early beliefs form without conscious awareness, you are asleep at the wheel of consciousness, as you are not awake to the fact that most of what you think and feel, perceive and follow up with action, eMAPs, is a mirror of initial caretakers' beliefs, or a reaction against these early beliefs. Besides parental and familial influences, we each are influenced by values and expectations from contemporary culture and social connections. We desire belongingness and adapt our social face, our conditioned identity, to be pleasing and accepting to others. This external focus neglects attending to our inner world for self-definition. The challenge is to change any beliefs which block out awareness, core connection, and joy.

Our brain relies on learned beliefs to understand reality. And perception is controlled by the ego. What the ego perceives is determined by your beliefs and becomes your subjective reality. Objective true reality is not perceived. Your ego brings your conditioned, learned, and accepted beliefs into literal physical reality. Beliefs generate thoughts; thoughts evoke emotions and the body expresses the thought and feeling weaving together an eMAP, which becomes your conditioned habits that assists in managing your everyday life. An eMAP is a habitual repetitive pattern of thinking, feeling, and doing. And it all occurs without your conscious awareness, within the subconscious realm. This is the amazing power of beliefs conditionally rooted in childhood forming the tapestry of your life.

The ego utilizes the eMAPs to choose your reactions to life situations to organize and simplify your life. Life is complex today, and eMAPs accomplish the amazing feat of simplifying life into understandable thinking, feeling, and visceral repetitive reactions. However, often at the cost of awareness of one's true, loving, spiritual identity and living in the present instead of the past.

You can recognize your eMAP habits when you commonly think the same thoughts, experience the same feelings, and act in predictable ways. You are living in a conditioned way, a repetitive life. And the beliefs that you have been conditioned to live by and define you are embedded in these cyclical eMAP habits. These beliefs represent the "M" of an eMAP. The "M" is supported by emotions, "A," and your physical behaviors or visceral reactions, "P." We have hundreds of eMAPs. But most of our strong beliefs are established within our birth family.

To understand the power of beliefs, I share the journey of a woman I refer to as *I'm a Patsy*. She took on others' responsibilities as a way to feel love. This client found her job as a custodian perfectly mirrored her childhood choice to clean houses for families in her neighborhood as her way to feel good about herself. As *I'm a Patsy* grew up in a family in which she was always blamed when things went wrong, self-blame became a strong belief for her. It rooted her personality, and it carried over into her adult life in her role as a school custodian. In the workplace, seeking to avoid the painful feelings and low self-esteem that accompanied he self-blame belief, *I'm a Patsy* did other custodians' tasks to gain approval and self-esteem. Her coworkers, along with a supervisor, continually berated her work, which caused her to try even harder and do even more. Although *I'm a Patsy* knew she was doing a good job, and in fact, the principal many times had complimented her performance, the strength of her core belief in being to blame and not good enough controlled her actions and self-feelings. There was no room for spiritual awareness. *I'm a Patsy* never confronted her coworkers about their beratement of her. Wanting to do God's work to feel better about herself, she convinced herself that accepting their criticism was part of being a good Christian, specifically, "turning the other cheek." Therefore, *I'm a Patsy* endured the treatment by telling herself that she was working on humility, tolerance, and acceptance, while cycling in feeling depressed and guilty.

One day, she was accused of stealing. This was her soul's way to answer her strong intentional prayer or request to feel better about herself as being labeled as a thief was not a belief in her personal knowing of herself. This perceived undesired event released her repressed righteous anger. Her tolerance for negative, self-blaming thoughts was exceeded by the accusation of thievery. However, her strong emotional reaction released a strong harmonized physical reaction; she developed a severe headache, which was later diagnosed as a symptom of a neurological condition. At this junction she entered therapy.

Entering therapy allowed *I'm a Patsy* to feel, without guilt, her justified anger as she finally recognized the truth: she was being treated unjustly. She filed a complaint and went on workmen's compensation because of the neurological issue. She worked also on throwing out her faulty beliefs and finding self-love.

I chose this woman as an extreme example of the power of beliefs. However, your core beliefs are as strong no matter how successful you are in building a conditioned self-concept. As *I'm a Patsy's* journey points out, beliefs form your conditioned knowing of yourself and your world. I also have a niece who set her goals early in life as to where she wanted to live, the income level her family would have, the qualities of the man she would marry and the ways she would raise her children. Her life has had bumps as we all do, but the clarity of her goals has led to her reaching these goals.

You are the builder of consciousness and breaking free of limiting beliefs programmed in through a conditioning process releases your core identity. For conscious awakening, build on unconditional self-love and care for self and others. Doing so is transformative. Unconditional Love has the innate power to undo hypnotic effects from parental child rearing beliefs regarding who you are. Doing so opens you to defining "who you are". Create your miracle path through the transformative power of love Again, what you believe and think, you create in consciousness. Beliefs that fuel behavior can breed disease as well as heal disease as you spread loving thoughts and feelings.

You create through imagination, insights, and intrinsic creativity, skills existing beyond conditioning. As such can provide access to higher spiritual realms of awareness, tapping into the guiding intelligence of your "I am" core self. Your core self always knows what you are thinking, dreaming, and desiring and complements your loving actions with loving actions. These are times when your unconditioned aspirations take hold. So, have "M" represent core mind not just the ego brain.

Ego Functions and Characteristics

The ego serves the mental function of maintaining eMAPs. Here is a review on ego.

- **Organization of perceptions**. The ego gathers the information from your five senses-all that you see, hear, taste, smell, and touch-notes perceptions, and produces reactions into predictable patterns referred to as eMAP programs to assist functioning.
- **Ego** monitors your automatic emotional reactions and generates the appropriate behavioral response. For example, based on incoming sensory data, the ego tells where you may safely place your foot on the ground. Ego will guide your response to all situations. Ego as gatekeeper of your perceived reality.
- **Creation of mental components of eMAPs**. The ego creates MAP programs specific to you, based on factors such as your conditioned learnings and genetics.
- **Repetition of behavior patterns.** The ego likes to follow the well-worn neural roads in the brain that keep life predictable. It encourages repetition of behavior patterns. In effect, the ego creates a stimulus-response playback system that uses eMAP programs to provide a sense of security and predictability.
- **Fears Change and Unconditional Love.** Ego fears change. The ego will cause you to think the same thoughts, experience the same emotions, and reenact the same responses, virtually in autopilot mode. It fears love as it is an emotion it does not understand and believes unconditional love threatens survival.
- **Control and conditioning of human will.** The ego fights to keep its center-stage role in your life. The ego chooses responses according to familiar and predictable MAP patterns as ego believes it can

control the outcome of events, both external and internal, through minimizing change.

- **Determination of conditioned self-identity**. Simply put, the ego maintains who you think you are instilled in you by responses of significant others, your community, and your culture. The ego shapes your identity, recognizing what works to provide safety, security, and self enhancement.

- **Constant surveillance for threats**. The ego always scans the horizon for danger or problems as it intently strives to avert or mitigate threats. This function is not inherently detrimental. The ego's job is to keep you alive. However, ironically, by overdoing its job, it keeps you focused on problems rather than mindfully choosing to basically feel safe and loved.

- **Preferred recollection of undesired events.** As undesired events are viewed as physically threatening to the ego, it remembers the survival threat of undesired events more so than positive events; it skews your outlook on life.

- **Lives in the past.** Ego's automatic responses are to reenact past experiences. It's eMAPs are based in past experiences. Ego places present experiences in to past learning matrices as much as allowed by the human side of soul, psyche.

- **Use of separation strategies.** Ego's follows separation strategies. It follows an *I me, mine* philosophy. In its reptilian functioning its first response is to attack, not accept differences between people and "you and me ego against the world of others." Me feels like self, but it is the ego at work

- **Assign blame.** When a problem arises, the ego seeks to separate you from the issue and cast the blame upon others. However, the ego is also fickle: if the ego cannot reconcile matters by blaming another, it will turn against you. To keep you alive it will blame you for the problem. This is the first response in rape situations, however illogical that may be.

- **Inability to rationalize**. The ego does not think; it cannot think abstractly or creatively. It can only surmise, perceive patterns, and repetitively apply your matching or closest-fitting eMAP programs to solve problems.

- **Ego invents problems**. If left to its own devices, ego will invent a problem to keep your mind preoccupied, perhaps to ensure its importance and control. At other times it becomes your worst enemy as it blames and criticizes. Keeping your attention focused on problems blocks out core connection.
- **Disinterest in objective truth**. The ego neither understands nor cares about objective truth.
- **Negation of the spiritual realm**. The ego does not have any control over the spiritual realm. Ego causes you to forgets spiritual happenings.
- **Ego cannot tolerate ambiguity, contradictions, or conflict**. It becomes subordinate to your core following your directives.
- **Ego** can transcend to functioning as the gatekeeper for spiritual awareness.

Thinking Blocks to Spiritual Awareness

Self-Doubt

Too often the ego has been conditioned to believe unhealthy self-thoughts such as *I am not good enough* and other self-doubting thoughts. Living in a chronic state of self-doubt is unhealthy. Negative thoughts are a common eMAP block to core connection. It is human to have self-doubt. When we try a new activity, it is normal to question one's ability to meet the new challenge. Self-doubt is meant to help you decide a course of action. We cannot usually exceed at every challenge and activity we try. To be OK with not being proficient or successful in some challenging areas is a natural happening. Knowing yourself, looking back over your life and noticing the types of decisions from your personal past that were productive and helpful, can give you the necessary inner strength to continue to combat the overuse of self-doubt. However, never doubt your core self's willingness to guide you. You are a spiritual being more loved than a mother loves her child no matter mistakes.

Rationalization

Have you ever convinced yourself that bad behavior was understandable and acceptable? You are rationalizing away your responsibility for your behavior.

Denial

When we cannot accept within ourselves behavior that goes against how we desire to view ourselves, we each can simply say no, I didn't do that, I didn't say that, hear that, or refusing to admit the truth.

"M" of MAPs

Takeaways

Mind ("M") is the builder of your life. Attention, a mental function, places you into earth reality in which you create your life.

Beliefs mold into thoughts that are governed by a conditioned self or by a consciously awakened self.

The "M" is supported by your emotions ("A") and your actions ("P").

The ego, a structure within the brain, is charged with maintaining eMAPs to govern one's life.

We have hundreds of eMAPs. But our strongest beliefs are established within our family, from birth.

We are all one energetically connected within a loving, unified consciousness or within the one mind of God.

Our mental intentions, with or without conscious awareness, create our lives.

Due to conditioning we can be on autopilot, repetitively thinking, feeling, and acting the same throughout our life.

Perception determines awareness and will expand with a change in motivation and primary identity.

Self-doubt, rationalization and denial are some of the blocks to core self connection.

imagination, insights, and intrinsic creativity, are mental skills existing beyond conditioning.

Springboard

- Identify negative self-beliefs and identify your beliefs regarding others that stand in the way of interior spiritual connection.
- Accept your limitations. Know what you can and cannot do.
- Own your spiritual identity.
- Replace negative thoughts with a thought that is more objective and realistic. If you desire, simply replace with acknowledgment of your spiritual inheritance.

> My thoughts have infinite organizing power. (Deepak Chopra)

> All healing and constructive thinking lies within the realm of your own consciousness. It is how you apply it that brings healing and constructive change. (Edgar Cayce)

Notes

_____

_____

_____

_____

_____

_____

_____

Beliefs to Own

- Can you believe that you at this very moment you are creating consciousness in which your beliefs, thoughts, visceral expressions, and feelings are molding your perception of reality, just as wind influences the day's temperature?
- Can you believe that you are consciousness itself, unseen consciousness, without boundaries, without limits, existing beyond space and time limits, eternal and a powerful creator?
- If you desire to be consciously and unconditionally loving, for one month, respond to all life happenings with a form of care and love such as acceptance?
- Can you be open and receptive, awake and alert to movements in your life, and movements within you that reaffirm a loving life path?

The Power of Self-Talk

> Your responsibility to yourself as well as to the divine law, is to keep yourself inwardly poised and to keep your thoughts positive and loving in spite of injustice or disorder around you. (Eric Butterworth)

To assist in creating a desired life it's important to recognize the power of thought including thoughts we are not consciously aware of. The ego, in its conditioned goal to maintain control for your (and its) safety, keeps you thinking, cycling around conditioned beliefs formed into eMAPs. It is a fact that each of us thinks throughout the day. This is free-flowing inner talk, and it strongly influences your self-opinions influencing self-esteem and self-concept. If you have developed a positive responding ego, likely with core connection, you work at maintaining positive inner dialogue. However, ego is always looking for a problem which may threaten survival and easily invests in negative thinking patterns. Negative thinking eMAP patterns will need to change for spiritual awakening. Remember you are eternal and powerfully creative.

Identify your inner thinking eMAP pattern for healthy change.

Whatever you think about repeats in your brain and consumes your attention. The net result is your unaware self-talk is defining you, establishing your self-concept, influencing personality and character structure. And all your thoughts are being written within unified consciousness.

Explore the feelings associated with the self-talk. Awareness of your thoughts also helps explain mood changes, knowing why you feel as you do on a certain day, as well as keeps you alert to the ego's maneuvering. Get to the roots of the eMAP to provide yourself a change opportunity for growth as a human being. Changing free-flowing thoughts to reflect your highest intentions, and changing activities to change your mood is a positive step on the journey to meeting your spiritual ideals and personal goals.

As you and your core are one in spirit to talk to your core increases connection, another form of self talk. As well you can listen for core communication just as you listen for ego maneuvering.

By noticing self-talk, you develop an objective observing aspect within self; you become aware. Awareness leads to awakening, being in more conscious control over your life, and awareness of the movement of spiritual reality. Invite your authentic Christ nature, your core self, to influence your thoughts. Allow self-talk to work for you.

Self-Talk

Takeaways

What you say to yourself without conscious awareness has a powerful influence on your thoughts. feelings and behavior

Your core self is always within earshot so remember there are no idle thoughts; all thoughts create.

Springboard

- To have conscious control over the "M" of eMAPs, pay attention to your inner chatter, stop every hour of your day, and notice what you have been saying to yourself through your inner dialogue. Keep track of your self-talk internal dialogue to promote necessary changes in thoughts for spiritual and human health and well-being.

- Write down your negative and positive self-talk. Choose to replace any negative thoughts with a self- love positive thought.
- Remember the ego likes control, so journal and identify your problem thoughts and feelings to work on positive change in thoughts and feelings.

Notes

_____

_____

_____

_____

_____

_____

_____

Developing the Observational Ego

Objective Observation: A Witness Stance in Life

Watching self go by. (Edgar Cayce, *The Sleeping Prophet)*

One of the tools to identify your unhealthy eMAPs is to objectively observe yourself as if from a distance. As you mindfully observe your conditioned self without immediate reactions, you are entering the flow of your life. Through practice of direct observation, you will experience a natural rhythm to all life. By learning to stop and look within for interpretation of happenings in your life, you learn to control your automatic thinking, feeling, and doing habits, moods stop sweeping you away from objective thought and emotional control, feelings are modulated so that emotionally you do not bounce around like a beach ball in the wind. No longer investing in strong emotional reactions, you remove the emotional drain on your energy. What a release! And objective observation keeps you out of the red zone of toxicity as your body is not releasing fight-flight chemicals. You are healthier mentally, emotionally and physically, and disease does not have a breeding ground. Once you stop automatic feeling responses and actions, let your thinking expand. Most important identify rigid thinking habits that block awareness of your spiritual "I am" core self and core movement in your life. Rigid thinking patterns are unhealthy eMAPs and need to be released. As a therapist would explain, by disinvesting, detaching, and disidentifying from ego interpretations, eMAPs, you allow your automatic response to go into extinction. You open your way of thinking to consider alternative interpretations of personal experiences.

Through objective observing, stop, look within, and listen for core wisdom, you provide a space for core communication. Consider the observation of Victor Frankl, Auschwitz survivor and founder of ego psychology. "Between stimulus and response there is a space. In that space is our power to choose our response. In our response lies our growth and our freedom." By producing this space, you become awakened to your own presence, beyond the limiting constraints of human conditioning.as you objectively see the good in the bad life events, and hopefully lovingly accept all components of self and others. Now, you have freed yourself from the pressures of the ego and its conditioned eMAP response habits. No longer do you distort reality to fit your eMAP protocol. Blocking unhealthy eMAP responses allows the holistic and integrative path to open. And with awareness you feel more real, more present, more awake, and more alive.

Holding attention with inner awareness brings about the ego mind's willingness to change in order to maintain its authority and central position as gatekeeper of reality. Ego cannot tolerate dichotomies. You suggesting new eMAPs based in truth, honesty and love produces conflict for the ego. It will find a way to integrate new eMAPs. Remember you are the boss with authority over all of self. As ego transcends, it notifies you of the intersecting of spiritual life and earthly life as ego learns to objectively observe. You no longer need to wear the limiting glasses of the reptilian ego.

The transcendent function of your core self takes hold when ego and your core align and you enter a nondual accepting world. As you practice objective observation, your feelings of inner peace and love will grow. As you stay the course, fears and insecurities dissipate as awareness leads to inner peace, knowledge of self as eternal, and fundamental well-being. You will attract more loving people and experience love, following the universal spiritual law of attraction "like begets like." You mindfully observe your life leading to managing your life based on conscious choices. Monitoring your awareness and intentions strengthens the mind and over time rewire your brain.

If on a quest for expanded awareness of yourself as a vital component of a larger and loving reality, ask yourself, "How do I maintain inner peace and calmness while experiencing a life problem, or how can I express care while holding someone accountable for harmful actions? How do I express my spiritual goals, such as kindness and care, at all times? What form of love, such as sympathy, mercy, forgiveness, and unconditional acceptance, do I need more of in my life?" You choose your personal and spiritual goals for building a conditioned free life.

While working on evolving bringing the superconscious into conscious reality, maintain your personal boundaries and positive attitude. You do not allow your ego, a situation, or others to negatively influence you. And there may be persons close to you who may be threatened by spiritual awakening and do try to pull you down to a negative energy level. You decide your reactions rather than ego or others. In addition, when you practice objective observation, it benefits a meditation practice as you have learned to quiet your mind and your emotions.

Objective Observation

Takeaways

Objective observation helps to identify habits that block awareness of your spiritual components.

Objective observation assists in maintaining your personal boundaries, limiting others' influences.

Objective observation helps you to control your feelings so you are not emotionally bouncing around like a ball in the wind.

Through observing, rather than immediate reacting, you are out of the red zone of physical toxicity.

Objective observation provides inner mental space and freedom to gradually assist the ego in recognizing core movement in your life.

The ego communicates spiritual happenings to regain its influence and position. In its expanded role, the ego promotes harmony between the human self and your core self.

Springboards

- At the end of the day, reflect on how you handled each of your day's experiences. Did you take time to observe happenings from an objective stance, and did you allow unhealthy eMAPs to pass by without responding?
- Consciously focus your awareness on being present to the moment and listening for core guidance.
- Visualize freeing yourself from conditioned thoughts, feelings, and actions, eMAPs, so that your sacred core can be heard.
- Repeat often the following phrase: "I choose to disengage from the 'myth of the given' and give myself time to respond to life from the wide-angle lens of my true core self."

Notes

_____

_____

_____

_____

_____

_____

CHAPTER 6

"A" or Affective: Emotional Aspect of eMAP Programs

> You know to do good is to just be kind, just be patient, just friendly, just loving to others! These are the fruits of the spirit, and they bear fruit in the hearts and the minds and in your soul of those you give such to.
>
> —Edgar Cayce

THE "A" OR affective state referred to in the abbreviation eMAP refers to emotional expression. We are emotional human beings experiencing a wide range of emotions. We seek, rage, lust, care, play, panic, and are happy, sad, joyful, or fearful, or perhaps we live consistently in a state of unconditional love, contentment, and joy. We enter the world to experience this wide range of emotions and doing so makes us each humanly real, not robots. Emotions validate our external experiences and motivate each of us to respond. Emotions are spontaneous awareness in motion. We grieve the loss of loved ones on the earth plane, we experience the shock of killing others unless television violence has numbed you emotionally, and we each emotionally experience the dying process of oneself.

Desire influences our emotional journey. We create what we desire.

Desires are ego or soul oriented. Ironically, due to conditioning, we are unaware that we create the stepping stones and stumbling blocks of our lives. We create through subconscious ego control.

One's creation wheel begins to move with emotional expression and in a harmonious way thinking and viscerally feeling is added, an eMAP is created. Your internal emotional state is triggered by one's ego and/or soul. Ego is the gatekeeper emotionally labeling what you see, hear, and experience. Ego links together the emotional-sensory information, screen happenings in the external world, chooses thoughts from past experiences, validates the cognitions- thoughts, forms a mental impression, and directs the body to viscerally respond in a harmonious way. One's emotion triggered the eMAP response. Our human system works this way to avoid being overwhelmed by life's complexity, for coherence, simplicity's sake, self-protection, and enhancement. As soul does not live in the past, but the present, soul can suggest new opportunities, new ways of experiencing joy.

Thoughts can also trigger the ego to respond to an internal or external event with a chosen emotion and physical expression; the response is likely based on opinions, judgments, expectations, and beliefs. It is a complex process simplified by the ego into a predictable and familiar eMAP. Because a response is familiar and predictable, it is desired; even when the consequences for doing so are negative. So, don't wonder why you keep choosing unlovable women or distant males. Thoughts we maintain from childhood through adulthood are based on early conditioning and are subjective, not objective. Thoughts and emotions can be wrong and counterproductive. So don't wonder why you easily feel threatened by someone whose opinions do not agree with yours, or feel anxious, worry about the future, or are obsessed with building a material kingdom. The ego needs a job. And culture, reinforced by your caretakers and significant others, emotionally conditions each of us to listen to the ego, which reinforces fear-based thinking, feeling, and actions. We are automatically programmed believing value, approval, self-esteem are based in ego conditioning. And conditioned emotions, chosen by the ego, also follow the rules of feeling easily physically threatened and too often responding with attack, which denies one's true identity and invites anxieties, fears and depression.

And who has started this downfall, the ego. The human you is hurt, angry or sad because the ego is hurt, angry or desiring revenge, though it feels like you. This does not produce long-lasting positive self-feelings or positive results. Herein lies our dilemma: we rely on the ego, a fear-based mechanism, to design our lives, but in doing so, we are designing our lives to manage fear! This may have worked well when humans were living in caves. Have we evolved from this fear-based conditioning today? Perhaps not.

To support integrative stable personal and spiritual health, emotions and opinions, judgments and beliefs will lift your spirit when reflecting core spiritual values such as kindness, compassion, and mercy. No matter the situation it is responding according to higher values, which produce feelings of internal stability, safety, security, and overall feeling good about oneself. As well learning to manage human responses through immediate non reaction helps. Wait until the strength of the hurtful emotion has passed and decide your response. Remind yourself that you are an "I am" part of the original, sustaining, intelligent force guiding the universe, the "I AM". This is your true eternal identity.

Love Emotion

We are also faced with another dilemma: to experience love in human relationships, one must meet conditioning-imposed requirements, some of which are necessary for society to evolve and some of which oppose the knowing of self as an unconditional loving, human and divine being. And yet, unconditional love is our inherent nature. Should love come with a metaphorical price tag? And it is ironic that the ego, a fear-based mechanism, presently controls how we know, give, receive, and withhold love.

We live in a world in which we depend upon one another for survival. We rely on others to provide goods and services, and also, we have a deep, inborn need for human connection. This means the inborn desire for unity resides *within each of us*. We need to feel loved. Can it be that some of the problems we face today are due to lack of acknowledging this inborn need to be a unified, loving people in favor of narrow self-interest pursuits? What do you think has promoted racial inequality, which growing movements such as Black Lives Matter seek to address and the plight of underprivileged with our citizens lacking food and medical care? Problems which will continue as food resources deplete. If we listen to our deeper self, would we stop before we act and consider how our intentions may affect others?

Interconnection with others makes us healthy emotional beings and actually evolves the brain. Yes, our brain develops through connection with others. Our relational experiences build neural networks within the brain. Yet we rely on the self-serving ego for managing emotions and relationships. Perhaps we come into this world to evolve through experiencing the depth and breadth of loving as we work out a life plan for ourselves and our global world.

We are amazingly emotional creatures, whether we walk a slow or quick pace on our journey toward knowing loving wholeness in mind, body, spirit, and soul. Is the next evolutionary step to wrap all emotions with the energy of unconditional love from your core self? The pathway to joy is to support and express unconditional love-based feelings in all situations. This is the gift within our spirit. On a societal level, each of us is charged with opening to the desire for unity and using his or her inherently loving nature to evolve culture and build a safe, secure, and unified world, thereby ensuring survival of the planet. This does not exclude accountability for harmful actions for this too is a loving act. Yes, we are creatures of habits, of eMAPs. But we can use our habitual ways to design spiritual eMAPs founded on nonjudgment of a person's worth and value based on external criterion and recognize God exists *within each of us*. We each can feel, think, and act with humility, patience and courage to express love in an unloving situation. Each of us can honor the face of another's divinity, knowing we all are on a journey but have not arrived at the destination of being one within a unified, loving consciousness or whatever divinely intelligent force it is that organizes the universe and assists in organizing each of our lives. And we can use our core loving energy to manage our fears, anxieties, angers, and frustrations, along with our addictions and desires to consume, and at times hoard, the resources of the world. In doing so we each are on the path for all people to be fed and have shelter.

Following this path can be fear producing, fears you may not have enough. We each must feel all our feelings. At a personal level, we can interpret all our negative feelings as signals that unconditional love within a situation is at risk. We can face our fears about negative or undesired feelings, the shadowlike underside of our nature. We can allow ourselves to feel unwanted feelings, such as guilt, shame, anxiety, worry, or protective anger, by accepting them while not believing in this illusion of reality, holding firm to keeping love in situations that produce these negative feelings. Doing so engages one's "I am" core self and breaks through conditional fears and negative feelings. You ensure fear cannot find a home within you. Choosing to think, feel, and act in a loving way is the only emotional choice that will free each of us from emotional imprisonment. Feel unconditional love emanating from your core self, which points out that your core is on a path of influence, assisting each of us to resolve issues and evolve spiritually through our choices. Health in mind, heart, and body is based on the true needs and wants of your human self, in cooperation with your spiritual core, which desires to love you and spread genuine love in the world through you. Not through self-gain, rather because you desire to spread the love you feel to others. What are the ingredients of *your* conditioning?

Emotional Blocks to Core Connection, Your False God

> Human fear is the last vestige of the natural man before
> he accepts God's grace.
>
> (Randy Becton)

Fear

The opposite of love is fear. Love rules your core self while fear is the emotional energy of the ego. As with all emotions, fear is a healthy, innate, visceral reaction that plays a legitimate role in interpretation of our world. As a built-in alarm system, it signals danger for you to assess. Or fear can simply be a reminder that something in your life is about to change, such as getting a new job, moving to a new location, or taking up scuba lessons. When you try a new activity, you will experience some degree of fear. Perhaps fear initially arises only to make sure you firmly want to move forward with a new activity. Yet it appears fear is always around the corner making it an underlying root of most of the ills of humankind.

Today, perhaps more so than at any other time in our history as a nation, Americans face the fear of potential physical harm virtually everywhere, from churches to schools and any place where crowds gather. And any one of us can fear the unknown or the unpredictable, fear what others think of us, fear losing power or status, fear poverty, including loss of wealth, which can lead to compulsively building a material world, or even fearing one's neighbor. Cycling in kinship fear states of self-doubt, living in a state of worry, fears of abandonment, rejection, or failure, feelings of shame, chronic guilt, continual obsessive-compulsive issues, or self-protecting anger responses are the result of the fear emotion. The ego has been conditioned to respond in an automatic and repetitive way according to the chosen fear state in which, ironically, the ego merely uses the fear energy to continue its search for threats, maintaining the beliefs that you are not safe and secure. Fear places each of us in a chaotic, reactive state to any sign you are not in control of the external world, to any life changes. Fear has become the false god that consumes your time and attention, having the qualities of a magnet with the goal of controlling your perceptions of reality. And reality includes self-perceptions.

When the ego's conditioned urges are at odds with your soul's more universal, loving concerns, a state of duality is experienced. With the lack of agreement between core self and ego, you experience internal conflict and can feel split in two. Fear builds a false reality of internal separateness, chaos, and conflict. "Am I good enough? Am I going to be harmed? Am I loved?" become issues in the dualistic search to define good and bad, right and wrong. To have faith and trust in a loving consciousness is nonexistent when fear is a chronic and controlling state of mind. Death is viewed as the final event you experience, without conscious life afterward. And emotionally as you give in to fear, fear takes over and this fear-based mindset can root with beliefs that, somehow, I or others are innately bad, evil, or inferior.

Complicating matters, a fear-based person may be unable to notice positive happenings, believing life is only to be feared as one waits for the next problem to arise. And such a person will find it difficult to generate positive thoughts or express gratitude. We may search for love and care to combat fear, but paradoxically, at the same time you can be consumed with finding things to fear following the habit of fear. The more you give in to fear, the more fear controls you. A fear-based orientation pulls toward oneself persons and situations, like a magnet, that energize still more fear as the natural law of attraction suggests. The more one looks for fear, the more things to fear are found. This is your self-fulfilling prophecy at work. What a paradox; we ignite fear while the desire for others to love us unconditionally burns brightly within each of us!

When fear takes over, not only do you lose personal autonomy but also the spiritual knowledge of self as a cocreating, timeless spiritual presence. You cannot hear the voice of the authentic core self, which points out the true path to safety, security, spiritual awakening, and soul evolvement. Without core connection and adequate healthy unconditional self-love and love for and from others, the self-involved fear focus remains. And so, regardless of the need to find the meaning and purpose of our life, when fear is your common mental-emotional state the fear eMAP habit is the response, further fueling fear. This is the power of the emotion of fear; it is your false god in control of your consciousness. If you rely on the ego, a fear-energized structure, to identify the path to health, happiness, safety, and security, your reasoning is faulty.

While it is healthy to allow yourself to feel all the feelings arising within you always, we each need to monitor these internal states, compare our initial reactions to responses on how we want to choose to deal with these internal feelings, and so respond with emotional control, clarity, and free choice. We need not allow fear to magnetize our awareness. We each can choose to think, feel, and act in loving ways, to promote personal autonomy and societal evolvement.

Could it be possible that knowing and feeling safe and secure is not based on the external world? What if feeling safe and secure is based on knowing oneself as an integral part of a loving, intelligent, unified consciousness and having faith in these creative forces, often referred to as God? How much are you willing to step out of your comfort zone and so believe? We each need to be willing to give up loyalty to the fear-based ego. It is possible that our fear, along with the chaos, dissension, and hatred that they produce, are creating evil and possibly our destruction. As president John F. Kennedy stated in his "Peace Speech," "We all inhabit this small planet. We all breathe the same air… we all cherish our children's future." These ideas have been echoed by all the great men and women of our world.

You can win the battle against fear and its many forms by holding firm to unconditional love, including accountability. The ego will eventually bow to your decision. When the ego clearly knows you are in control, it allows awareness of spiritual matters. And an open loving disposition feeds your core. Right action follows. So simply use fear feelings as a warning signal. Do not live in fear. Remember what you perceive, you intend and build. Walking through fears provides inner strength. Replace fear with love, and you will never be lonely and helpless.

Fear

Takeaways

Fearful emotions are meant to trigger awareness that change is coming and that you may have reached the edge of your comfort zone.

Fear leads to state of chaos, overprotection of self, anger, anxiety, shame, guilt, chronic worry, obsessive compulsive issues as ways to combat fear while paradoxically strengthening fear through these emotional avenues.

Fear is likely the underlying root of many of individual ill health and societies problems of today.

Fear blocks out your core self and its wisdom as well as blocking out joy that comes with core connection.

Fearful feelings can be controlled by you by maintaining your spiritual goal of being a loving being in thought, word, action, and feelings.

Springboard

- When you feel afraid, stay with the emotion, breathe deep into your groin, and imagine opening your loving heart to jump-start the relaxation response. Remember old patterns run deep in the survival mind. Activate love, and confront fears with the knowledge that you are an integral part of a unified, loving consciousness.
- When fearful feelings are felt, you can acknowledge them and then let them pass. Do not energize with feelings or thoughts. Learn to let them pass knowing fear is not an objective, appropriate feeling. Without thoughts building fear, the physiological state passes.
- It is best to replace fear with positive feelings and thoughts and explore what thoughts, feelings, and actions will be needed to keep you in a calm, core state.

    The only thing we have to fear is fear itself. (Franklin Roosevelt)

Notes

_____

_____

_____

_____

_____

_____

_____

_____

_____

Shame: A Fear Tool of the Ego

> Shame is the warm feeling that washes over us, making us
> feel small, flawed, and never good enough. (Brené Brown)

Adam and Eve, in the biblical story of Genesis, were Christians' first
teachers about the feeling of shame when they covered their genitals,
feeling vulnerable and unworthy, knowing they had disobeyed God. At
some point along our journey, we each have experienced shame.

Shame is a strong emotion. In its positive form it is meant to
remind one of poor choices which do not fit into the conditioned
identity. You have acted in wrong ways. A conditioned identity is
commonly based on being a labeled a good person, acting in right
ways identified by one's social group. When shame becomes a
chronic feeling, it prevents a person from feeling natural self-worth.
Chronic shame generates intensely painful feelings suggesting one is
inherently flawed and does not deserve to be attended to, cared for,
and loved. A shamed person can feel underlying anger and depression
and perhaps hate and envy. Such feelings are in disagreement with
your core self and can lead to feelings of being split apart internally,
unable to reach core connection as well as having an unhealthy self-
concept. Eventually inner turmoil can then lead to feelings of being
inherently evil.

Emotional security is nonexistent when a person lives in a shame-
based state, which causes an inability to bond with others, as the journey
of *I Am Nobody* illustrates. He is a thirty-five-year-old single man who
entered therapy for treatment of long-term chronic depression. He
initially viewed himself as a nobody and thought that this was his fate
in life and change was not possible. Yet his spiritual desire was to feel
love; he desired to feel genuine feelings of care and love for himself. And
his personal goal was to share genuine, felt feelings of love with others.
However, being raised to feel ashamed of himself, he did not feel he
could ever feel safe enough, or trust enough, to genuinely connect with
others. His spiritual strength of faithfulness was misdirected as he was
loyal to the ego and its nobody beliefs. He lived without felt love and

joy. And likely the hidden anger regarding his inner beliefs kept him from making positive change.

Unfortunately, *I Am Nobody* was raised to negate any internal desires resonating from within his core. Living was a chore for *I Am Nobody*, and he conditionally believed his job *was* to be what others wanted him to be as his only way to come close to feeling loved. He always felt like a fake and unsafe.

The ego of *I Am Nobody* was rigidly developed and powerful as he strictly followed his belief of being a nobody. When he swayed and did something for himself, his ego released fear and internal battering self-talk, which was intense and accompanied by more intense feelings of being inherently worthless, unlovable, and incapable of doing anything right. Although feeling "not good enough" is a common human feeling, it is meant to occur when we try to become proficient at something that is not in our skill set. And having an internal dialogue that reminds us of this fact is healthy, so long as the inner critic is not punitive. However, *I Am Nobody* had to work moment to moment to ward of the punitive criticism he received from his inner critic. Needless to say, *I Am Nobody* had much difficulty maintaining the belief that he was a powerful, intentional spiritual presence, nor could he hold onto the belief he could create a meaningful life. He trusted no one, including himself, was devoid of emotional connection, and was emotionally numb-that is, without felt feelings. Whenever he desired to open up to others honestly about any thought or feeling, this consistently set him up for more internal battering as his ego was shame focused believing this was the path of safety and survival for him. He stated he had learned to connect with others in an unemotional way, as if they were only representations of people, such as the king and queen of a card deck. Certainly, he was one of the saddest clients I had worked with in my then forty years of practice.

However, his personal goals in alignment with his loving soul continued to produce inner conflict, as it knew his true desire underneath his conditioning was a man who desperately wanted to love himself and be in felt personal connection with others. I'm sure his soul, in connection with the unified, loving God consciousness, had difficulty finding a way to answer his true desire for personal connection. And yet, it did find a way, through a perceived undesired event: his employment became unstable, which forced him to put up a loving intention for himself. Specifically, *I Am Nobody* wanted to remain at his present place of employment, at his present salary, and perform more challenging work. And he wanted to have a supportive boss. This was not a small request. The position he was leaving paid well, although he lacked the requisite educational background for such a well-paying position. Fortunately, when one is working within the spiritual dynamic of one's core self, earth reality limits do not apply.

To activate his intention, *I Am Nobody* was asked to believe he was important and loved by his own interior core and believe that his needs would be answered. Believing was not easy for *I Am Nobody*, and many months passed, with consistent reminding from me that an open heart and belief are needed to ignite a request and attract a different outcome. He continued doing his interior work, undid much of his conditioning blocks of fear and beliefs of having no control over his life, and finally felt a touch of self-love and asked with belief for a desired position. *Immediately* his request was answered and almost exactly as he had requested, except with respect to the desired salary; he received $25,000 less than his prior salary. You would think he would continue to trust and have an open heart. However, the ego is powerful, is often in charge, and does not like spiritual matters it cannot control. Ego has you forget the small and large miracles that happen. And so, his ego suggested to *I Am Nobody* that the job was somehow just fortuitous, while the inner critic attempted to ramp up the conditioned cyclical reasons supporting his being a nobody, not good enough, not important, and not cared for by anyone. But he now had skills and beliefs to rely on to quiet the inner critic, providing momentary breaks from his depression, and it enticed him. He had connected with his core self, which assisted him in attaining an employment position that met his requirements.

The new job was easy. And *I Am Nobody* enjoyed the new work environment, started sharing his spiritually kind nature and genuine self with others, and had two supportive bosses who recognized his abilities. Within a year, he had a promotion and salary increase commensurate with that of his former job. During this time of change and transition in therapy, *I Am Nobody* worked diligently to maintain control over his inner critic and its attempts to have him feel like a nobody. He began walking in the woods as his mediation practice and started remembering how much he loved the woods of Colorado. He dreamed of moving to Colorado to walk in the woods there, although this idea produced anxiety and fear of change, including the loss of his job and the loss of newly formed social contacts. These intentions became the ingredients for his next soul movement. With the depression less intense, as he had broken through the constraints of conditioning, his next intention was answered, down to the specifics. Today, he lives within walking distance of his tree path in Colorado, where he moved with a mate and was able to keep his job, salary, and supportive bosses. His thirty-year clinical depression has lifted. I now call him *I Am Somebody*. His journey reminds us of the power of early experiences and parental conditioning, the persistence of the ego mind to maintain its learned eMAPs and the power of core self connection based on a desire to believe in one's core self.

When you chronically feel shame as an adult, the conditioned ego sends out shame signals suggesting you are different from others and are at risk of being trampled upon by others. Personal alienation from the necessary social networks results in stunting personal growth, which further reinforces shame feelings. As well, it is not uncommon for Americans to live with shame or its counterpart, anger, if they live in poor communities or if someone in their family suffers from mental illness or drug or alcohol abuse. I have both issues in my extended family and was subjected to witnessing the consequences of my extended family illnesses during my childhood and teenage years. I decided to accept this happening and learn from it. Acceptance is a healing path and it guided me to a blessed career further defining "WHO I AM" IN God's world.

If you identify yourself as a flawed human being because you differ in some way from cultural standards or social group norms, you are turning away from accepting the complete package that is you. Always your authentic, primary identity resides within the profoundly loving force field of God, in whose eyes self-esteem and self-worth is a given. Brush away feelings of shame like a bothersome fly, and do not allow shame to possess your consciousness. Connect with your godly core, and rely on its wisdom. Shame has no place in the ascended-conscious state.

Shame

Takeaway

When actions are not in alignment with one's ideal of self, natural shame can be the resulting feeling.

When conditioned to feel inherently flawed, feeling a lack of self-worth and self-esteem are outcomes.

Personal alienation from a necessary social group is lacking as trust in others is deficient.

Owning one's primary identity helps to work through the conditioned feeling of shame.

Springboards

- When feeling shame, find ways to be OK with imperfection, without believing your limitations mean that you are inherently flawed. Having a weakness, such as lacking a particular skill, makes you human and yes, an imperfect being.
- Think of your weakness or differentness as a person, your particular weave pattern in the complex, closely knit fabric of spiritual and human life. Recognize these are not a confirmation that you are inherently flawed or deficient.
- Push shame away like a bug.
- Write down the ways shame expresses within you. Write down a positive and rational thought to replace the shame-based thought.

Notes

_____

_____

_____

_____

_____

_____

_____

_____

Guilt-Blocking Effects in Children and Adults

Within each of us, feelings of guilt begin in our toddler years. This emotion, part of the human socialization process, is an obedience tool that parents implement early in a child's life to promote cognitive, emotional, and relationship development. A toddler developmentally passes through the two-year-old phase in which the child says no to parents' requests! This reaction is the first step of discovering self-identity. At the same time, guilt erupts, as the child loves his or her caretakers and is socially dependent on being cared for and loved. Guilt helps the toddler to manage negative feelings and learn self-control. When the child's conscience has developed, which is connection to one's core self, and the child has internalized the social rules as to what is right and what is wrong that guide behavior, the guilt response typically diminishes. And then guilt is replaced by a sense of personal responsibility, which comes from one's conscience, the soul.

With respect to adults, continuously living in a state of guilt is an unhealthy internal signal that one has identified self as imperfect and sinful, pushing aside one's innate spiritual nature as one's identity. The

"I am" core self understands that although we make poor choices and undesired decisions, mistakes are not one's true self-definition. And no other person should define your worth. Identifying self as of less worth because of sin and the guilt the ego suggests can maintain an unrelenting guilt grip over adults' behavior. The ego has been conditioned to use the powerful guilt tool to cause a person to believe that he or she is somehow harming or is disapproved of by a loved one for not doing, thinking, or feeling the way one "should." The person may fear that as a result, significant others will withhold care, approval, or acceptance. In fact, if you have fallen into the ego's trap, you are withholding love from yourself, specifically self-compassion and self-acceptance.

The rule is simple: you are primarily a spiritual presence and as a human being are on a path to tame your human conditioning and own your inherited spiritual nature. Yes, at times, we do harm ourselves and others. We make mistakes. However, if you lose love for yourself or others, your core signals that now you are harming yourself. And when we do harm self or others, your conscience will hold you responsible and suggest corrective action. But always within your core you are a loving, eternal spiritual presence. What a conundrum living in a dual world of self-esteem based on right and wrong when not one of us is always right. Listening to your core will unify your life. What becomes important is self-love not being right or wrong.

Accountability is always at play. Sometimes, we can sidestep feeling a sense of responsibility for wrong actions or inaction. For example, we can pretend not to be aware of the massive poverty of others. But if you do not correct your actions or inactions, the *I, Me, Mine* desires of ego will eventually cause you pain.

Adults who remain trapped in childhood guilt-conditioning eMAP programs will continue to interpret life events through the guilt-based, survival-ego framework and identify self as sinful, unable to use their free will to combat powerful guilt conditioning. Guilt will keep you living in the past without a future to look forward to. And in the steel grasp of the ego, whose number 1 fear tool is guilt, you are blocked access to your core self. Ultimately, the fight to combat guilt feelings from the perception that one is never OK can cause psychological harm in the form of mental health issues. I recall an extremely nice, intelligent, and financially successful man who placed himself in relationships where he consistently felt guilt. This client had an emotionally boundaryless mother and easily felt that he was mean, selfish, and cruel if he distanced from Mother and became intimate with others. This left him feeling continual guilt and living in an ongoing state of inner conflict. I call him *I Am Always at Fault*. His intention was to be a good, loving, honest person. He activated his core self with these intentions, which called out for right thoughts and actions. This led to inner turmoil caused by the disagreements between his conditioned, guilt-based ego and his loving soul. This led to his seeking therapy. While *I Am Always at Fault* felt guilty, his wise core self was also communicating that he had nothing to feel guilty about and that he needed to not believe anyone who expressed otherwise, even those he loved. Perhaps this was his karmic pattern needing healed.

In therapy *I Am Always at Fault* came to accept that his mother was not a mother when teaching him to feel guilty when he did not do what she asked or was intimate with others. And *I Am Always at Fault* started listening to the advice and feelings coming from his wise core self. Over time, he followed the wisdom of his core self and learned to allow and choose loving relationships in his life. Though he never had the courage to confront his mother's guilty ways directly, he did develop healthy, loving relationships with intimate others. I now call him *I'm OK* as he has taken a healthy step toward honoring himself as a loving human being.

Your core self will wrestle to bring about an awakening within the human "guilty" self. Your core self, concerned with its purpose of loving, will be screaming no when your actions are harmful to yourself or others. You will feel internal conflict in the hopes you will hear your core. When your soul and the human self wrestle, guilt will deplete your energy. According to *A Course in Miracles*, a book by Dr. Helen Schucman that contains a curriculum for spiritual transformation, guilt is an illusion. She observes, "Without guilt the ego has no life."

If guilt is allowed to embed itself and cycle, the ego expands its fear-based control. It snatches away your self-authority, compels you to self-identify as a less-than-worthy person, has you viewing self as selfish if you act in self-care ways, and robs you of the energy to act in positive ways toward yourself. The conflict between the conditioned guilt habit and the real self often leads to underlying feelings of anger and resentment fueling depression, as often we have layers of feelings. Unfortunately, without core connection, feeling angry and depressed leads to feeling more guilt. When these bedfellows join forces, you become mentally and emotionally conflicted and bounded. Your enjoyment of life diminishes. And you have difficulty in feeling unconditional love toward yourself and others, which further fortifies the obstructions that guilt has placed to block your path to spiritual awareness. The door to spiritual freedom remains locked, and you are compelled to resume cycling in guilty states. You are a prisoner of the ego, destined to spin round and round on the wheel you have created, with the same thought patterns, without logical end. I recall the following wise words from a client when she understood her guilt eMAPping:

> I've developed a self-destructive coping strategy of assigning guilt/blame to myself that allows me to sidestep reality and impose what I believe is a logical interpretation on an illogical event. I think the way my mind works is I try to assume guilt for an event, then I own it, and if I own it, then in theory at least I can correct it. My mind seeks to gain control and makes me guilty to do so.

From a human perspective, guilt is an illogical feeling. From a spiritual perspective, it is inaccurate; you are inherently guiltless according to your primary identity. Gain firm mastery over guilt, for you will not connect with your core under its influence. Accept that life's journey can be difficult and that sometimes you may make poor choices or unwittingly find yourself caught in guilt. Mirror unconditional love toward yourself. Remember feelings can be wrong and counterproductive. If you have done something wrong, as we all do, the spiritual core self signals you to correct your thoughts, feelings, and actions in a quiet, supportive way. By listening, you will intuitively "know" corrective action. Simply correct your actions. Use your energy for positive self-change, and break free of your guilt. Following a loving spiritual framework in your life provides an easier, conflict-free, truth-filled life path. Live within a spiritual vortex.

Guilt

Takeaways

Living in a state of guilt past the toddler age is energy depleting and keeps you paralyzed to living and reenacting the past.

Guilt can prevent developing an autonomous self and blocks one knowing one's spiritual identity.

When guilt has become a chronic way of feeling, one identifies self as sinful, imperfect, and selfish while living with underlying resentment and depression.

Springboards

- Accept your imperfect human nature.
- Recognize you are on the earth to build your life as an authentic, autonomous, spiritual, and human being.
- Loving self at all times, no matter the circumstances, heals.
- Follow your core conscience with correct thoughts, feelings, and actions.

Notes

_____

_____

_____

_____

_____

_____

_____

The Face of Anxiety and Worry, Spirit-Blocking Emotions

How do we each maintain control over anxiety against the backdrop of global and national terrorism, financial struggles to meet economic needs, and child care needs. Complicating matters children need one-on-one parental time and a special place in a parent's heart when time is often unavailable. There is the changing job market with AI involvement, against the backdrop of a faulty education system and overall lack of care for our fellow citizens due to lack of equal social and economic opportunities. Is it a wonder we are an anxious group of people? As humans we prefer stability and predictability yet live in a world of constant change.

Forty million adult Americans are living with anxiety disorders, and clinically, it is not uncommon for panic and depression to accompany anxiety. Six million adults experience panic disorder and 15 million have social anxiety. These numbers have skyrocketed since the COVID-19 pandemic to approximately 1/3 of our citizens feeling a need to have mental health therapy. Stress can be overwhelming. There are many social and economic factors that contribute to stress and persons in a position of authority and power fail to make change to assist each of us in decreasing the reasons supporting stress in our democratic, "freedom-based" country. Do we have answers, the richest country in the world? Perhaps freedom needs to be universal valuing and accepting all persons of all faiths, color, national origin and provide for one's health care and safety needs.

Anxiety can place you on automatic pilot by always expecting the worst to happen and focusing on being prepared for the next anticipated problem. Or avoidance of anxious feelings sometimes by a continual focus on being busy. The end result when anxiety comes to the surface it overwhelms.

Worry

To deal with our anxieties we can turn to worry as a solution. Like anxiety and other spirit-blocking emotions that only produce irrational, disordered thinking, lies worry. Worry is a fear-based, anxiety-driven emotion that blocks access to the problem-solving prefrontal cortex and to knowing one's true creator potentials through connection with one's core self. Worry occurs as a way to control happenings in the external world, an irrational belief. The ego has been conditioned to believe that doing something, such as worrying, will gain control over anxiety, magically averting catastrophe. If a catastrophe does not happen "today," worry is reinforced. Yes, this is "magical thinking" at work.

Although worry does not feel rewarding, it distracts from the distress of anxiety and offers the illusion of control. And anxiety and worry keep you reacting to past happenings with beliefs that work against living in the goodness and beauty of the objective present moment. One lives a life believing and fearing change, as the ego prefers. Change is avoided as ego has the worrier living in the belief that perceived "physical" danger is around the corner. This belief rules your life if you are a chronic worrier.

Worry can develop in childhood, when a child perceives harm and does not have enough trust that adult caretakers will protect and provide for him or her. Also, a child who is intellectually gifted can perceive fearful possibilities before having developed the emotional capacity to address the potential harm. The gifted child conjures up thoughts and images of danger, and as a result, he or she worries as emotional development of defense mechanisms, which follows a predictable time path, is not available to release the anxiety and worry. If a parent is not available to reassure the worried child, worry can become a way of life. Children who raise themselves are also subject to worry.

Free-floating anxiety and worry habits also develop when an unpredictable undesired life event happens. Chronic anxiety and chronic worrying become an emotional eMAP habit response to the uncertain or the unknown. You lack trust in yourself to handle life changes, although you survived the trauma, and lack faith and trust in your core having a plan for your life. Worry simply breeds more to worry about, and rumination takes over, a never-ending cycle following the natural law of attraction.

What will help each of us to feel free, fearless, and joyful? The answer lies within. We cannot control the external world; we can control the inner world and influence the external world through our actions. We choose what we create.

Anxiety and Worry

Takeaways

Anxiety and worry are natural responses to unpredictable happenings.

When being anxious or worrying becomes the chronic state, it is accompanied sometimes with magical beliefs that by worry you are preventing a negative outcome.

Worry distracts one from the physiological discomfort of free-floating anxiety.

Worry blocks the problem-solving prefrontal cortex and prevents core self connection.

Springboard

- The antidote for anxiety and chronic worry is neither to fight it nor listen to it but simply let it speak and pass by.
- Never try to repress a negative feeling; it will not work. Breathe through the body location where anxiety manifests. Feel love for yourself, be kind and gentle with yourself, and stay present to both feelings until calm takes control. Then trust in and listen to your core self for guidance, and act accordingly.
- Replace your worry and anxious thinking patterns with a rational thought.

Notes

_____

_____

_____

_____

_____

_____

_____

_____

_____

_____

Protective Anger Blocks Core Self Connection

Within each of us, the human emotion of anger is a survival response when a threat is evaluated by the ego. In a healthy way it is an affective ("A" of eMAP) emotional response signal that asks you to be alert to an unwanted change in your environment. However, the ego interprets survival threats broadly, such as when one's feelings are hurt, others do not live up to our standards and expectations, or when one loses control over a situation. Too easily, the ego interprets threats as *physically* dangerous when such danger is not present. An unhealthy cycle begins if you respond with protective anger as a defense against perceived self-esteem attacks in a cyclical way. It is the ego who feels the attack and pushes you to respond. Who is in control?

It is difficult not to respond with anger when one interprets danger. Unfortunately, protective anger never resolves the underlying issue but does build separation between self and the other. Not only does protective anger rob you of your inner peace, but it also gives another control over your emotional expressions to the other. Yes, at times people can harm, but what is the most effective response to another's wrath? Know that retaliation, holding grudges, or being resentful simply keeps you cycling in anger. Recognize these feelings can cause inflammation in the body, autoimmune disease, high blood pressure, sleep disturbances, and potentially cancer. Your heart is closed; you are not listening to your soul's advice. And you may end up and become a victimizer, and at other times feel like a victim or martyr. These three feelings represent the dynamic of victimhood. If you remain stuck in the dynamic of victim, victimizer, or martyr, you become an injustice collector, live in the past, and likely are profoundly unhappy. What eMAP, usually from the past, is supporting living in an anger state?

From a spiritual perspective, is your survival being threatened? Likely, it is not. Your ego is under attack. And as mentioned ego is hypersensitive to threats. To use anger for spiritual growth, recognize this human emotion is a signal that the person threatening you is stuck in emotional pain. And he or she is also an integral part of human consciousness and is on a journey as are you, perhaps still working on the spiritual strength of emotional control over anger expression. The goal is to bring about right action and accountability. As a client simply stated, "When I listen to myself and tactfully speak up instead of blowing up, I feel empowered, and my chest does not hurt because I am not holding in my anger." Intend a form of love, such as nondefensively relating to others, maintaining personal boundaries, accountability, and being mindful and in control of your emotional reactions. Use the energetic loving capacity within your "I am" core self, and the unifying love surrounding each of us to resolve grievances and produce positive change. Doing so keeps you healthy and lifts your awareness into the higher realms where joy resides.

And don't run away, try to repress, or avoid your anger. Running away from conflict never resolves the conflict, and as the ego will have it, likely the conflict will repeat as ego continues to set your life circumstances, often without your awareness to reenact the conflict. The ego likes problems and will have you set up situations subconsciously to keep problems repeating, although ego may think it's solving the problem; it's not. Label the supporting eMAPs. I recall a client I call *I Want to Please Others* who entered therapy for low self-esteem. She consistently walked away from her angry feelings but did not think that had anything to do with her low self-esteem. We could also call her a codependent, common lingo for anyone who places others' feelings above their own. In the case of *I Want to Please Others,* an elderly aunt became homebound and needed her assistance. In her desire to please others, she provided car rides to doctor appointments for her aunt, brought dinners to her home, and picked up her medications. Yet her aunt acted as if she did not want any care and was not appreciative of the effort, *I Want to Please Others* extended. And *I Want to Please Others* felt angry but thought it was a wrong, unchristian feeling and worked at repressing it. How often each of us represses anger, calling it wrong. As *I Want to Please Others* genuinely cared for her aunt and was doing the chores out of love, as well as a need to please others to boost her own self-esteem, she felt inner conflict every time she provided assistance. And she could not understand why she was experiencing conflict over her "nice" actions. For *I Want to Please Others,* her conflict was a repetitive eMAP response, yet a longtime indicator of core movement. By not listening to her anger, she did not understand the guidance coming from her soul, which was calling her to speak out about her hurt feelings. Possibly doing so would have led to understanding within this relationship and renewed closeness, as well as personal health for *I Want to Please Others.* Anger can be the god-self moving within you.

Group Norms Affect How We Conditionally Learn to Express Anger

We humans are social creatures, born into social groups, and we desire to create and share with others. We each become part of a group. Initially the group is our birth family. Group process dictates that one identifies with the values and norms of the group, and a norm can be anger and hate for others outside the group. The internet promotes awareness of many diverse groups. Each has specific values, norms, and agendas, which form its boundaries. Doing so fosters a sense of belonging. Group membership provides acceptance of members of the group while rejecting outsiders.

An outgrowth of groups is the development of bias. A group identifies itself based on its biased beliefs in which core members believe their rigid beliefs represent the correct ideal for humankind. Beliefs, such as discriminating and hating non-group members, that bind a group. Anger regarding bias issues reinforces group boundaries. When protective anger and hate reinforce group boundaries, this serves only to embed the problem and rigidly freeze up thinking capacities as conformity with rigid thinking boundaries are part of the group dynamics. This dynamic feed acts of violence. As previously stated, when you introduce a spiritual strength, a form of unconditional love into a difficult situation, and you assertively speak up for accountability, right action, and change, you successfully manage the difficult situation. Yet such groups can be difficult to influence. As we negotiate difficult emotions and situations, the "I am" core self reminds us that while we need to stay alert to survival concerns, we also need to pursue the right course spiritually by extending love and promoting fellowship for *all* others on earth. This steers us toward opportunities for personal, spiritual, and global evolution. We are urged to not allow the forms of fear to control us.

Protective Anger

Takeaways

Anger is an inborn survival signal to the ego.

Ego interprets anger emotion as physical harm.

Don't avoid, run away, or repress your anger. Wait until the anger passes and act with a form of love, such as nondefensively relating to others, maintaining personal boundaries, and being mindful and in control of your emotional reactions.

Recognize it is a loving response to hold people accountable for wrong actions.

Anger can be the god-self moving within you.

Hate groups are readily available on the internet and promote a sense of belonging, which can lead to acts of hate against individuals and groups that do not share similar values.

Springboards

- Identify how you express anger: passive, aggressive, or assertive?
- Recognize that fairness and right action are not automatic on the earth. It is a loving response to hold people accountable for wrong actions, yet doing so with care, empathy, and consideration.
- Act on the anger, not in the anger.
- Recognize we each are a journey and don't always know the exact way. Open your heart to all others. Use the love in your heart and the love surrounding you and send love to the person who has harmed you.
- Remember we each are divine beings at our core and God lives within each of us.
- When angry, if for approximately eight minutes, you can protectively block the ego from interpreting the anger event, you will find the anger physiological flight-fight response will pass. Do not strengthen your anger by thinking about the issue that caused it. After the physical anger response passes, channel the energy for positive means.
- Learn that responding to another with anger is giving the other control over your emotions.
- Mercy and forgiveness heal you and potentially the harming other.

Notes

_____

_____

_____

_____

_____

_____

_____

_____

Pulling Free from the Quicksand of Depression

> When we completely lose our way, we become one with
> loss. When we become one with loss, loss embraces
> us. *(Tao Tĕ Ching,* verse 23, interpreted by Ralph Alan
> Dale)

Being human means that we will experience loss and grief, natural human emotions. It is quite acceptable to cry, be angry, and perhaps feel hopeless for a period of time such as when a loved one dies. However, the love bond remains, crossing through the boundaries of everyday reality. Hold on to this belief as you process your grief. And be on the alert because the ego can interpret life challenges an undesired situation as a sign of the intelligent force guiding the universe is not caring about you, increasing susceptibility to clinical depression. We are each on a search for unconditional love, and we function best when expressing and receiving love. Perceived lack of unconditional love empowers the ego, and we end up caught in eMAPs that cycle around unhealthy beliefs, conditional eMAPs.

When not feeling loved, any one of us can cycle in unhealthy eMAPs to deal with human emotions. If angry and depressed we can hurt others or harm oneself if there has been a loss of genuine care and concern for yourself or others. One can also invent a personality around taking care of others and not oneself. And it is depressing to think one is alone, not loved, and "unable" to create a satisfying life. Clinical depression can deplete your life energy as lethargy sets in along with difficulty problem-solving due to blocked thinking patterns. These unhealthy expressions feed depression and block change, and one's self-concept is devoid of spiritual truths regarding being loved. Ego is energizing an internal suffering matrix. You can end up feeling like life is against you as you do not feel a sense of belonging or being cared for. Rather you are a victim to life. And believing in being a victim further opens one to being a victimizer, and at other times a martyr. You are stuck in this suffering relating triangle, stuck in looking for causes of problems everywhere except within one's conditioned self.

Depression also works against longevity. Recent research tells us a depressed person is four times as likely to experience physical issues. And experiencing depression early in life is causally related to certain types of dementia. Mental and emotional choices impact the energetic vibrations created within the body, which brings health or illness.

According to the National Institute of Mental Health (NIMH), at this very moment, an estimated 16 million adult Americans are suffering from depression. And the NIMH estimates that 35 million people will experience depression during their lifetime. Professionals who treat depression believe the figures are much higher. Dr. Norman Shealy, holistic guru and founding president of the American Holistic Medical Association, believes we clinically know that at least 30 percent of Americans are depressed enough to need therapy. And he suspects that another 30 percent are depressed enough that Freud's idea of a "death wish" is alive and well. Thoughts and feelings fueling depression can be powerful and extreme negative thinking is placing our powerful will into creating and maintaining depression. In the same manner we can create a fulfilled life. We each create what we energize.

As depression physically robs you of energy, don't expect to reach the higher-energy plateau. And core self is a loving vehicle who does not buy into depressive beliefs. I'm not sure the core self understands irrational beliefs. You may be on your spiritual path, but not negotiating the conflicting issues supporting depressive feelings keeps you in depression's clutches. I recall a client I call *I Don't Feel*. She entered therapy because she felt no emotions most of the time, and if she did feel, she felt either anxious or angry and depressed. Though she had a family and many friends, *I Don't Feel* was emotionally numb, unable to genuinely experience her friends' joys just as she could not feel joy for herself. Yet *I Don't Feel* could not admit that she needed attention as she had a core belief that therapy was a sign of weakness or pathology.

The conflict for *I Don't Feel* was between her higher self letting her know she needed unconditional love and attention versus her human core belief suggesting she was not lovable with proof being the physical and emotional abuse from her husband. She was angry about these occurrences, but expressing anger was not allowed by her ego-controlled self. She kept her needs and her anger buried, which eventually led to the burning out of all feelings. And, her journey points out that not attending to anger can take the anger underground into the subconscious arena and contribute to depression.

Fortunately, *I Don't Feel* had a strong desire to feel better, decided to enter therapy, and through our relationship, she worked on viewing herself as a sacred and love-deserving person. Anger rose into her awareness, including anger at God. Memories of not feeling loved during her childhood and adolescence came to the surface. As well she was beginning to understand how she subconsciously participated in choosing an abusive husband, the ego reenacts our learned ways of being. She understood she married a man who acted in familiar and predictable ways, although not desired ways. It was a difficult faith walk for her to acknowledge the lack of love from her parents, and it was difficult for her to see how she repeated the not deserving of love belief in her marriage, as it can be for any of us. Eventually, she realized that the whole emotional dynamic of her relationship with her parents, which also existed in her marriage, also existed in her relationship with her son, grandchildren, and friends because she created it. Of course, she married the perfect man to recreate this belief. The insights regarding family patterns, allowing herself to feel all her feelings, connecting with her core to decipher if feeling angry was justifiable, and learning that self love and acceptance is a path to healing herself.

As of this writing, she remains on the faith walk to becoming an *I Feel* person. She realizes that her love for her family is part of her spiritual and human life walk and an indication of her core goodness and holiness. Slowly, her depression is lifting as she owns and empowers herself to stop toxic patterns of relating. She is listening to her core self, and she is experiencing moments of joy.

Love or fear: which is your primary emotion? When the human desire for personal growth and autonomy and your core self desire for individuation unite, soul evolvement and spiritual awakening are in alignment and spiritual growth, health, and individuated autonomy occur.

Depression

Takeaways

Grief is a component of earthly living. However, the love connection never dies and remains after physical death.

Clinical depression is built on faulty beliefs regarding not being loved.

Viewing yourself as a victim, victimizer, or martyr simply keeps you cycling within all of these roles or ways of being.

Shame, anger, anxiety, panic, depression, and worry can be managed by believing that your core self can guide your life to live as a joy-filled being.

Living in negative emotional states blocks out your core self connection and requires change on your part.

Springboards

- Recognize each of us is important and loved by the most intelligent force guiding the universe, God.
- Practice positive self-talk.
- Exercise lifts the spirit within self. Do it!
- Eat your vegetables.
- Express gratitude daily.
- Identify eMAP patterns to understand the situational and emotional dynamics at play.

Notes

_____

_____

_____

_____

_____

_____

_____

_____

Meditation Method Number 1

Give Life to the Inner World

1. *Set the intention* to achieve an inner-centered state of peace and relaxation to energize your body for "I am" core self-connection. Intentionally focus on breathing into the center of your body. Breathing deep produces a state of calmness, yet heightened alertness if chosen, which is necessary for connecting to your core.
2. Diaphragmatic breathing is inhaling down into the base of your lungs and filling up your chest cavity with air. Breathe as a baby breathes, with your lower chest expanding and your upper chest remaining stationary.
3. *Focus attention on your breath.* Where breath goes, energy follows. Focus your attention on the lower lung area, which reaches down to the belly button and abdominal area, the center of your body. Breathe in.
4. Keeping your attention on the abdomen, slowly exhale. To release stress as you breathe out, imagine that you are breathing out your stress, filling up a balloon with all that you want to discard. As you

release your breath, concentrate on your goal: increasing relaxation or increasing psychic energy.

5. Practice breathwork five to ten times, until you have entered your intended state of peace, while yet feeling energized. Stay in the quiet mind-activated body state for as long as desired.

6. Upon leaving the quiet state, reset your intention with a centering phrase that represents a spiritual ideal or goal, such as achieving core connection, inner strength, or inner peace or increasing psychic energy for healing.

7. Think about your spiritual centering phrase throughout the day.

Opening the Heart Meditation
Method Number 2

1. Place yourself on a comfortable chair, sofa, or bed in a quiet room where you will not be disturbed for twenty minutes.

2. Sit back or lie down, whichever is more comfortable, and breathe deeply into your abdomen. Pay attention to your breath movements, breathing in and breathing out.

3. When you are comfortable with your breathing and it has regulated, repeat, "I am love."

4. Visualize an energy-based opening, which is the shape of an ice cream cone at the apex of your heart, the lower left heart ventricle. Imagine the cone extends outward from the apex out into the space in front of you. The smaller part of the cone resting on the heart area and extending outward into the space in front of your heart.

5. Think about your "I am" core self's profound love for you. Your core knows everything you have ever said, done, thought, or felt and always loves you, understands you, and knows all the ingredients that went into every thought, feeling, or deed better than you know yourself. And still loves you. Invite this feeling of love to open your heart.

6. Visualize your heart opening like a rosebud opens to the sun. The love from your heart enters the cone and extends out into the universe of all living things. Feel the joy. Breathe through your heart and imagine the loving/energy of your breath opening the heart rosebud from the air-energy inside the lungs and pushing out,

through the cone, to the exterior. When you breathe in, imagine you are breathing in love and sending love to your heart. And when you breathe out, breathe love out through the cone. As you return to your daily activities, remind yourself that you will take this feeling of peace, love, and joy with you through the day.

To Strengthen the Meditation

As you direct the breath to come in and out of your heart, and you think about love, imagine that you are sending love to your core, and your core sends it back with the outbreath after it fills every crevice on your innermost being.

Remember an event in your life when you knew and felt God's love or you felt love from another. Or think about a spiritual or religious service and its meaning for you. Think about this love experience at other times during your day to challenge and direct your ego to remember love. Doing so keeps your heart open, a step toward health. Recognize the more you practice this opening-the-heart exercise, the greater the benefits you will receive.

Building a Path to Unconditional Love through Unconditional Acceptance

Within each of us lies the ability to achieve emotional security and lasting inner peace and joy. We simply need to *choose* to cycle owning the inherently loving nature gifted to each of us known through activating the fruits or strengths of the spirit and listening to the soul's wisdom. When you have a clear image in mind of who you are and how you want to be in the world, your desired ways of thinking, feeling, and acting are strengthened.

On the spiritual path it is important not to get side-tracked by the bad events in one's world. Unconditional acceptance is a human and spiritual tool helping each of us to be consistent within oneself no matter external events. Unconditional acceptance is easy when "things are going my way." The difficulty is to lovingly accept all happenings when things are not going one's ego-based way. The ego's dual perspective on life, convincing you bad things are punitive, seeds suffering and causes you to think, feel, and act from that mind-set. And what one thinks, consciously or not, is the reality one creates. Suffering becomes your core belief upon which you build your life. One's negative thoughts are controlling one's consciousness and empowering negative happenings, according to the natural law of attraction.

Perhaps it is time to accept all events as a way to initiate or maintain unconditional love in your life. Acceptance of all life events is the way to inner peace and world peace. What does it mean to be a citizen of the world? What is right action? How do we solve the problem of harmed persons living in jails or unhealthy dictators controlling countries? Certainly, when I was asked to return to my spiritual event, the event did not appear to be what I considered beneficial. Yet in a spiritual millisecond, I was taught the power of unconditional love from my benefactor, Jesus Christ. I integrated his love for me and allowed love, which exists within all of us to lead. I reentered the harmful situation and intuitively sent love to my abusers. The event stopped. The results were not all good. They usually are not. I was left with some "bad" psychological effects which I have had to work on my entire life, as well as being gifted immediate access to inherent intuitive abilities. It may appear paradoxical to offer love in a hate-filled event, particularly while knowing I might well die. However, as I accepted the prospect of my human death, my higher core self, in communion with the Higher Spirit of Christ, provided me a way to live. An event I did not perceive as of divinity became of divinity. I accepted his challenge to return to the event with love and acceptance. Again, the spiritual encounter contained a mix of good and undesired happenings. Life is a faith walk, with spiritual forces always dynamically giving shape to ordinary reality. Sometimes, we each must embrace the uncertain for the eye of higher awareness to open.

Since there simply is so much going on underneath and beyond this surface layer of reality, within consciousness, the simplest and most positive response one can have to life events is acceptance. Acceptance recognizes that in many situations not one of us really or absolutely knows what "should" be happening.

Though this manner of thinking goes against common sense or rational thought, lovingly accepting all events keeps you within the flow of your spiritual life preventing an event from blocking out your spiritual nature and consuming your attentions. Spiritual matters, and all events are spiritual matters, require uncommon sense and perception as your core self exists beyond the commonplace. I know of no better examples of how difficult loving acceptance can be then the mothers of deceased children. I recall a woman who lost her daughter in an airplane accident. I call her *Oh My God!* She and I witnessed God acting through the disruption to their family, which opened the door for many personal and relationship changes. Each event could be reasonably interpreted as another horrific event, events in which anyone would respond, "Oh my God!" Whether it was her having to accept the inability to get out of bed all week or accepting her deceased daughter's ex-husband moving across the country with her only grandchild. She believed her grandchild was her only reason to live. Would you view her faith walk as extremely difficult? *Oh My God!* was amazing as she worked at stepping out of shock, disbelief, anger, and sadness and accepting somehow this was all a part of her healing process for her and her loved ones. Often the way we humans tend to spiritually awaken is through dark-night experiences. And just when I believed *Oh My God!* had a handle on her life but could not handle one more crisis, soul did the unthinkable; her husband was diagnosed with a life-threatening heart condition.

Once again *Oh My God!* had to hold onto the faith and trust step of loving acceptance and the belief that all was happening for good reason, for love. She did not want to fall into the pit of believing she was a victim. *Oh My God!* kept her faith. Events dramatically unfolded within the next week. Husband's cardiac issue was addressed, and she grew closer to her stepson.

As she and I were discussing these tragic appearing events in therapy another event unfolded giving her the courage to continue, a small miracle, not uncommon for the discerning eye to witness at difficult times. *Oh My God!* glanced through my office window and pointed out to me two white butterflies-in Pittsburgh, in December! This was significant for her for she had been associating butterflies through the summer as a sign that her deceased daughter was present.

But in December! She felt her daughter was smiling upon her, letting her know she was not walking alone and that all would be all right. The sighting empowered her as she worked through the events and issues with firm, loving authority.

Oh My God! accepted the spiritual intervention. It was an amazing spiritual pickup, lifting her from depression in a most unusual way. Instead of being ego active-angry, victimized, afraid, and depressed-*Oh My God!* gave her God loving acceptance and in so doing managed through the difficult feelings and events.

To maintain your peace of mind and remain within communion with your core self accept that many factors are operating to produce an event, some seen and some unseen. To lovingly accept is your best step to dealing with life problems and events. Doing so is adding a form of love to life happenings.

To accept life happenings, maintain inner authority by not accepting as truth what your human, ego self interprets. By doing so your awareness does not become magnetized to the problem or the perception, which keeps you from falling into the pit of despair or illusions of self alone importance. Conditioning chains are broken with love; the "always looking for the enemy" ego is disarmed. Its "divide and conquer strategies" of the ego judging mind, which schisms your awareness away from your sacredness, is blocked. To lovingly and unconditionally accept life, surrender assumptions of how life *should* be and go with what life has to offer. This is going with the flow. It is surrendering to what is, a nonresistance attitude in which you lovingly accept events and situations in your life with belief in your inner guide's dynamic capacity to lead your life path in alignment with a unified, loving consciousness. For divinity to be at work, personal and spiritual growth requires shattering of the old ways to make room for the new.

Loving acceptance does not omit right action. Rather, it prepares you to do right action. Loving acceptance unites the human and the sacred. Over time this attitudinal set provides entrance into knowing truth, giving a wider-angle view of life, beyond the contextual and feeling framework of ordinary life, survival reality. And you remain within the spiritual and earthly flow of your life.

I know of no one whose journey better exemplifies the difficulties of learning to accept the consequences from negative actions in the present lifetime than a client I call *No Legs*. He was a fifty-year-old man who viewed himself as having the requisite good looks, charm, and physical strength to justify acting in entitled ways. And indeed, he had done so in his adult years. But *No Legs* entered therapy to obtain help in coping with the reality that he was physically losing his backbone and facing the loss of ambulation. He had a sordid career of harming others for money. Eventually he lost a physical fight, which led to surgery to repair a disc. The initial and subsequent surgeries were unsuccessful. In fact, *No Legs* was allergic to the substance used to strengthen his back, and by the time the allergy was discovered, his bones had deteriorated to the point that he literally was losing his backbone and use of his legs. He felt he was being punished for his life choices. I suggested that he was fortunate to be able to pay back and meet his karmic debt in this lifetime. That is, *No Legs* was being offered an opportunity to make amends for the harm he had caused others. I suggested he accept his loss and redeem himself. Then *No Legs* became perplexed and confused.

Fear often overcame *No Legs*. He suffered strong panic attacks, which is ironic as formerly he was a man who knew no fear. And he was already experiencing unrelated medical issues for the unhealthy life choices he had made. He developed emphysema from his two-pack-a-day smoking habit. And he had heart issues caused by steroid use during his bodybuilding years. The difficulties continued as his wife left him because of his incapacity. Next, *No Legs* struggled with unrelenting anger at himself for getting into this predicament. He cycled in an eMAP-driven world of self-blame. Anger, depression, and debilitating anxiety fueled his creation wheel. Caught in this dark-night world, his ego bowed as the ego can do in hopeless situations, and *No Legs* chose to walk the hard path of acceptance. *No Legs* accepted his cross and worked on self-love. He began to intuitively hear the loving voice emanating from his "I am" core.

Eventually, he did lose the use of his legs. But he accepted the opportunity presented by this loss to ignite positive karma and make amends for his wrongdoing by volunteering at an agency to help the physically disabled. He was giving back likely releasing any karmic debt. And volunteering also lifted his spirit. I now call him *I Walk in My Life with Love*.

Loving Acceptance

Takeaways

Lovingly accepting life events ensures you will not get caught in an event in a way that blocks out your spiritual nature.

To honor and invoke connection to one's core, recognize that free will exists on the earth plane and place your will into acceptance.

Step into your sacredness with a self-definition as a divine being walking a human and spiritual life path.

Springboard

- Own this belief, as St. Paul says: "All things work to the good." I add "if you so intend."
- When an event grabs you, lovingly accept it as a first step, which maintains inner authority.
- Do the Joel Osteen move and simply "shake it off." Let go and shake off criticism, not allowing others to take away your joy (interpretation of Matthew 10:14).
- Learn not to take life too seriously, allow yourself to have fun, and be joyful at times even though a situation in your life is difficult.
- Practice the mindfulness state of "just being." Being present, not wanting things to be different, and accepting what is.
- If of a Christian faith, practice holy indifference.

> The appreciation of wholeness comes only through acceptance. *(A Course in Miracles)*

Notes

_____

_____

_____

_____

_____

_____

_____

_____

Release Suffering

We Americans know how to suffer, as evidenced by the high numbers of anxious and depressed people in America and persons who are afflicted with diabetes and autoimmune issues. And in America, if your life does not lend itself to a "Facebook" happy image, you can consider yourself a "poor me" victim of life. Feelings and thoughts about being a victim block core self connection. Victimization comes in many forms. As a victim, one can suffer from "not having" and "if only" beliefs, which are narcissistic ego desires. When we do not have what others have, it is quite easy to believe we are a victim and are suffering. As well, one can become a victim of life if one is forever waiting to have everything just the way one wants life to be, perceiving this as the only path to joy. For some of us we suffer if we don't have the right job, the right income, children who meet one's expectations, a devoted spouse, and perfect health. And while you wait for the perfect life, you are suffering in your unhappiness. "If only I had everything I want, then I will be happy." These beliefs can consume your life and keep you from appreciating the now moment with feelings of inner peace and contentment.

Safety and security come from the hidden hand that loves each of us. Looking at life happenings over the years, it is easier to see the hand of God at work. How is it that our forefathers gathered together and formed the US Constitution? How is it that President Lincoln came at the right time to manage the Civil War and free slaves? And President Obama came at the right time with his ability to financially stabilize America while providing access to health care for the disadvantaged. Perhaps Donald Trump was needed to uncover and heal the animosity some Americans feel. And who could be better at managing NATO alliances than the well-versed and internationally respected President Biden at this critical time in history? These are just a few examples of the manifestations of the intelligent form of love that is guiding America, commonly known as God. Look at your personal time line. How is it that at times you made right decisions? Likely intuition from your core guide you?

Coping with pain is a challenge. Pain robs you of energy and potentially of a contented life. It is as we age that the physical issues accumulate from the choices we make. As well, pain can be a message from your core alerting you to change your path. It is likely your core self, in coherence with the body, is asking you to make a growth step toward loving acceptance. For example, a woman who falls as she rushes to her husband's side and breaks her leg on the ice later finds out he doesn't love her. In her core, she knew he didn't sincerely love her, but she listened to her ego and was dutiful, although unconsciously angry. Perhaps her "accident" was a wake-up call. I recall a car accident I had while I was stopped at a red light. My car was hit by an elderly man. He stated I did not move fast enough when the light turned green. I assumed it was my or his mistake, but I was wrong. In hindsight, I realize I was being told to move quicker in my children's lives. The accident was meant to open my awareness to and prepare me for upcoming issues in my family life. When negative events happen, it is perhaps best to own the idea proposed by Caroline Myss in her champion book *Sacred Contracts*. She suggests that inner conflict is the divine motivating through spiritual suffering. The aim is to help each of us return to an authentic life path. The idea validates that love from your core self is molding your life at this moment, under the surface layer of ordinary existence. And you will gain resilience and inner strength as you do not allow the pain to control your consciousness.

We all experience unwanted happenings; no matter what external circumstances appear to be. Dealing with difficulties with loving acceptance of the problem, and being patient and learning to listen to your core to heal the underlying issue, is an evolving spiritual path. Difficulties can lead to a more meaningful life. Herein lies the paradox for each of us. Yes, pain can be a consequence of being human and divine, and unconditional loving acceptance of this reality keeps each of us on the path to spiritual awakening. Take the Buddha's advice. "The way to nonsuffering is to learn to accept the reality of living." Recognize that while accepting pain is part of the reality of living on the earth, being a victim and suffering is a choice. Stop investing in beliefs that support suffering.

The ego says you are suffering. Why not recognize the need to relabel and stop suffering by simply acknowledging you have pain or something had not gone the way you would like. Your core self does not follow ego-based beliefs. Instead, it acts according to your soul's job to meet human needs and wants that agree with your spiritual path, to move you forward in expressing your authentic spiritual identity and autonomous human self. When you perceive you are suffering, ask yourself if you are *really* suffering or experiencing pain along your life journey. Do not believe the ego. When you follow the ego's beliefs, it is difficult to connect with your core self to spiritually awaken to the reason for the problem. Yet within spirit lie our hope and resilience.

When you decide that no matter the pain, you are no longer going to suffer, the ego will notice. You can rise above pain by reminding yourself, with certainty and conviction, "I am" love and "I am" loved. I exist in the loving relationship between my human self and my core self. And I exist through spiritual connection with all others, as an integral part of unified, loving consciousness. You will not suffer, no matter what perceived undesired events may befall you, when you understand and trust that you are loved, are a loving spiritual presence, and that the powerhouse soul constantly works on your behalf. Of course, this concept is not easy to accept. But I wouldn't ask you to trust in anything that I don't personally know is true, from knowledge gained through my life experiences and further validated by the life experiences of many clients I have counseled. For example, my latest physical issue pointing out disharmony between my core and human self is neck pain. Not only do I have the natural osteopenia in my neck area, which I do not feel, but I also do notice intense muscle spasms. I drink more water, take electrolytes, and the pain remains. Finally, I asked my soul's reason for the pain. I received information upon awakening in the morning that I still needed to forgive a few relatives in my life. I was totally surprised. Yet on closer examination forgiveness is needed. I look forward to the forgiveness journey as doing so will metaphorically, if not literally, help me hold my head up. Perhaps my spasms will diminish as my soul will be freed of this anger burden. Yet they may continue as I am human and aging. Yet I am comforted knowing my soul is designing my life journey for eternal joy.

Yes, we can more easily believe in soul-designed events when life is going our desired way, and so we label desired happenings in positive terms, even sometimes mistakenly referring to them as coincidences or good luck. Yet perceived undesired events often are stepping-stones to human and soul evolvement. You choose the path, strictly human magnetized to earth creations, believing undesired events are a sign of not being loved or a victim to life, or trusting undesired events can be placed within a soul-evolving spiritual path.

Suffering

Takeaways

Experiencing undesired events that produce pain is part of human life.

When you experience pain, the ego tries to make you believe you are suffering. However, suffering is a human choice. You do not have to honor the ego's belief. The best choice is simply to acknowledge that you have pain.

Sometimes your soul causes the pain to alert you to a need to change something in your life, which will lead to well-being.

Remember that you are on a journey and remain an integral part of a unified, loving consciousness. This thought may help you to manage pain.

Springboards

To gain inner authority over pain do not believe the ego's interpretations that you are suffering.

Look at your time line of unpleasant events. Did you cause those events through negative thoughts, feelings or behaviors? If not what is the spiritual message?

Notes

_____

_____

_____

_____

_____

_____

_____

_____

CHAPTER 7

The "P" or Physical Aspect of eMAP Programs

> If you change your perception, you change the experience of your body and your world.
>
> —Deepak Chopra

Thoughts and Feelings Become Physical "P" expressions

A PERSON'S PASSIONS OR problems, which may range from feeling a sense of vitality and joy to experiencing muscle aches, headaches, and heart issues, to being afflicted with cancer, are often the result of the quality of mind-emotion-body and "I am" core self-connections. We have all heard common expressions that acknowledge mind-body influence, such as "dying from a broken heart." The heart carried the burden of emotional and mental pain, likely soul heard the pain, decided nothing more can be achieved in this lifetime, and agreed with leaving the earth plane.

The human body serves as a sacred receptacle for the "I am" core, just as the flesh of an apple encases its core. Soul enters the body and the struggle between human thoughts and emotions focused on survival alone versus one's loving core self begins. When a psychological issue exists, it can create physical issues. Your thoughts, attitudes, feelings, and perceptions are held and actively expressed within the body, which in turn directly influence your health and well-being. Yes, your attitude, what you think and what you feel, not only directly influences the health and well-being of your physical self but reflects the joys and struggles of your core self. The body coheres and hangs together with the mental-and-emotional self, and the effects influence the human and soul self. This is the mind-body-soul connection. A client feels pain in her chest. She visits the doctor and is told that her heart is fine and that she is in good physical shape. The doctor tells her that her chest pain is anxiety. She and soul are not in good connection as her fears need addressed. Another client has intestinal problems and knows he has a hard time "digesting" family issue. If he is to become healthy, these family issues will need to be addressed. Another client has sore throats constantly while hearing her core asking her to speak up and assert herself. Her human and the core self are trying to work together. Yet another client holds a grudge against people who will not wear masks during this time of COVID-19 infection and one day discovers that his feet, the point of contact with the earth, are swelling. I discuss how his walk on the earth has become uncomfortable from the anger and resentment he carries toward others, which his true self is telling him through the physical problem. This is another example of human self within the body and soul trying to work together. And living with anger as a constant bedfellow is toxic; the kidneys may have a hard time discharging. It is not easy to tame the human self with its animal nature. The physical issues of these clients reflect the energetic mental and emotional blocks which occur between soul and human self and are expressed in bodily illness.

All the emotional experiences we have chosen, consciously or not, actively chosen or permitted, are integrated into the body. If you have minimal self-worth and have not taken good care of yourself physically, the body expresses through discomfort leading to disease. In particular bad health habits accumulate and express with age.

Our bodies express negative thoughts, angry and fear-based

feelings, which eventually produce sickness or disease. If you have an unhealthy habit of not taking care of yourself and have excessive attachment to food, particularly fats and sweets, medical research points to this a root cause for disease. And, the body is made for movement so don't be surprised if you have weakness or illness if you avoid regular exercise.

Of particular interest is what feeling fear produces in the body. When the body resides in fears it expresses through acid-building physiological responses. The body and mind and emotional-visceral reactions harmonize to a state of physiologic alert, releasing stress hormones and chemicals in the body. The mind has to choose between flight and fight. If threat is real the body can reach a paralyzed physiology state. And all systems of the body are involved: the nervous system, circulatory system, skeletal system, muscular system, and the powerful hormonal system. If you live in this state, stress has an opportunity to root. And stress works against longevity. Of course, if you are in an extremely dangerous situation, such a response is appropriate. However, how often are you in such a fearful situation? Yet how often are you unable to sleep longer than a few hours because of lingering fears and concerns? How many times have you found that relaxation escapes you? Are you living in a disease-provoking, stress-filled state? We all know that high stress causes burnout and when not treated can lead to disease and death. The "always on the lookout for threats" ego interprets all threats as a *physical* threat. It believes your life is being threatened. We also know that stress is part of living, and when one maintains a positive attitude, a potentially stress-filled event is simply the next task to tackle. This attitudinal set leads to positive feelings and successful outcomes. This is a loving way to handle stress.

Health and healing occur through love, loving thoughts, feelings, and loving actions. thoughts, feelings, and actions produce health in mind and body. Tuning your ego mind, heart, and body to your loving "I am" core self is the best choice for health and happiness. Think, emote, and act with love toward self and others brings soul and human self together, leading to be at ease-at one-within one's own body and better health.

The Body Remembers

As an amazingly alive instrument, the body possesses "body memory." You can walk outside after the COVID-19 pandemic and without conscious thought be on alert due to your body remembering COVID-19. Even when the pandemic passes and years go by, there can be environmental triggers, "e" triggers, which the body will automatically pick up and communicate to your mind. Triggers such as a person walking close to you can trigger a visceral change in your body; it switches to flight-fight mode, alerts your brain, and a decision occurs based on your beliefs. You may not know why you are feeling stressed; look within.

It Is also not uncommon for dates to trigger responses without your conscious awareness. About a month before an unhappy happening, you can start to feel stressed, depressed, or anxious. Your body, remembers the unhappy event before you consciously do. As well, you can feel happy when a positive event memory is occurring.

Although love is a healing energy, sometimes loving actions are not powerful enough to change the disruptive energy pattern in the body. A threshold or tipping point of disease has occurred and much change is needed to halt the disease course. For example, you may have an unresolved issue noted in the name given to clients and their spiritual journey such as *Why Me?* on page 46. The ego will set up your present situation to reenact the past as a way to heal. This does not work. Ego needs to be conditioned to change in beliefs, feelings, and attitudes, and diet must accompany self-love for a change to health to succeed.

Even when the soul and ego mind are on a loving path, fear is powerful and the body may succumb to its predictable fear-based pattern and hold the illness. And even after the body has been taught to de-stress it can quickly return to its stress-response habit, just as easily as an adult remembers how to ride a bicycle, even though he or she might not have ridden one since childhood.

Fortunately, memory serves us for positive experiences as well. As an example of positive eMAP cycling, remember how relaxed you felt on vacation. The memory takes you down a few stress notches. This is the positive power of mental conditioning. The more attentive and alert, the more control you have over the body, mind, and emotions. Take authority and quiet the mind's chatter, which is groundwork for spiritual connection.

We also know that rest and relaxation, achieved particularly through being time, breathwork, positive thinking, guided imagery, meditation, prayer, attentive awareness of one's emotional and mental attitude, and desiring to care for all humans, are healthy practices and on the pathway to healing illness. You know that what you think and feel is what you create in the body. As mentioned, we can create our physical issues through poor lifestyle choices and chronic negative eMAP patterns; we can reverse the process and increase longevity through the opposite mind-emotion-body-soul-spirit connection. As you activate the loving strengths of the spiritual self and use your soul's guidance, you have ignited your will to follow a loving path. As you intend, so you create.

Fortunately, we each carry within us spiritual healing power, which is based in love. Only love heals. Jesus's miraculous abilities demonstrated the amazing inherent healing power *within each of us*. If you strongly believe in love and your ability to heal yourself, repetitively practice new, healthy habits of thinking, feeling, and caring for your body, release all negative thoughts and feelings, your body chemistry will respond to your intentions, and you will change your body's vibrational expressions. We each are gifted Jesus's superhuman capacity and can regulate the body's physiology, down to the cellular level. Soon it will be commonplace for people to use their strong intentions and core self connection to heal from a variety of illnesses such as cancer. For healthy change to occur when a deadly illness has inhabited the body, there are a few ingredients to produce health. Loving yourself fully is required. Awareness of and resolution of negative feelings, along with healthy eating and thinking habits, and movement as we are born to move, and it is not time for you to pass on to another plane of existence and leave the earth plane, are necessary along with full belief in your God-given capacities and spiritual connection.

"P" of eMAP: Physical Responses

Takeaways

The body is a conscious human vessel that holds your soul and is energized by your spirit.

What one thinks and feels is created within the body. The body holds and expresses one's thoughts, attitudes, and feelings, which in turn directly influences health and well-being.

The body also initiates a physical eMAP response based on a past situation.

We each carry within superhuman spiritual healing power to regulate the body's physiology, down to the cellular level.

Breathwork, positive thinking, guided imagery, meditation, and prayer are key tools for rest and relaxation, which are necessary for healthy living and core connection.

When guided by the "I am" core self, the body fosters health and well-being.

Springboard

- Imagine that just as the spirit of God fills the earth, God's spirit fills every cell in your body. Breathe in God's love and power.
- Vagal Nerve Activation for Relaxation

The body's healing potential is notable. Recent research is particularly highlighting the stress-reducing capacities from activating the vagus nerve. This nerve is quite long as it begins in the brain and goes through the face and thorax to the abdomen. The vagal nerve can dysregulate stress effects throughout your body and regulate your internal system for relaxation. A type of psychotherapy polyvagal theory, developed by Stephen W. Porges, recommends connecting activities with a vagal state. Through activities this nerve is activated, such as singing, humming, walking in the woods, belly breathing, and chanting *om*. In the Indian religion of Hinduism, the word *om* is the most sacred and primordial sound of creation, believing chanting this word calms the mind and brings energy or vibration into the body. When chanted the body vibrates, or more specifically, the vagus nerve is activated.

Mental Imagery for Healing

• Imagination penetrates the conditioning wheel of everyday life and can present a pathway for healing if so intended. A healing pathway brings mind-body-emotions-soul and spirit into harmony. Your core uses imagery to symbolically or metaphorically communicate particular emotions, thoughts, or experiences that stand in the way of physical and mental health to assist healing. Your core communicates what needs to change for well-being. Healing can begin when a physical symptom is displayed through an image. I recall many clients who were blessed with clear images to guide their path to healing. One client straightened his back by working with an image of unevenly stacked dinner plates. As he restacked the dinner plates, his back pain decreased. Upon self-reflection, he realized he allowed people to be the pain in his back as he felt he was taking on too much responsibility for others' jobs. Another client, working on his colitis, received an image of fire in his intestines. He learned to control the colitis by imagining he was reducing the flames with a fire hose. Unfortunately, the colitis client never stopped his emotionally inflammatory feelings and thoughts. He had to keep working on the imaginary level to reduce the flame, thereby lessening his colitis symptoms. I recall another client, whom I call *I Am Overwhelmed*, who spontaneously received an image of a beach scene in which she noticed she was moving her hand very slowly in the water. She began laughing at herself and imagining having fun with the water. For *I Am Overwhelmed*, this image was a gift telling her to slow down in her ever-too-busy life and to relax and enjoy her life. Her core was giving her guidance on a way to achieve self-love along her road to becoming a joy being. Stop, look, listen, and honor the image gifts you receive. Images open the mind, the mind affects the body, and healing can occur.

Inner Sun Guided Imagery
Method Number 3

After identifying a quiet place and setting an alarm for ten minutes, sit or lie down, and attend to your breathing.

1. Allow yourself to imagine a warm, gently radiating, small, white sun at the base of your spine. Feel its loving warmth.
2. Slowly allow the sun to move up your spine, at your own speed. As the sun moves up, notice it becoming larger and larger. Notice how it radiates its healing warmth to all areas of your body that surround the spinal area. Feel the warmth.
3. As the sun reaches your midframe-stomach area, it is now large and fills up your entire midframe.
4. Your sun continues to travel upward in the body, toward your heart. Imagine the sun's warmth is like feeling loved.
5. The sun moves up into your facial area, relaxing the many muscles of your face.
6. Then the sun envelops your brain with its loving warmth, and the brain and body are in a warm, embracing harmony. This is a natural loving connection between mind and body.
7. The sun warmth exits your skin pores, surrounding you with loving warmth. Allow yourself to sit in this warm, loving state.
8. When you leave this guided imagery session, imagine the warm sun whenever needed in your daily life.

Circulating Energy Meditation
Method Number 4

This is a powerful meditation that can be used to increase your psychic energy flow or to direct this energy for healing. All creating begins with intention. Intention directs the life energy, which manifests the intention. Set your intention to explore your energy circuits for continued health.

1. Do steps to relax breathing in and out and having your attention follow your breath until you experience relaxation. Follow method number 1.

2. Now let's activate psychic energy by controlling the flow of breath. With concentration and your quiet mental state, as you breathe in, bring your energy up your back, and lift the kidneys as if lifting the water in your kidneys. Place your tongue on the roof of your mouth.

3. If there is a part of the body needing healed, place the energy in that area. For example, bring energy up through the back and enter the back of the heart, allowing the energy of the breath to enter your heart. Imagine collecting love from the heart.

4. If not going to a specific area of the body, continue taking this breath up into your brain, placing your tongue to the roof of your mouth as if closing an energy circuit.

5. On the exhale imagine breath is concentrated manifesting energy. Through focused attention, drop your tongue, imagining sending the air/energy down the front of your body as the physical air exits your lungs, depositing energy. Or imagine dropping the energized breath into the affected body area, or send the energy up through the top of your head.

6. Visualize, feel, and think peace spreading through your body with every circulating breath. Imagine each cell opening, cleansing, releasing toxins. Take your time. Attune and harmonize.

7. Repeat phrases describing your unchanging, authentic, sacred, "I am" core of self.

8. After several breaths return to regular breathing and stay attentive and in the quiet for ten to twenty minutes. Take note of anything you experienced. If you have a request, ask. Be alert and listen.

A Note

*   To enhance activation of your life force, you can also add visualization, such as the Sadhana practice of imagining currents of air traveling within the body.

*   Or you can imagine your breath as a glowing inner sun that grows brighter with each breath you take.

> Breathing in I calm my body, breathing out I smile.
> (Thich Nhat Hanh)

The body must not, should not, lose courage to carry on, but working in patience knowing that all healing, all help, must arise from constructive thinking, constructive application, and most and first of all constructive spiritual inspiration. Use body disturbances as stepping stones for higher and better and greater understanding. (Edgar Cayce, reading 528-529).

Notes

_____

_____

_____

_____

_____

_____

_____

_____

CHAPTER 8

Neurological Tools for "I Am"
Core Self-Connection

OUR NEUROLOGY IS an aspect of "P," physical eMAP programming. Today science is mapping the brain and developing neurological based tools for mental and emotional health. Therapists are using a neurological-based therapeutic technique called ABS (alternate bilateral stimulation) to tap into spiritual resources. ABS and a similar technique called brain-spotting are two key neurological tools that can help you to relax the brain; they consciously reduce stress and anxiety and replace negative, unwanted eMAPs with empowered love-focused MAPS. And if you so intend, these tools can ultimately strengthen your connection with your core self. I recall a client who used the ABS technique with breathwork while praying. I call her *Breathe, Tap, and Pray.* She entered therapy with a solid spiritual foundation; she viewed herself as a child of God, as she had been taught. She routinely meditated and prayed to God, and this communication often provided the answers to her life problems. However, when a life situation became overwhelming and meditation and prayer were no longer providing answers, she felt she had lost her connection. And so, she entered therapy with me. She had difficulty in controlling her stress, which compromised her ability to hear and understand the answers to help her regain interior connection.

To help relax and calm her mind, she added tapping when she prayed. And so, *Breathe, Tap, and Pray,* over time, once again began intuiting answers to her personal dilemmas. She also developed greater inner strength to deal with life situations. Recently, she began viewing herself as a portion of divinity, using ABS, breathwork, and prayer for spiritual self-connection. Another client performs ABS simply to rekindle happy feelings. He calls ABS "happy tapping." Try it! This is positive conditioning at work. The more you relax, tap in a positive thought and feeling, perhaps by using a snapshot of a happy past memory, which will increase positive feeling, thoughts, and a relaxed body.

ABS is a component of eye movement desensitization and reprocessing (EMDR), a therapeutic tool discovered by Francine Shapiro, PhD, a Canadian clinical psychologist and luminary of our times. During a walk in the woods, she began thinking about problems that upset her. And she realized that walking, a natural ABS activity, helped her find cognitive solutions. This excursion literally began her journey of development of EMDR as a psychotherapeutic tool for eliminating the symptoms of disturbing life events. Today, EMDR has additional therapeutic applications.

Activating the Brain's Hemispheres

The brain consists of two hemispheres or lobes connected by a bridge that enhances processing of life events using both rational thought from the left hemisphere and basically feelings and sensations. When the bridge is open, the hemispheres work together. And when they work in congruence, whatever new chosen eMAP you are attempting to program is strengthened by applying ABS.

Alternate Bilateral Stimulation

ABS is tapping on one side of the body alternating with tapping on the other side of the body. As you tap you repeat a self-reaffirming phrase. ABS can be tactile, visual, or auditory. And you can do it no matter where you are. You simply tap your hands on alternating sides of your body-for example, alternating on both arms or on both legs. Actually, even though you may not realize it, you already move bilaterally each day; every time you walk, you alternate from one foot to the other. Just add a positive self-reaffirming phrase to feel an emotional lift.

Understanding Our Neural Wiring

Canadian neurologist Donald Hebb proposed Hebb's law, which says, "Neurons that fire together, wire together." From birth onward, the brain collects and wires in life experiences. When thoughts, feelings, and actions harmonize, the brain develops interconnected neural pathways or well-worn neuro roads, wiring together the eMAP. You can visualize these neural pathways in your brain as a system of frequently traveled roadways.

ABS helps you to rewire neural roads so that you unplug from unhealthy eMAPs and connect with consciously chosen eMAPs. In addition, the more you apply ABS in accessing a new chosen MAP, the more often the new eMAP fires, and the easier it is to access. And ultimately, over time, the new eMAP becomes your well-worn, neural road.

If you so choose, you can use the healing and transformative power of ABS, through activating your neural networks, to access your core self. ABS is a useful tool in your spiritual self-empowerment toolbox.

I view ABS as rocking the brain, like one rocks an infant. For new programming it is important for the brain to be relaxed. Relaxation helps the brain to be receptive to new programming, including programming to enhance spiritual connection, help you manage emotional issues, and provide guidance on health issues. The more belief, will power, or intention, the more effective ABS and the clearer you know right paths for yourself. ABS helps you achieve a state of hemispheric congruence in thoughts, emotions, senses, and perceptions following your intention. You are now choosing your well-worn neural roads.

You choose what thoughts to tap in. If you choose to feel love toward your neighbor and desire to act in loving ways, with mind-body in agreement, the response has manifesting power. However, this interhemispheric coherence feels right and good, regardless of the moral and ethical content of the thoughts you are thinking while doing ABS. Use this tool wisely.

Neurological ABS

Takeaways

When neurons fire together, they wire together.

ABS is a tool for relaxing the brain, increasing feelings of internal peace, and increasing the brain's receptivity to new programming.

By using ABS to connect with an eMAP that is based on feelings and thoughts of love for self and others, you can access your "I am" core self.

Springboards

Bilateral Stimulation for Self Love
Method Number 5

1. Decide where on your body you will perform ABS. The only requirement is that you alternate between right and left sides. Some people move their feet or hands, others tap on their thighs, and others hug themselves and tap. You choose.
2. Add an "M" (spiritual) component such as a self-loving thought. An example is true happiness resides within me. While alternately tapping, repeat your affirmation. Your mind will proceed on the beginning thought.
3. Notice an "A" (affect) component when you repeat your phrase and feel happy. Feel the peace or joy and perhaps a sense of belongingness and connection.
    *   Take a mental sensory snapshot of how you feel internally, from the top of your head to the tips of your toes. Notice how you feel when you reside in feelings of love. Most likely, you will become aware that your breathing is regular, the muscles in your body are relaxed, and your mind is focused on personal connection.

4. Lastly, set the intention to focus only on your chosen positive, love-focused experience.

   • Start tapping, alternating from right to left for five to seven tapping rounds. Adjust the pressure and speed of tapping to your comfort level. After you have tapped or squeezed approximately seven times, take a breath, and stop for a few minutes. Then start again. Do three to five sets or seven sets at once. Then stop. This is an important component.
   • At another time, repeat these actions while focusing on the same thoughts and feelings of love. The more frequently you apply ABS while focusing on a particular eMAP, the stronger the eMAP will become.

5. Now that you've learned the technique, apply ABS frequently to strengthen your neural network.

Stress-buster
Method Number 6

The following is a two-to-five-minute stress-buster meditation:

1. During the day, when stress or unwanted feelings enter your consciousness, apply several sets of ABS.
2. Take a few deep breaths, repeat your affirming phrase to refocus your day, and apply ABS.

Imaginal Bridge to Connect with the "I Am" Spiritual Core Self
Method Number 7

Visualize the place that you consider to be your personal safe and sacred haven. For example, if the beach is your sacred place, imagine hearing the rhythmic rush of the waves and the calls of shore birds and feeling the firmness of the sand and the warmth of the sun. Choose an affirming thought. Now breathe, focus, and apply ABS while remaining in your safe place.

Choose one of two options.

- Focus on your heart, and think of its warmth. Think of the love your heart feels for you as it beats and sends warm, oxygenated blood throughout your body. Feel the warmth from your heart as it spreads throughout your body. And apply ABS while focusing on these feelings and your affirming thought.
- Recall the comfort of rocking back and forth in your favorite rocking chair or on a porch swing. Virtually all of us have enjoyed such an experience. Do so while thinking positive, self-affirming, core-energizing thoughts, and perform ABS several times.

Notes

_____

_____

_____

_____

_____

_____

_____

_____

_____

Brain-Spotting

Where the eyes look, the heart is directed. (Buddhist saying)

When Eastern meditation practices came to the West, the movement introduced a variety of ways to meditate that can help anyone to calm down, relax, make clearer decisions, and if desired, reach enlightenment. Meditations range from laughing to moving your life force with your breath to simply sitting still and focusing your eyes on a candle flame. Today, ministers are taught to "go within, feel your peace, and hold that eye position" to maintain peaceful feelings.

Brain-spotting is a technique that uses concentration and our eyes to access our brain for neural programming. If you have ever had test anxiety you will enjoy the journey of my client. I call him *I Am Smart* because much of this young man's self-image was based on his intellectual abilities; therefore, much was at stake. He was a young college student who very much wanted to succeed at his studies but had debilitating test anxiety. In high school, he achieved excellent grades and rarely needed to study for tests. But after he began college, he developed test anxiety. For the first time in his life, he questioned his self-image of being smart. During a brain-spotting session, he was shocked by how relaxed he became as he thought about test taking. He called it "weird and almost magical." His test anxiety dissipated. Now I call him *I Am Smart* as he has owned his gifted abilities.

Brain-spotting involves visually holding a position and mentally focusing on that spot until you experience calmness. The technique requires patience and persistence, but the rewards are many. Brain-spotting sharpens mental alertness, enhances the capacity to be mindful and regulate emotions, and most importantly, releases negative wiring and rewires the brain for positive neural networks. It increases one's sense of peace and ultimately assists in attaining higher levels of consciousness. The technique was developed by David Grand, PhD, another luminary psychologist of our times, who found that eye position, combined with mental concentration, heals emotional issues and stress-related medical disorders and promotes personal integration. Dr. Grand's method releases the neurology that holds the problem.

In today's fast-paced, often chaotic, and stress-filled world, brain-spotting is a quick way to help you find inner strength, inner wisdom, and peace, thereby ensure that you remain within your solid spiritual foundation.

ABS and Brain-Spotting

Takeaways

Both ABS and brain-spotting are neurological tools that remove negative, unwanted eMAP programs and create new, positive, healthy, desired eMAP programs.

Both tools actually change the brain's neural structure or "wiring," such that the new healthy eMAPs become your well-worn neural road.

Both tools enhance physical relaxation and increase mental and emotional inner peace.

Both tools can be applied in brief sessions and as frequently as desired. The more you practice, the greater your results.

Springboards

Brain-Spotting Meditations
Experiencing Unconditional Self-Love

To use brain-spotting to experience unconditional self-love, you must have unconditional self-love as your intention and a desire to think of and believe in self as a loving, spiritual presence while concentrating on the image of yourself as a spiritual being and holding your gaze steady. As you do so, you will turn your attention inward, reprogram neural networks, and strengthen your capacity for insight and healing. Deep, regular breathing seems to help the process.

Brain-Spotting for "I Am" Spiritual Core Self Connection
Method Number 8

1. Set aside twenty minutes to think about the loving qualities you have activated, or wish to activate, within your spiritual core, such as peace, love, joy, and contentment.
2. Close your eyes, and think about a time when you were acting in a loving way, automatically aligning human self with your core. Then open your eyes, and hold the eye position for a few minutes.

3. Make sure you are sitting comfortably while holding the brain-spot and thinking about your core self.
4. Hold the brain-spot until you feel relaxed. You can close your eyes, but hold the brain-spot.
5. When you feel peace or an internal lifting, perform a few sets of ABS for this experience to permeate your mind while holding the brain-spot.
6. Do a body scan, and notice how you feel.
7. As you return to the everyday world, set the intention to remember all of these learnings, perceptions, feelings, and visceral sensations.

Now that you have learned the techniques of ABS and brain-spotting, do these activities frequently to strengthen your chosen neural network. With practice, you will strengthen the connection to your "I am" core self. And if you prefer, as you seek connection, you can always brain-spot on an image of God, Christ, Buddha, other higher master, or a loved one and end up feeling connected.

A Note

I recall my search for the neurophysiological underpinnings of the "I am" core self, which culminated in a conference I "happened" to attend, a lecture with Dr. Dan Siegel, a guru for understanding mind-body-spirit connections. He believes you are in the flow when in a harmonious state across the layers of the brain. When there is coherence across the two lobes of the brain, you energize a feeling of inner peace, freedom from inner conflict, and joy. Dr. Seigel's research further suggests that you feel "larger than your usual self," as if you have crossed the limits of space and time. Dr. Siegel notes when you are in this harmonious and consistent-flow state, you achieve "transpirational consciousness." You are "in the flow" and have developed core self neural pathways. I believe this gives you access to cocreating your own miracles as a fully human yet fully divine being. His lecture confirmed for me that I was on the right path and explained my own expanded-horizon experiences. You can program your brain to attend to your miracle path, and with a loving intention, watch your requests being answered.

SECTION 4

Spiritual Tools for Core Self Connection

CHAPTER 9

Faith, Trust, and Belief in Core Self

NEGATIVE BELIEFS AND fears surrounding one's concept of God give the ego mind control over your way of knowing, or not knowing, God. Just as a toddler does not understand the no when asking for candy before dinner, the ego does not understand the reasons for the bad events, perceived unanswered prayers, and unmet expectations except to say what the toddler says. "You don't love me." And at times, "I hate you." It's a monumental task to have faith and believe God loves you while the "rational" ego mind uses fear to build more fearful thoughts. This ends up turning the happenings of a "bad" event into proof that "I am not lovable, deserve bad happenings, am being punished, am suffering," etc. The presumption that I have evoked God's wrath or am simply not loved by the loving consciousness is an idea that keeps one in the dark of not knowing self. In our conditional life, we each do make mistakes and follow poor judgment at times; however, God sees us in our spiritual nature. Doubting in a loving, unifying God consciousness speaks to the powerful force of the ego. Our "rational" labels not only do not work, but they also work against our trust and faith in our God gifted inborn ability to create our lives. We may live in a secular world, but the unseen loving consciousness is always present and we do receive the present of a soul and free will.

It is fear that surrounds our image of God when God does not act as we humans expect. Yet paradoxically it is when we are at our darkest moments that we turn to God as if somewhere inside there is a knowing that a loving consciousness exists and cares. It is at these times we go within and with utmost heartfelt sincerity and belief, use our creator skills and activate God's message to each of us, "ask and you receive, knock and the door will be opened." Beyond rational thought exists *within each of us* the power to create our lives using truly "free" will. You are a loving intelligent force, a portion of God which is who you are. Faith is not denying or belittling our spiritual identity or the tragic experiences we encounter; rather, faith helps us to bear the experiences we encounter.

Even if you religiously, and spiritually, believe bad events are meant for your betterment, the ego can't easily hold an atypical thought. After all, the ego does not want a secondary role that a divinely instrumented world provides. Our "rational" theories fall short in explaining God's love as seen through "bad" events of life or the unanswered prayers. To change our assumptions about our lives, to find the good in bad, to see light in darkness, to believe in a unified reality *always* desiring to work toward a loving oneness is a spiritual perspective reaching beyond our casual-based, rational minds. We can call bad events the mystery of faith. But is it really a mystery? Do we create our lives and our world? Perhaps it is possible that our gifted "free will" is ruling our lives creating many of the bad and horrific events experienced. Can it be that God so loves us that even when we are not listening to his inner voice we are still loved, still allowed to create what we desire?

It is this faith and belief in who you are that can be relied upon. Even if you do not have faith and belief in a God available to you, as a first step I'm asking you to have faith and trust in your relationship with your inner guide. Notice the intuitive connections. Have faith in your authentic core self in the same innocent way a child trusts a parent. I am asking you to have faith that within you exists a spiritual and soul manifestation that has direct access to knowledge, wisdom, safety, and eternal security. Through the springboards, guided imageries and other recommendations experience your inner self. By desiring to connect with the "I am" portion within you, attunement to one's core self as a human being occurs. Do not be afraid to fully depend on your "I am" core self for life guidance. Trust, discern, and believe you can negotiate all the twists, turns, and events in your life road as if life were dancing with you. Rooted in the experiential connection with your core roots faith. "I am" love and I have faith in my own self-love to guide my path.

As mentioned, faith does not exclude the occurrence of undesired events. Clients' journeys begin with a perceived undesired experience. Fortunately, choosing a soul-evolving, spiritually awakening path with faith and trust provides inner strength to handle disappointment and change as it strengthens your faith. To accept and endure weariness and pain, as well as change the course of bad events such as illness, is recognizing events as opportunities to change and grow. That's why we turn to the mystical when in crises; we know we need to change. And as the Christian Bible reminds us, "Your faith has saved you." Remember you have the capacity to choose a joy-filled miracle life no matter external circumstances.

As you experience helpful ways of your core self, a desire for conscious connection with your true core identity likely will expand to knowing that each of us is unconditionally loved and has a unique and necessary place, and position, in a unified, loving consciousness as you open up to such beliefs with a humbled heart and allow truth in. This was clearly at work with a client I called *I Live in Panic*. She is a striking example of the healing power of faith. She endured a series of anxiety-producing events, further fueled by memories of past harms, which unexpectedly disrupted her once serene, problem-free, faith-filled life. The difficulties began when her husband had a heart attack. He was the rock upon which their marriage, family, and finances were founded. And with this heart issue, *I Live in Panic* feared losing her husband as the family rock. Her fears began her journey of having panic attacks. She believed that God was not paying attention to her and allowing her to have these attacks. Her faith, trust, and belief in God's love for her and her place with him was being challenged. She believed God was supposed to protect her and provide for her, without problems. A trick of the ego is to believe that we each are special and should not have problems to deal with. And if we do, we can turn on God saying he is hidden, silent, remote, and perhaps punitive.

As *I Live in Panic* drew upon her faith, trust and hope, her anxiety lessened, and she reported that she felt her God was walking beside her after all. Her core connection grew, and she became stronger than her fearful ego.

Life went on and she felt relief from the panic, anxiety, depression, and anger when her husband lost his job. New employment was not forthcoming. And they were not savers yet they both wanted to move out of apartment life and into a home. The couple still wanted to buy their first home. Even amid this turmoil, *I Live in Panic* turned within and relied on her core self in connection with her God for comfort. She not only managed her anxiety but had times of inner peace.

The couple fell in love with and bought a very old house located near her childhood home. The house needed major repairs. Although *I Live in Panic* was not worried about their financial issues, as her therapist, I felt concern regarding the number of repairs needed and their lack of experience in this area. Buying a home that needed repairs seemed unwise to me. But I, too, had to honor her faith walk.

This new life walk was nonetheless fearful and difficult for her at times. Change is difficult for us humans. She kept her "I am" core present and relied on her faith in God's care for her and her husband. It was the way *I Live in Panic* could disarm her fears as their new home was close to the neighborhood, she grew up in. As *I Live in Panic* encountered people and revisited places from her past, traumatic childhood memories surfaced. Soon, *I Live in Panic* began to recall the harms and tormenting fears of her youth with clarity. Yet *I Live in Panic*, walking where she had walked as a child, felt empowered by the thought that she had survived her childhood. She noted that returning to the places where she had been emotionally wounded helped her to become a stronger person as she learned where and how her panic began and recognized she need not be afraid in the present. She felt that God had led her back to these places where, as she stated, her "fences were broken" so that she could mend them.

I Live in Panic recalled a dream that she had experienced at the beginning of this anxiety-filled journey. In the dream, she rescued a young, frightened child. She now realized that she was the young child. She then remembered a time two years earlier when upon awakening she heard God say to her, "I AM preparing a place for you." She at last understood God's message. God had prepared the very place where *I Live in Panic* grew up to give her the priceless gift of revisiting the past and healing herself from childhood scars. And as so often happens the moment one experiences God's grace, *I Live in Panic* released all the resentments from her childhood, which were instantly borne away, heavy logs of burden swiftly carried downstream by the powerful current of her faith. Her panic vanished. I now call her *I Am Alive and Happy*.

Notably, *I Am Alive and Happy* received grace through very difficult life experiences as an adult and as a child. Her husband's health issues turned into blessings that ultimately, over time, empowered her faith walk maintaining her human-and-divine self. She ministered to herself, trusted her capacity for self-definition, and become her own rock. And she trusted her God, following her intuitive perceptions. God also guided her husband, who found employment, also well-timed. And just when I thought I was done with this section of the book, she visited me to tell me of her husband's job, which provided the idea for and blessing of adding her story for your understanding.

I know that having faith and trust in your god self is worth the work because of the spiritual journeys of my clients but also my spiritual encounter with Christ when I was a toddler and stopped a sexual assault (page 4). The experience left me knowing I always am being watched over, cared for, and absolutely loved. When, with full belief, I called for a savior that day, Christ appeared. God is always within earshot.

My encounter and the spiritual journey of *I Live in Panic* point to the need to accept, as a surrendering process, undesirable events while having spiritual faith or psychological trust that your life can be fruitfully guided by one's core self if so chosen. The god force within will guide your life and help to negotiate the more difficult times as your core provides the way. Hold on to the knowledge that not one of us walks alone and this divine consciousness is always available to help each of us along the way. Direct the walls of the ego to dissipate and allow faith and belief interior room in your thoughts, feelings and actions. Follow the wisdom of your core self, you will be directed to the best possible path. And sharing the love and wisdom you receive with others is providing hope and helping others move into the light and become aware of God's love and indwelling within each of us. Your core always has your physical safety and emotional well-being in mind. Make these beliefs your known reality, including some situations that are very difficult to accept the belief in core self or God having one's best interests at heart. Focus your awareness on believing in right happenings, and believe you do not walk alone even through the difficult passages on your human-and-divine journey.

Faith, Hope, and Trust

Takeaways

Faith is trusting that each of us is unconditionally loved by our own interior "I am" core self.

Because your core self is unseeable, faith, hope, trust, and belief will guide your footsteps.

Have faith that you have a unique and necessary place, and position within eternity.

Trust in your inherent connection to loving consciousness.

Believe this loving consciousness always responds with your best interest.

Recognize that faith does not exclude the occurrence of undesired events, which are opportunities for soul evolvement and spiritual growth.

Springboard

• To build faith, think this thought consistently over a six-month period: "I am first and foremost a loved, eternal, divine, spiritual essence." Set your intention to know yourself in this way. At the end of this time, if you have *not* experienced an expanded sense of who you are and more stable feelings of contentment, you can always return to your present way of thinking, feeling, and acting.

> Put hope and trust and faith in the divine within—the revivifying, the rejuvenating of that spirit of life and truth within every atom of the body. This will put to

flight all of those things that hinder a body from giving expression of the most hopeful, the most beautiful. (Edgar Cayce 572–45)

Notes

_____

_____

_____

_____

_____

_____

_____

_____

Patience, Fruit of the Spirit

Patience is an unbounded form of Love. (Edgar Cayce)

Patience is a Christian fruit of the spirit. Like all spiritual strengths, it is transforming. Sometimes, the loving unifying consciousness needs time to orchestrate events for your betterment. And sometimes, psychological stepping-stones need to be traversed before intentional requests can be answered. You only need to drive on America's roads to know patience is a quality much needed. I came to recognize the value in patience in my life when a request I made as a child was answered in midlife. When I was a young child, I used to play in my grandmother's attic. I recall one time running down the attic steps to go home and saying to myself that I hoped someday I would have my own attic room like the one I was playing in at my grandmother's house. Some thirty years later I was walking through my new office, which is a small house I had been directed to buy through a dream. When I remembered saying this wish to myself, I realized I now had my own attic office that looks amazingly similar to my grandmother's attic. And as a sideline, I bought the property from a friend who said to me at the closing that when my friend first bought the property eight years earlier, she was thinking I would move into it when she retired. Plans were in the making to make my wishful intention come true. Incidentally, neither my friend or husband knew about my grandmother's attic wish. I had been looking for a few years to purchase office space, but my architect husband never liked any of these other properties. And when I bought this property, I had not initially recalled my request some thirty years earlier. Clearly, requests are answered within spiritual time and earthly time as in my forties I had the financial ability to make such a purchase. If you pray for a particular happening, know that it may come much later than you humanly desire. We each are subjected to the rules on the earth and need to do our part in making our dreams come true. When your spiritual self, a loving desire, is included you increase the opportunities on earth for yourself as well. However, keep your request in the front of your mind and keep a lookout for answers. Change requires awareness with keeping a focus and at times repetition.

When requests are answered and you become aware of the loving universe attending to you, you may become afraid. Not to worry, your core is aware of everything you have ever done or said and loves you. It is a blessing when requests are answered, reminding you that you are cared for and loved. Research by Sarah Schnitker, PhD, associate professor of psychology at Baylor University, confirms that patience is positively associated with life satisfaction, hope, self-esteem and negatively associated with loneliness, depression, and anxiety.

However, society does not look favorably on patience. We live in a fast-paced technological world today and multitasking is socially rewarded over patience. Research repeatedly points out that multitasking on cognitive tasks shows an IQ decline, reduces comprehension, overall performance, and can lead to mental blocks. Surrender your need for quickness even if doing so initially causes anxiety. Learn to be patient with yourself even if doing so causes you to do so kicking and screaming. Take your time, and by doing so the dynamics of time changes. As you mindfully slow down, your perception of time changes as you feel in control of the flow of your life. Time no longer has a foothold on your consciousness. Instead of time running your life, you and your core self have the foothold over your life. Patience, like everything in life, is a choice.

As you continue to patiently await movement from within your core self and perhaps guidance from God, blessings do occur, even blessings you have not consciously requested. You witness your "I am" core self guiding your footsteps. I recall a client I call *I Am Dying,* a remarkably beautiful woman who was a victim of surgery gone wrong. She suffered an undetected perforated intestinal wall and almost died in the hospital recovery room. A few years later, she found herself dying again, this time emotionally from an unwanted divorce initiated by her perceived soulmate husband. Still suffering from the physical damage of the surgery, *I Am Dying* lived on a very limited diet. It was clear her body was in a depleted condition. However, she initially focused on dealing with the divorce and making certain their son adjusted to the divorce. She never gave up faith and trust that God would answer her prayers for a passageway out of her divorce situation and depleted state. Over the years, she had many dreams in which she received guidance regarding inner strength but felt she did not receive answers for her physical issues.

Still, patiently she continued to wait, until one day, while experiencing some relief during a Reiki session, an image of a yellow lion appeared to her. At first, *I Am Dying* didn't think much of the image. But as she drove away from the Reiki session, she tuned into a Christian radio station and heard the preacher advise his listeners to be as bold as a lion. Here were synchronous blessings at work! Now *I Am Dying* felt that she was being reminded that she has the strength needed to walk the difficult divorce path, not as a creature forced to face an upsetting situation but as a loving creator of her own future. And *I Am Dying* began praying to receive the courage to follow the lion's path as it applied to being firm with her estranged husband regarding the emotional needs of their adopted son. She decided to focus on her divorce and simply maintain her poor health and to stop looking for an answer to her health issues as she believed this path was the chosen path for her. She followed this course with patience. She went through the divorce and continues to speak up for her son. Then she felt herself losing her physical and emotional strength and determination. In her prayers, she asked for something to hold onto. A few days later while in her bedroom, an earring dropped from her ear. She called me to see if it had fallen in the office. It had not, but I immediately knew this event would be significant to her. The earring had fallen under her bed, and when she reached for it, to her surprise, she pulled out a thank-you card from the Salvation Army that had a picture of a rainbow, a strong symbol for her as it reminded her that she and God have a contract of eternal love.

The blessings continued; a thought came to her mind to use the phrase "God in Christ, Christ in me, perfect unity." This phrase became *I Am Dying's* daily reminder of her god's unconditional love and continually gave her lionhearted strength. Two years later, *I Am Dying* stopped by to say hello to me as I was writing this section of the book. Here again, synchronicity manifested itself in the timing of her visit, evidence that we live in a unified field. Synchronicity continued; three years later, as I was editing this section, *I Am Dying* called me to say that she had been thinking about me, an intuitive, core self connection as I was reading my writing about her. She told me that her patience and courage had paid off. She had another round of surgery with a preferred doctor, and he had helped her.

As I reflect on her inner journey, it is clear that she was being asked to build up her courage and resolve divorce issues before an answer to her health issue could present itself. She now realizes her courage and patience led her to visit one doctor after another until she found a doctor she trusted and whose recommendations felt right to her. Today, she has moved through her divorce emotionally and mentally. She feels joy in being alive. And she continues to receive messages from within. I now call her *God in Christ, Christ in Me, Perfect Unity*.

Her patience teaches us to accept God's timing rather than trying to impose our own even when the path is difficult and the blocks to solutions appear numerous. It is OK to keep trying, but have patience until the right time and the right sense or feeling of something being a right choice occurs. This is a surrendering practice. And as you surrender, the loving consciousness exposes itself to you. And know that today's cultural fear of missing out on something makes no sense. If an event is meant for you, and you are in communion with your core, you will be guided so as not to miss out on something important in your life. The universe of God knows the perfect timing for you, and you cannot really miss out on anything that is meant for you to experience. Recognize this fear of missing out is your ego mentality speaking-the author of your struggling and suffering. Step into the flow of your life; accept that any need to wait is an opportunity.

Patience

Takeaways

Patience is a fruit of the spirit that is a form of unbounded love.

Patience has many blessings, including life satisfaction, hope, and self-esteem.

Believe in your own self-importance and position in eternity, knowing you are not time limited.

Research shows multitasking is detrimental.

To believe that you could miss out on something important in your life does not make sense for the loving universe is in harmony with your core, which has perfect timing.

Be patient for requests are answered in spiritual time not ego-driven earthly time.

Springboards

• Be guided by the rhythmic timetable and ways of nature. Each tree waits for its time to blossom and bear fruit. And each will bear fruit for many seasons in your lifetime. A tree does not push the sun to rise and shine. It awaits and receives the sun's light and bears its fruit in a season. The wind stirs waves in the ocean, just as the sun opens the delicate tree blossoms. All work in harmony, automatically, according to the right time. When you maintain a humble attitude and have patience, God's core within you will present the path that spiritually fulfills you and meets your true intentions.

- Honor this idea: I am on a human journey and I can patiently allow myself to know who "I am" more fully, moving toward a deeper appreciation and understanding of my journey.
- Learn to stay in the present moment. Though you spiritually live forever, learning to live in the moment is a healthy human step. Spiritually, the past and present, and even the future, as influenced by free will, are available in the moment. Live in the moment. If the past comes up in the moment, accept and deal with it. Keep the following poem in mind.

> I was regretting the past and fearing the future.
> Suddenly my Lord was speaking,
>
> "My name is I Am."
>
> He paused. I waited, He continued,
>
> "When you live in the past, with its mistakes and regrets,
>
> It is hard. I am not there.
>
> My name is not <u>I WAS.</u>
>
> When you live in the future, with its problems and fears
> it is hard.
>
> I am not there.
>
> My name is not <u>I Will Be</u>.
>
> When you live in this moment, it is not hard. I am here.
>
> My name is <u>I AM</u>. (Helen Mallicoat)

Notes

_____

_____

_____

_____

_____

_____

_____

_____

Empowered Spiritual Humility, a Fruit of the Spirit

Humility subdues the ego's voice so that you can hear the quiet voice of your "I am" core self. Humility enables you to discern if conditioned illusionary beliefs are in play due to the ego's desire to control reality and to feel important. When you understand the ego's fascination with itself and its selfish ways and break its grip on your consciousness, your awareness shifts towards recognizing we each are but a cog in the universal whole. Now being humble feels right.

Humility is a difficult step for human beings. Our animal instincts require us to be empowered and act in empowering ways, to ensure that we remain on top of the food chain. We take authority over the earth and its creatures and selfishly use up earth's resources while not caring how our desires and addictions affect others as well as the earth. Being humble can be perceived as a humiliating step, working against being the best, on top, selfish, powerful, and in control. In contrast being humble means you are not loyal or hypnotically magnetized to these conditioned ego desires as a primary goal to your life and identity.

Supporting the belief that we are in charge of the Earth, we have developed rules enforced by the lower ego mind. For example, believing in one's narcissist-based self-importance above others is an American illusion and we quickly defend our importance while easily feeling threatened in our competitive oriented society. We all too often refuse to treat others with regard when their values, opinions, or life circumstances are different. An example of this today is the differing values and opinions regarding COVID-19 mask-wearing and vaccinations as well as political divisiveness. And we separate self from others based on an ism, such as racism, Catholicism, Christianity, spirituality, and authoritarianism, just as we turn our backs to the poor.

We seem to be on a journey of eliminating differences rather than seeking equality. We seek sameness rather than equality as a driven value. Yet we all are unique and here to spiritually evolve, which means respecting others journey with tolerance and care, building a shared sense of safety and self-value from the foundation of social connection and sacred unity nondefensively with warmness, openness, compassion, and vulnerability as well as mutual respect and reverence for all living things. These are the ways of humility.

We do best when we work toward accepting differences on the path to equality. It is a difficult step and requires quieting the ego and connecting with your wiser core self. Have you ever responded humbly? When we recognize we each are here to be of service to all others and not to empower ourselves as the top animal allowed to be so at a cost to others. Recognize that feeling superior to others, arrogant, or self-righteousness is a path to inner separation and darkness.

We each are inherently precious and deserve to be respected and esteemed as portions of God. Our position cannot be affected by any outside consideration, including power, social standing, wealth, political affiliations, or vaccination status. We are all equal. That means each person is as important, as significant, and as worthy as the next person. There is no need to be perfect or right. There is no need to equate sameness with worthiness.

Healthy humility is a pathway to knowing and expressing to all others unconditional love and care. Doing so provides attunement with another, which builds relationships. Humility, in the deepest spiritual sense, provides awareness that you are humanly small yet profoundly a part of a larger human consciousness and a unified universal loving consciousness. Yes, each of us is important though not in control of all happenings and not more loved or more important than the next person, although ego thinks differently. And realistic self-love is never at bay when humility is present. In fact, when your actions and inner self follow the path of humility an oceanic feeling of self-love is the end result.

All healing comes from attuning yourself to higher values such as the many forms of unconditional love, and humility is a form of love. Loving yourself unconditionally is a necessary ingredient for healing illnesses. Fighting an illness does not assist the healing process. Rather, humbly asking for spiritual assistance and energizing yourself through accepting and acting according to your godlike position as a cocreator. You can heal mind and body. We can heal society in the same way. Society evolves through our higher, loving-core nature. Through relational attunement, a desire to connect with others with care and compassion, the world will become a safe and secure place for all. It is possible, for our creative capacities are limitless. As always happens when you patiently, humbly, sincerely, and lovingly surrender your ego will, you will receive spiritual strength. Where do you think unconditional love and joy reside? They reside in staying the course of humility.

Spiritual humility also is acknowledging that each of us do not know all the reasons for happenings in our personal life or the life of others. There is much going on underneath the surface layer of ordinary reality. We each may be an integrated portion of God, but are not God with total understanding. It is best to practice loving acceptance of all happenings, all peoples.

You may find it helpful to reflect on the following thoughts:

I do not have the vision of God, but I am incarnated in his image. I am a creative, loving, intentional being, and I have faith in God and my core self, to design my human and spiritual life path. I humbly ask for guidance as I bow my ego and await guidance. I forgo immediate self-defensive posturing and help others always with respect and dignity, no matter their position in life, even while knowing that my ego is threatened by doing so. I realize my ego needs to be nurtured into trusting my "I am" core self. Fighting for dominance and control over ego mentality and over others will not work! Humbly expressing unconditional love is what works. I am the person of my destiny and am evolving as a human-and-divine being. To experience the peace and light of spiritual evolution, and avoid the chaos and darkness of inner schism and separation, I unconditionally love all of myself, including the fear-based, conditioned self. I embrace others. I search for the face of God in everyone I meet. And I recognize I am equal to all; I am superior to no one. I realize I am here to bring unconditional love into the world. And "thy will be done" is, in fact, my highest will, in direct connection with my core self and my god. This path will lead me to clarity, inner peace, abiding love, and joy. I will humbly initiate all my actions on earth with unconditional love of self and unconditional love of all others, honoring my innate holiness as a spiritual creator. No longer will I be directed by and suffer from the familiar, socially conditioned thoughts and feelings that negate a humble nature. I humbly recognize that each of us is a traveler on the journey of becoming an enlightened joy being, with a unique individual path, graced by individualized blessings, and likewise, hardships. I respect the core entity of each human being. And I act compassionately as I understand that we are all on different levels of the learning curve for spiritual progression. Although we are individual physical beings, we are all one in spirit. Acknowledgment of this truth frees each of us from worry, guilt, and other spirit-blocking feelings and enables us to experience inner peace and joy as we each act responsibly toward ourselves and others.

Humility

Takeaways

From a spiritual perspective, humility is not a humiliating practice.

Humility enables you to gain authority over the self-defensive ego.

Humility requires choosing to self-identify as a loving, holy, eternal, creative, and intentional spiritual being.

Humility acknowledges that we are each precious and deserve to be respected.

Humility enables you to live with joy and create a safe and secure world.

Humility recognizes that underneath the surface layer of everyday reality much is happening and it is best to accept that we are a portion of God while not God with His greater understanding.

Springboards

- Do not view any job as menial as all jobs are a way of building a loving world.
- Do not attack another or otherwise defend yourself because of unjust criticism. Instead of creating a barrier to keep others away, find a way to build a bridge to connect. Acknowledge unifying oneness by being respectful and listening to others, even if you do not agree. Yet when your core voice within tells you to speak, grab hold of the moment with the strength of the mountain lion and climb the mountain to spread loving justice and rightness in the world.
- Choose to see the other person as they are, not as how I want the person to be, and have respect, concern, and care for the other.
- Practice opening your heart to all others as St. Teresa of Lisieux.
- Consider these phrases:

> Pride is concerned with who is right. Humility is concerned with what is right. (Ezra Taft Benson)
>
> The world tells us to seek success, power and money; God tells us to seek humility, service and love. (Pope Francis)
>
> True leadership is humility combined with compassion and power. (Lankton Ford)

Jesus as a Role Model

Jesus expressed his feelings with humility and firm authority. He was not arrogant or prideful. Upon the cross, he expressed care and compassion by asking God to forgive those who harmed him, a humbled stance. This man, born in a manger, capable of igniting unconditional love in others, transcended his human self to reveal the Christ figure we know today. He is a guide for each of us.

Notes

_____

_____

_____

_____

_____

_____

_____

_____

Spiritual Logic: Touching the Mind of God

> Trust in the LORD with all your heart, and lean not on
> your own understanding; in all your ways submit to him,
> and he will make your paths Straight. (Proverbs 3:5-6)

What the ego perceives you believe, and you create based on your perception. As perception is determined by the ego mentality in most situations, let's reach beyond the ego and find the unity in all things. Spiritual logic is a unifying your thoughts spiritual tool. It is a way to break away from the dual mind and find the positive in the perceived negative happenings in life. You will no longer use dualistic thinking, such as right versus wrong, good versus bad, black versus white. By thinking all events are, or can be fundamentally changed to express unity within life leads to lasting feelings of safety and security, inner peace. As a loving acceptance tool, practice the skill of spiritual logic by believing in a good potential behind a perceived negative event. Not that the good reason takes away the harm and hurt but helps to accept a difficult happening in life and live within a lasting contented state. It also changes your beliefs to view life from a nondual perspective, which strengthens your ability to be humbled and patient.

For most of us, causal logic, which is cause-and-effect thinking, and dual judgmental logic, such as good versus bad, are the basis of mental interpretations to explain life happenings. The ego likes to believe it has control over life and likes to find the 'bad' culprit to blame when bad experiences happen. Yet, when the ego is quieted perceived undesired events can move us forward on our spiritual path This is the belief underlying the tool of spiritual logic. It is viewing all of life events from a nondual perspective. Such a belief does not fit causal thinking or judgment patterns. However, follow the spirit of life and view negative experiences as simply what is next on my soul's path. Awakening requires intentionally allowing yourself to adopt a different viewpoint. It requires a willingness to understand yourself, others, and the events of your life from a spiritual self, nondual perspective. Doing so requires believing that sacredness exists within each of us and we each are on a path to being an integrated expression of unified consciousness.

Although some of us choose an ego-directed path of self-interests, we each are best served when working in alignment with one's evolving spiritual path. This is difficult to do when the other is perceived as harming you and when personal problems erupt. We may not be able to believe in the other as a spiritual being when it cannot be directly observed. And personal difficulties defy thinking from a spiritual perspective. Yet your goal is to use loving-kindness for clear seeing while holding another accountable, and spiritual logic for staying within a spiritual vortex that keeps you on the path.

As your soul resides in a nondual, nonjudgmental reality, it's time for the human you to accept the reality that nothing that happens to you by another primarily meant to hurt you. Rather it is an expression of a person who is stuck on his or her life path and needs change for spiritual evolvement. For example, I recall many women who have entered therapy to cope with divorce. Not recognizing the power of extended family issues, or a spouse's incompatible desired lifestyle, they often feel betrayed and abandoned. How does one view such ego-interpreted harmful situations without dualistic separation strategies? Can it be possible that in a nonjudgmental, nondualistic perspective a spouse can become aware that his or her spouse is simply being who he or she has always been? And is it possible that you, as a soul, are helping you design your own life for personal and spiritual fulfillment through a divorce? Believing so is the challenge of spiritual logic. This is more than thought replacement; it is replacing ego mentality with nondual belief. To believe that experiences chosen by you (and your ego) can be counterproductive for your self-awakening and spiritual progression on earth can be difficult. Yet soul will guide you to a fruitful outcome if you listen to soul and not the judging ego. Through acceptance of your sacred connection to your "I am" core self, and willingness to accept "perceived" undesired experiences, you will remain on a path of fulfillment.

Yes, we live in a free will zone and at times what appears to be a right choice, whether a marriage partner, job relocation, etc., turns out not to work out as anticipated. And bad events do happen, sometimes chosen by oneself. For example, when I was around eleven years old, my mother spirit guide told me I would marry a man at the end of a street my family was driving by. I thought, *No way. This is a poor urban area and I live in the suburbs. I do not want to be poor.* But I took note of the information at the time and over time forgot about the intuitive information following my ego's desires to forget. When I was seventeen, I worked in a restaurant at an amusement park a few hours' drive from my hometown. My inner guide told me to tell the other waitresses to call me if someone came in and opened the doughnut case on the counter. I did so. Close to the end of the summer season, a person opened the doughnut case and ate the doughnut. The waitress informed me. In talking with this attractive man, I learned that he lived at the very end of the street my guide mentioned when I was eleven. And he was the only one that summer season who touched the doughnut case. I did end up marrying that man and we also divorced. Neither he nor I grew to the spiritual state that we could negotiate a healthy marriage at the time.

Now it's time to look at thinking patterns and apply spiritual logic through identifying option A, B or C thinking patterns.

Option A

Option A Is your usual way of processing bad events, your eMAP interpretations. It is your automatic mental assessment of the reason that an unwelcomed event occurred. Your response interpretations for why an unwelcome event occurred have innumerable thinking and feeling pathways, such as responding with self-pity, anger, thoughts about being a victim of life, how you can take advantage of the situation for personal benefit, or beliefs that you are unlovable and unloved, to name a few ways we process unwelcomed events. As an example, let's consider a divorce situation in which a spouse has cheated. In this situation the woman is cheated upon, feels betrayed, abandoned, and humiliated. Perhaps her ego interpretations have her stuck in feelings of anger and despair-her automatic option A response. Next, a spiritual logic step is to release her anger and despair and follow option B.

Option B

Spiritual happenings are not easily understood in the limited logic of the ego, which fears love and prefers perceiving life as threatening. When you apply spiritual logic option B, you are reorganizing or recontextualizing thoughts, a mental shift away from the ego's sole focus on self-enhancement as the critical axis point for reasoning. Spiritual logic option B is totally detached from cause-and-effect ego-mind logic, which attempts to analyze, fix, find a reason, build on events for self-gain, or place an undesirable event into a framework of thought that blames the other. In contrast, spiritual logic involves viewing an event from the spiritual-evolvement perspective of an opportunity to work with one's core self to understand and heal from an undesirable event.

Spiritual logic challenges the ego-harmed person to process the disturbing event according to the belief that the happening is what is the next challenge on her path. To aid thinking from this perspective, find reasons supporting this belief. For example, how is this divorce going to help her? A difficult step. Or what is the couple to learn from the entrance of an affair into their marriage? To assist option B spiritual logic step, it can be helpful to reflect on how the higher force of soul is guiding one's life through the event by asking, "What am I to learn from this experience? What is my soul communicating to me through this happening?" Surprisingly, answers are uncovered though usually over some time passing. Don't fall into negative, option A ego thinking patterns.

As you practice option B disempowering negative beliefs and eMAP thinking patterns, the ego mind will release fear signals to stop you from thinking from a spiritual perspective. Can you interpret fear as simply a warning sign of a change in thought processes and perhaps ego challenging your decisions and not allow negative interpretations to be a deciding factor in your life? The ego fears that a change in thinking will lead to its loss of control and, ultimately, your demise. So don't be surprised if you struggle against guilt feelings or hear a recriminating voice inside. The ego is pushing your emotional buttons and releasing negative self-talk. And know that the ego, fueled by fear, employs separatist strategies to convince you that others are either "for you" or "against you," that is, are your enemies, or that you are a victim, are guilty, are to blame or need to attack for self-esteem, which is really ego esteem.

Can you let go of dual-thinking patterns? Can you switch to spiritual logic and believe that many negative life events and happenings can be stepping-stones, not stumbling blocks? For the writer, the last happening I wanted in my life was a divorce, yet it ended up saving my spiritual life and ended up assisting my former husband. Can you view events in your life by believing that *all is happening to serve or has the potential to serve your growth as a divine-and-human being*? Spiritual logic helps you overcome mental and emotional blocks as you work at loving yourself through the acceptance practice of spiritual logic.

Difficult experiences, such as a job loss, divorce, living during the current COVID-19 pandemic, or even interacting with others who have a different viewpoint or different political affiliation, require *courage* to accept an undesired event as a mysterious way of promoting spiritual awakening. It also requires you to *lovingly accept* the event. Loving acceptance does not mean giving up and saying there is nothing you can do to change a situation. Perhaps you can't get your old job back or work at mutual growth in the marriage. If you follow the flow of your life, without paralyzing emotions, you can view difficult situations as an arrow pointing out what is next for you to address on your life path to spiritual awakening and joy. Perceived undesired events can be answers to your higher desires. A divorce is difficult, but it can lead to a better-fitting life partner, for example. And believing your core expresses God's love for you and has your best interests at heart leads to entrance into the transforming level ground of Christ's consciousness, which leads to becoming an integrated divine-and-human being living as a joy being. Reach beyond human logic and use spiritual logic as a reasoning tool.

You can do it! But you must break through the ego's interpretations, your automatic first beliefs that you have been harmed or are harming another and God is punishing you or does not love you. My willingness to follow my core self and identify spiritual logic occurred when in my career I was intuitively directed to ask a client who had lost her five-year-old daughter to cancer to find a good spiritual reason for her daughter's death. Option B. Her eMAP, option A, told her she was somehow at fault and doomed to feel low self-esteem and chronic depression in her life because her toddler daughter died. Subconsciously she believed she somehow harmed her daughter and caused the cancer. She probably thought I was crazy to think there could be a good reason for a child's death. And it was a difficult request for me to make of her. Yet I knew my core was answering her request to find a way out of clinical depression. I had to trust that one's core self looks beyond the face value and surface effects of events and knows all the factors at play in an experience. I had to trust that one's core knows best. And from following core guidance, I personally know that the inner voice becomes clearer and increases one's knowing capacities.

Trusting in my core, I made the request. Fortunately, this client believed in God and could accept that there was a good reason. She left the session with the intention to uncover what God was saying to her through her child's death. Two weeks later, this client reported that finding a good reason for her child's death was a challenge for her. Yet she did so, and the understanding given to her immediately lifted her depression. She realized that she knew best how her daughter was feeling, and she was able to provide maximum comfort for and personal connection with her daughter throughout her daughter's dying cycle. This released her guilt and gave her back loving connection with her core self and God. She believed her daughter was now in God's hands.

This mother also used the message as an indicator of the purpose of her life, to be a nurturing blessing to dying children, helping them along their spiritual path. The knowledge did not take away the loss of her child, but the truth helped her to survive the loss of her daughter and in fact to thrive throughout the rest of her life. She continued to help dying children for many years. This mother, like each of us, had to break away from conditioned, casually linked ego-mind thinking and release guilt feelings to find the spiritual purpose of an undesired event-in her case, her daughter's death. She did not invest in the conditioned, causally linked ego interpretations of undesired events, option A, and instead found the spiritual meaning of the undesired event, option B. And choosing option B has the additional blessing of personal integration providing her the blessing of thriving with a purpose in her life. Allowing one's loving core to guide oneself is always the right way. If she could find a "good" reason for her child's death, any of us can find alternative or spiritual reasons for perceived undesired happenings! Accepting that each of us is here purposed to bring the blessings of love for all on earth helps us understand how one can give even though it hurts, risk one's life for a loving cause, as did Martin Luther King Jr. Or die on a cross for the salvation of others, as did Jesus.

To change our conditioned assumptions about our lives, to find the good in the bad, to see light in darkness, to believe the sun is above the rain clouds, and to believe that a unified reality is always working to promote loving oneness is a spiritual perspective that reaches beyond our casually linked minds. This is the way of the mystical and the way of spiritual logic that leads to joy.

When you choose option B, the results will deepen your awareness of self as a valued and cared-for member of loving consciousness. And doing so will open new neural pathways in your brain through which the ego will bow, transcend, and point out your miracle path.

Option C

However, the ego is powerful and it may be difficult to accept and believe in spiritual logic, option B, including the idea that higher forces are granting your true intentions. Or perhaps you just don't feel comfortable changing your thoughts in alignment with option B. Turn to option C, which will help you create a happier life.

In option C reframing, you accept that in every event there is good in bad, even though you may find such a thought as uncomfortable. You look for an alternative, everyday reason for an event that does not place you in a victim position or any other negative position. You assume there is a good reason for an unwelcome event, and option C challenges you to find the good reason or faithfully accept that a good reason exists even if you cannot conceptualize it. For the divorcee with a young child, it may be recognition that the ex-husband did not desire to be a father and really only wanted to play and have fun as they did during their courtship and early marriage. For the marital couple experiencing an affair, it may be to increase intimacy in the couple or clarify limits and boundaries, which may include a divorce. Finding the good in an undesired experience balances your feelings and thoughts and places you on a level emotional field, which is needed to spiritually evolve.

Spiritual Logic

Takeaways

Spiritual logic is logic based on nondual belief and trust in your core self, believing your core holds your best interests as paramount at all times.

Option A is your usual, negative ego-eMAP interpretation of the reason for an undesired event.

Option B is believing that the "I am" core self can guide you through a perceived undesired event through acceptance, which can lead to insight into the reasons for an undesired event.

Option C is identifying a good reason for an undesired happening (i.e., divorce) today leads to a better spouse in the future.

Spiritual logic challenges you to consider, "What is God saying to me through this event today?"

Cognitive Steps to Spiritual Logic Thinking
Method Number 9

Briefly describe an unwanted or negative event you experienced.

_____

Identify and write down option A, your ego-driven eMAP interpretation of the event.

Consider what God may be saying to you through the event. Write it down (option B).

If option B is too big a leap, choose option C, in which you simply accept the event at face value but reframe your thinking to identify at least one positive aspect of the experience. Write it down.

Practice spiritual logic by writing down the good and undesired aspects of the COVID-19 pandemic.

Springboards

- A spiritual framework for thinking, rather than a learned, conditioned eMAP, reflects your true nature.
- A challenge. Research tells us we are a country that imprisons. Some prisoners are evil possessed and need to be imprisoned. However, many persons are imprisoned as they were raised in PTSD environments, experienced trauma and have PTSD, or have self-esteem issues and an ego that tells them selling drugs is all they can do. Accountability is important; punishment is not helpful. What do you think and what would you like to think?

> We will never be aware of all the things of which we are not aware. But recognizing this allows us to reflect on our assumptions and to hold them with greater flexibility. In this way we may become more conscious collaborators in an emerging new story that full embraces our collective well-being. (Marilyn Schlitz, PhD)

Notes

_____

_____

_____

_____

_____

_____

_____

_____

Seeking Lionlike Courage and Determination to Be a Joy Being

To make the changes from unhealthy, self-focused, fear-based, or entitlement-conditioned ways of living to a spiritually centered life requires courage and determination. Because the ego is powerful, knows you, and will do whatever it can to prevent change in your personal consciousness, courage and determination are needed to move you forward on your spiritual path. Courage, with humility, bows the ego and helps prevent unhealthy, selfish, and fearful eMAPs from controlling your life. And it is in believing and having faith in the inner guide leading your path, in alignment with the universal God, that gives us the courage to let go of what is not really working in our lives and to determinedly choose to walk a path of peace.

We each desire to know the course of our life plan. When you are driving a vehicle, it's always easier to plan your trip along familiar roads because you know where the twists and turns lie ahead. Having an idea of what is ahead on your life path would be a nice way to live. Of course, as discussed earlier, the ego's goal is to make your life predictable so it, and you, can feel in control of life happenings. Yet many times, events happen without a heads-up or warning.

As human beings, we certainly have some say-so as to how our life evolves. Along our life path, we make many decisions. And many happenings are unexpected and out of our control. To navigate the difficult twists, sharp turns, and downhill slides of life, it helps to have faith and trust with courage and determination that your spiritual core is always working to guide you, if you have so chosen. Unfortunately, sometimes our decisions are based on the advice of the conditioned ego rather than the wisdom of your core self. We cannot control outside events, only our inner choices.

Process of Change

Changing eMAPs can be a scary proposition. As ego-controlled humans, we don't like change. And the master controller, ego, can produce inner conflict when you make conscious choices that are not in agreement with its selfish agenda. The inner ego fights for control leading to conflict as it fears initiating change. The ego is powerful witnessed when it separates out the human race producing social, economic, political, and racial divisiveness among people, global ethnic abuses, dictators, nations at war, and abuses of Mother Nature. Sometimes, it may seem that even Mother Nature is against you. For example, it is hard not to listen to the ego's suggestion to be anxious and perhaps angry at God when one's survival is threatened by a hurricane, flood, earthquake, or pandemic illness. Perhaps these are the only means Mother Nature has available for rebalancing itself and change is always in operation on the earth. We know ocean and gulf waters are warming surrounding America making the cool winds of Africa a threat. Yet Mother Nature may need to be cooled for global survival. As well, soul can release conflict and inner turmoil when you are off your soul path. Some of the most difficult life challenges are part of the learning curve toward spiritual progression.

The ego's way of producing conflict is many and varied. It may send you disturbing dreams. Your dream life is a time when the ego can take control over your thoughts and feelings and do its fear-based work. You may experience nightmare images of demons and dragons or dream a scary dream about a life event. At other times the ego may give you dreams about becoming seriously ill. Do not energize these ideas with your attention.

All your faults, poor decisions and unloving acts may appear in your mind. And that's OK. No one is perfect, nor can a person be skilled at everything. Thoughts and feelings of self-doubt, shame, low self-worth, not being "good enough," may enter your consciousness. Think about these thoughts and feelings. Are they valid? Or are you simply acting, feeling, and thinking differently? Guilt, panic, anxiety, or worry may rise to the surface of your mind suggesting any change in eMAPs and conditioned personality places you in physical danger. Again, is this valid. Are you truly in danger, as the ego believes? It takes courage to be willing to change your life patterns and trust your core, and to believe your god has a plan for everyone in this world who desires to be guided.

It is difficult to believe in a life plan when faced with life-altering events or circumstances, such as divorce, financial chaos, job loss, the death of a loved one, or children who are having serious problems. The ego is busy supporting unhealthy feelings, such as anger or anxiety, as a response to a happening or a desired change on your part, reflecting its distaste for any form of change. As a global plan but we each have free will and are not predestined. Yes, it may be time to admit wrongdoings responsibly rather than to run away and hide or pretend. It takes courage to admit your weaknesses and likes and dislikes. Or it may be time to speak up about injustices. It takes courage to peel off the protective mask of the conditioned self, with its habits and routines that provide a false sense of safety. It will take courage to tear up the roots of unhealthy MAP programs based in fears, desires for retaliation, to heal past injustices and overcome selfishness.

Take firm authority by not fighting with your ego, and gently soften the ego's rigid ways to help you deactivate fear-based eMAPs. Use the springboards in this book that resonate with you. You must be willing to go through the process of change, which involves conflict and fear of the unknown. However, the challenge is worth it as worries, protective anger, and fears block your spiritual beacon's lens. Through detailed self-examination, take note of the aspects of your life that need to change! Choose to manage your thoughts and emotions and stay committed. Know that every step you make toward change, no matter how small, is a step in the right direction. As mentioned, your core self is always in earshot and is your support.

And it takes courage to believe you exist within a spiritual foundation and are being cared for through your own inner "I am" core self at all times. Know that your soul will never suggest change that will harm you or others. When you choose to act with courage, you will respond to conflict and chaos with courage. Hold on, for your core self will move you beyond conflict and bridge the gulf between real and imaginary happenings. Yes, many of our fears are imaginary.

It is said the opposite of fear is love. What would be different in your life if you did not allow fear to possess you? To support fundamental well-being, keep in mind that you are an eternal, holy spirit, always connected in the heavens, and you are an important part of the larger "one reality." Your true identity is a spiritual being, not a conditioned self. Choose to respond to all events with this knowledge and be courageous. Know that when the ego learns you are going to build a spiritual life, the ego follows your commitment to maintain its control. You will feel whole and joy as the two worlds of ego and core self come together.

It also takes courage to follow a hunch without worrying or being afraid of the outcome. You will need courage to act on the intuitive promptings coming from your core. Trust and at times determined patience are needed. For example, I had an ongoing, sincere intention to find courage I needed to publicize this book. I believed I was not a courageous person. About one year of setting my intention, my request to find courage was answered on what turned out to be a fate-filled day. My core placed me in a situation that required choosing a courageous path. I went on a vacation with my husband to Yosemite National Park. The intention to find my courage was ever-present in my mind. On a brisk and sunny early spring day, my husband and I decided to walk along the shore of Mirror Lake. Upon entering that part of the park, we came upon a sign stating what to do if you encounter a mountain lion. Immediately, intuitively, I knew that if I proceeded, I would encounter a mountain lion. I turned within and asked my "I am" core self to explain. I automatically recognized my soul speaking through the lion-courage association of one of my former clients, and I knew that proceeding on the path was part of finding my courage. And I thought I was on vacation! I knew I could choose and not honor my soul's intention. But I knew if only I could walk this path, I would be taking advantage of a great opportunity presented to me. I also took solace in the fact that I am not a small adult and that there were many other tasty foods available to mountain lions that early in the season. Being conscious of myself and my courage intention, and having aligned human intention with spiritual unconditional acceptance, I proceeded on my path. Knowing the power of intention wrapped in spirit, soul, and human self, I knew the likelihood of an encounter was great. And while I knew I was at risk, intuitively, I felt I would most likely be OK.

My husband and I walked along the path for a while, enjoying one another's company and the scenery. When my inner voice stated it was time to rest, I had forgotten about my intuitional awareness of the possibility of encountering a lion. I sat down by the water while my husband journeyed on. Time passed. Although I do not usually pack food on such trips, I had an energy bar in my coat pocket. As I pulled it out and unwrapped it, I remembered the potential for a lion encounter. I also recalled telling my core that on this journey, I would stay on the trail and that the lion would have to come to the trail. I thought this would somehow protect me. It was my attempt to control life. And I was hungry, so I began eating the energy bar. As I ate the power bar, noticing how good it tasted, I was awestruck: a mountain lion came out of his sleeping den on the water's edge of Mirror Lake less than fifty yards away from where I sat. Panic ran through my body.

Not being a "visual" person, I was first amazed by how clear my vision became. I saw every leaf on every tree limb and sensed every living creature. Panic physically paralyzed me while I felt a strong urge to run. Both of these responses are common physiological hind-brain responses in all animals who can be prey for a larger, stronger animal. I told myself that I had predicted this occurrence, that there was a lesson in this experience, and that I needed to be present to it even while my mind and body pulsated with fear. I was reminded how difficult it is to change, to step away from fear and respond with firm self-mastery. I forced myself not to move hastily, as I wanted. My eyes were glued to the lion's huge paws, waiting to follow his movement. His paws appeared large and firmly planted, giving me the perception that he had definite ownership of earth and power in his paws to maintain his kingdom. He stretched, and I knew he was just waking up and beginning his daily journey up the mountain to roam for his breakfast. And I had awakened him with the smell of my energy bar, food to tempt the lion and unwittingly become his prey.

During my fear-filled reaction, I felt the ego desire to blame myself for eating food. But I stayed continuously present to the situation, and while still facing the lion, I slowly began moving back to the path twenty yards away. As I backed away, I made minimal noise, against the written advice of how to handle a lion, reasoning that as I don't like to be bothered by noise when I wake up, likely neither would the lion. Though I was very close to the lion, he never looked my way. I felt he knew I was there but did not want to be disturbed or perhaps tempted. I continued to back away until I reached the main path. Then I ran down the path in search of fellow humans, knowing there is physical safety in numbers.

In reviewing the experience, the surefootedness of the lion resonated within me. I knew that I had to approach all of my fears in the same way, or I may experience anxiety attacks. The image continues to speak to me now. It reminds me to be lionhearted, to passionately speak up for spiritual evolution in the world, and to remember who I truly am, not a creature on a human journey but a cocreator on a soul's faith walk within my human self, allowed to be as bold as a lion. I am grateful for the "logically awe-filled" mountain lion encounter.

When danger is on the doorstep, responding with courage may appear counterintuitive. At times, not running away, avoiding threatening situations or not responding with anger goes against the "rational" ego. Certainly, I could have said no to the lion encounter.

But my inner request had been to find courage. I felt the lion encounter was the way God and my core self were answering my request. When I checked within to see if my decision to attempt this lion meeting was a good idea, I felt at peace with my choice, confirming the intuitive advice. I also know we never walk alone, that my core would correct the path in front of me, and I intuitively felt it was not my time to die. And I knew taking this faith walk would develop my inner strength, which we all need to effectively handle the storms of life with minimal physical or emotional pain. Fortunately, most likely your path will not be to encounter a lion. And I never recommend placing yourself in harm's way. I share this journey to point out the need for courage to stop ego control over one's life. Be willing to take risks and accept pain and disappointment as part of your journey; setbacks and sorrows are a part of life. Know as you address all life events with unconditional love it will make you stronger and steadier. Let your spiritual ideals regarding desired ways to express unconditional love guide your actions. No matter what presents, assume and trust that there is an inner road to owning your soul passage that will lead you to becoming a joy being. Have the "courage to be" all that you are meant to be in the spiritual world as well as the human world.

Courage

Takeaways

Courage requires hope, trust, and faith that your core self is lovingly guiding your life.

Courage requires willingness to work through conflict to reach inner peace.

Courage recognizes that soul progression often does not follow a "rational" approach.

The "courage to be" means accepting all happenings, without letting the ego and its fears guide you.

Springboards

- Allow your inner lion to speak to you. Imagine a lion resides within you, and it encourages you to speak up in lionhearted ways for taking right action in the world.

  Embrace a Bible verse that speaks to you about courage such as "I am the light of this world. Whoever follows me will never walk in darkness, but will have the light of life." (John 8:12).

Notes

_____

_____

_____

_____

_____

_____

_____

CHAPTER 10

Intentional Connection with Your Core Self

Intentional Dreaming

> There is an inner wakefulness that directs the dream,
> and that will eventually startle us back to the truth of
> who we are.
>
> Rumi.

F OR EACH OF us dreams provide a portal to the "I am" core self bringing forward clear answers to life problems; personal issues are made clear, solutions to health concerns provided if intended. Dreaming brings each of us closer to an ongoing, intimate interpersonal relationship with your own higher self.

The ancient ones knew of the power of dreams. Ancient Greeks traveled to the Oracle of Apollo at Delphi with the intention of entering a dream state for prophesy. Beethoven credited inspiration for his music creations to his dream life. The Lakota Sioux Indian, Sitting Bull, had a dream the night before the battle now known as Custer's last stand telling him of the battle's outcome and future of his tribe. He was told his Indian nation would win this battle, but it could lead to the demise of his nation if his warriors defaced and stole clothing articles from the dead soldiers. Articles were stolen and the nation did crumble. His dream, down to the details, came true. In today's time I have heard that Jack Nicklaus changed the way he held his golf club due to a dream. The good news is we all have the capacity to touch the inner core of self through dreaming.

Dreams are a necessary component to healthy living and each of us dreams throughout the night even though you may not remember those dreams. Dreaming provides the mind an opportunity to sift through the day's events, keeping what is important and needs remembered and discarding what is irrelevant. Clearing out mental clutter provides internal mental space for coping with tomorrow. Once the analysis on the day's events is completed you move deeper into dreaming, delving into long term, ongoing problems for resolution. To keep you asleep, unknown people and places will filter into a dream of a familiar circumstance that needs resolved. The unfamiliar is used so you do not awaken. Symbols are a way for soul to communicate. A symbol reveals and conceals information, planting the seeds for future understanding while giving an answer for today's issues. Feelings are also the conversation tool of your soul as feelings allow a broader interpretation base overriding limitations of words.

Soul dreams are most easily remembered in the last dream cycle before awakening, though any dream remembered is significant. An intentional dream works like a phone call in which you can literally place the call by setting your intention as you fall asleep and your call is answered with a dream. It is the hypnogogic time-when you are falling asleep, which is believed to be quite a receptive time for soul communication. This directs the sleeping ego to stay asleep. Receiving answers through dreams is another example of ask and you shall receive. For example, although my husband thought intentional dreaming for problem solving was an ability which did not belong to him, one day he lost his wedding ring in his truck. He had looked everywhere and was planning to remove the seats when he went to bed with this issue dominating his thoughts. His intention to find our ring was strong, and he received the answer. He awoke the next morning with a clear image of where the ring was in his truck. He found the ring right where the dream had instructed him to look. Most recently he dreamed he was in an accident and that afternoon was hit from behind similar to what his dream predicted.

Begin by setting the intention and directive that you want your soul to connect with you through a dream. Set an additional intentional that "only my soul is to communicate though my dreams." Intentions you choose to dream about, whether a problem in your life, a prayerful request for yourself or another person, a request for an intuitive heads-up on the upcoming day's events; be determined, clear and precise about your intention. Believe in the power of your dreams as a communication tool to your wiser self for life problem solving. Waking up rested is an important component of a healthy life and to receive access to dreams. Patience is needed as it may take time for a specific request to be answered. Patience insures you truly desire an answer to the request. It strengthens the energy of the request and your belief in core connection as patience keeps you awake and attending to your request.

Place a pen and paper next to your bed so you can catch the dream as you awaken. Once fully awake write down as many details as possible. Then start the interpreting of the dream. Know that no one knows the dream interpretation better than you. Feel the differing feelings associated with the dream. Soul prefers to communicate through feelings and symbols. Analyze symbols and note how the dream feels to uncover its meaning for you. Sometimes fear feelings are felt. Work through the fear and do not allow fear to paralyze and grab hold of your consciousness. Know your higher self will assist you in moving through the fears. The good news is solving a dream related to a life problem assist the resolution of a problem. For example, I had a bad day, feeling low energy and somewhat down, and I did not know exactly what was bothering me. I went to bed setting my intention to understand my lethargy, that night I dreamt I was dancing with a kind elderly man. At first, I wanted to stop dancing because I am not a good slow dancer. I forgot I was dreaming. Then, I looked into his eyes and sensed he was someone I know but didn't know who he was. We continued to dance. I look at life as a dance. I once again looked into the eyes of this gentleman as we danced to the edge of the universe. He asked me if I wanted to cross over to where I thought nothing existed; black-like emptiness, without light. He then told me without words, this is where "I am" heading. My dream ends.

There are many levels of dream interpretation. At a concrete level Life is a dance for me. At a thematic level the theme is, "I dance through life, even the blackened times." Symbolically for me blackness represents depression and surrendering one's human life to integration with God.

Takeaways

Dreams are a guidepost for life.

We dream throughout the night with the last dream often being a guiding dream.

Setting a clear intention, believing in its fulfillment, being rested, and patient for an answer are necessary conditions for intentional dreaming.

You are the best interpreter or your dreams.

Dreams can be interpreted concretely, thematically, symbolically and based on the feelings the dream evokes.

Springboards

Start a dream journal, purchase a dictionary of symbols and analyze your dreams.

Sacred Place Imagery for Core Self Connection

We all benefit from having a place of refuge where we feel safe and secure. Now let's create, from memory or imagination, a comfortable, safe, secure, and sacred place where your "I am" core self and your human self will meet. Choose any place you wish, such as a beach, a mountaintop, a stream in the woods, or even your backyard. Allow yourself to imagine your sacred place so it can be brought forward when you need to de=stress and relax on your path to healing and personal and spiritual transformation.

Sacred Place Guided Imagery
Method Number 10

1. I want you to imagine your own unique, personally designed, safe, calm, external sacred place. This is a place made by you and your spiritual core self that evokes a feeling of deep calmness. It can be a real place, even somewhere you have visited, or an imagined place. If it is a place you visited, change features or aspects so that it becomes your very own creation, where only you and your higher self can go. Examples of peaceful places include a beach, an open expanse of sea and sky, an island, an exquisite garden, a meadow, a clearing in a forest, a beautiful cavern, a mountain-top, or a church. Just as easily, your sacred place could be simply open, loving hands.

2. Next, to the extent possible, visualize to the smallest details your external sacred place. And experience it, using all your senses. For example, if you imagine being at the beach, feel the perfect temperature of the day, the sun on your skin, and the sand between your toes. Hear the gentle waves rolling, and see the puffy clouds in the sky. You can sit on a lounge chair, lie on the sand, or walk along the shore. Choose a landmark where you and your higher self can meet, perhaps a large sand dune. If it is a forest scene, perhaps the landmark is a bench near the stream.

3. Remind yourself that this is *your* place, created by you and your "I am" core self, and no one can enter without permission.

4. Take a few deep, relaxing breaths as you place yourself into your imaginary sacred place. Let the rhythmic rise and fall of your chest balance itself into slow, deep, even breaths. Set the intention to connect with your core to strengthen your awareness of being within the boundaries of your core self in this sacredly designed place.

5. Imagine that this sacred place is where your higher "I am" core self wants to be with you. Attend to, breathe in, and feel the peace.

6. Notice anything that presents or changes. Be certain to feel your entire body.

7. Ask for guidance, perhaps on a specific issue.

8. Remain in your sacred place for ten minutes to twenty minutes.

9. Open your eyes to return to the present, while still carrying back with you the inner peace and perhaps love or intuitive answer you experienced on your journey.
10. Take detailed notes of this experience for later use.
11. If you desire, before returning to everyday reality, "shrink" your sacred place and move your attention into the midframe or solar plexus area of your body. Now you can incorporate within and carry around with you the safety, comfort, and peace of this special place. The power of positive conditioning can lead to your merely thinking about your safe, external place and achieving immediate peace and centering.

When you are in the inner space of abiding peace, the image of your sacred place may expand. Or your mind may "automatically" shift to another image. Your image may involve movement such as visualizing yourself at the seashore making circles in the water, or it may change colors. When an image presents, allow, accept, honor, and express gratitude for it. Notice every detail of the image. And honor it by thinking about it and apply any understandings attained to your life. For example, if the image turns from gray to red, think about what red as a color means to you.

Imaginal Bridges

Invest in the powerful energetic resources where you live by connecting with a higher-energy place. These higher-energy places often are near water and mountains. Or they may be known as higher-energy planes, such as the Sedona's Cathedral Rock and the Black Hills of Dakota. Another example, Pittsburgh, is known for its three rivers. It is a high-energy plane. When meditating, you can visualize being at the center where the three rivers converge. Water, like fire and air, is a substance for movement. Imaginatively allow the three rivers to drench you, move you about, and uplift you. I have imagined the rivers moving me upward as if I were supported by a plume of water rising from a fountain. The imagination helps me to release inappropriate control needs and provides practice with the feeling of being physically uplifted, which you may experience when you are within higher spiritual realms.

There are many sacred places, such as churches, synagogues, and forests. Meditate in such places and set an intention, which is a form of prayer. Or connect with a holy figure in your imagination. Choose by thinking about the holy figures' history and what it means to you.

Attention directs the flow of energy, so pay attention to images and numinous experiences. The ego wants you to forget such experiences, so write them down, and refer to your personal experiences when self-doubt in your capacity to live as a joy being grabs hold of your consciousness.

Intuitive Soul versus Ego Discernment

Tracking Divinity Moving Within: Stop, Look within, and Listen

Your soul can help you tap into your unlimited creative potential and provide you clues, spontaneous hunches, and intuitive knowledge as you enter the flow of spiritual reality through quiet listening for discernment. Perhaps soul speaks quietly to allow you to choose your path, honoring your free will.

Through developing attentional-mental space to intuit the inner voice, you become aware of soul communication. To make inner room allow part of your attention to focus on the day's activities, while in the mental background you are quietly keeping alert, waiting, and listening for guidance. You are looking within for unexpected interior signals, while you also attend to the day's activities and at times hear the ego's voice. Soul is always listening to you and ready to answer.

Listening to different streams of mental life is a skill we each possess. Your brain can track two stimuli at the same time: ego pushes and pulls and soul communication. Always you choose which voice you are going to listen to. And as you follow soul guidance, your soul's voice becomes more distinct.

Your core communicates through the same human channels of thoughts, sensations, feelings, and perceptions used by your everyday ego. To intuitively discern your soul and its divine reality, which reaches beyond the realm of ordinary perception, be physically relaxed and be able to identify the ego's eMAPs. Invite spontaneous images, and notice vague inner stirrings and intuitive hunches that present throughout the day. Make a note of them as they can be your core communicating. Then during the day or evening, take time to befriend your inner self to determine what your higher self was saying to you during the day. If you need to, request a second event to confirm what you are thinking or feeling.

The best way to discern soul communication is to notice when feelings and thoughts step out of usual eMAP programming. For example, a former client of mine is asked to talk to groups on an almost daily basis. She maintains an inner state of dual awareness, which is awareness of ego and core communication. She has learned to clear out her unwanted anxiety eMAPs, and then, as she says, "I wait until I feel right about agreeing to give a presentation I'm being asked to give." At other times she says no to invites feeling that it will lead to unproductive arguments knowing presenting to a particular group would be unhealthy for her. She has learned to discern and follow internal core communication. In doing so, she reports benefits, such as being at the right place at the right time, acquiring substantial wealth, as allowed on her soul path, and living in a state of internal peace. Once identified, you can choose to ignore ego's eMAP advice while you wait and listen attentively for soul communication. Stop, look, and listen to become aware of interior movement and to follow your core suggestions for life-path guidance. Regularly set your intention to ensure that your thinking is open to core movement. As you are the boss assertively direct the ego to be quiet to assist discernment.

You can actively ask for and receive specific answers to life dilemmas as you watch and wait, maintaining an inner state of peaceful awareness, which is strengthened by meditation. Give your soul a specific way for your request to be answered. When I am faced with a situation, or when I need to make a life-path decision, I like to request specific action from my soul. I go within and ask for an image; as for me, my soul communicates symbolically, that is, without words most of the time. And I simply request a specific action like send me the right person, guide me to a helpful book, answer me through my runes. I trust and know soul will move my inner and outer worlds for my benefit. If I need confirmation, I ask for a second time for people or events to corroborate the correctness of my soul communication. At times, I'll ask for three confirmations to make sure the guidance is really coming from my soul and not my ego. When you make a request of your soul, specify the particular way that your soul should answer the request, such as an image or an action. For your soul to communicate it is important that you believe your soul has the capacity to move all things in the material world for your betterment.

Soul provides advice for physical health, emotional needs, and material needs. However, your soul *also* communicates through what we call negative emotions. Anger can be a signal coming from your core that right action is needed. At its base it remains a love action. Screen and discern your motives for feelings, thoughts, and actions. For example, I can be angry but not have a malicious motive. I recognize that my feeling of anger can be sacred communication from my "I am" core working within me, letting me know I must act assertively, with right intent, and bring care and compassion back into the experience that is causing me anger. This is not easy for me as my ego stays on guard when I begin to feel angry. A part of me always believes my anger is justified, yet many times it's my expectations for others, and ego need. Learn to trust yourself, even when you feel angry, inpatient, and desire to act arrogantly. And intuitively discern so you are not allowing the ego and its need for importance and control causing the disturbing feeling. Trust your intuition, moments of clarity, and spontaneous knowingness, which are really sacredness in communication within you. Remember the ego only knows its own eMAP content. Fully expect that your core will communicate to you. This is a way of being in the moment within the human frame to experience sacred communication.

Through subjugation of the ego, one becomes what author Eckhart Tolle calls a multisensory being, referenced as the "I" behind awareness. Or as I would refer to as the "I am". One is no longer rooted in conditioned, relationally programed feelings and thoughts, one becomes a conduit for knowing the spiritual universe of your core self within.

Connection via your core lifts your awareness into the spiritual rhythm of consciousness. In this higher level of conscious awareness, you feel a sense of belonging and oneness, and you reside in love and inner joy. These are the feelings resulting from listening and following core advice. The more you connect and invest in core connection, the more guidance you receive. And as the poet Rumi reminds us, the presence within is a friend.

Soul is not limited to discernment only to benefit the individual self. Because you reside in a universe of oneness, you can receive inner communication in service of others. We all know or have heard of mediums who connect with a client's needs and receive intuitive perceptions to help him or her. You may remember a time when you gave advice to a friend and didn't quite plan to say all that you said, but your expanded message helped your friend. Spiritual communication at times is mysterious and does not follow our rational rules for communicating. However, communication from your core self always has the same message: you are loved beyond your wildest imaginings, and you are a loving being with unlimited creative potential.

Discerning soul communication is setting an intention, and doing so follows the law of creation as what you believe you create. When you intend to be aware of core connection, you receive core connection. As you set your intention, so it happens.

Intuitive Soul versus Ego Discernment

Takeaways

Each of us has the capacity to distinguish the different streams of mental life and sensory experiences occurring within.

Intuitive discernment is attending to and discerning typical eMAP programs from core self communication.

Intuitive discernment requires quietly attending to thoughts, feelings, perceptions, and interior pulls that are not part of typical eMAPs while functioning in the everyday world.

Intuitive discernment lifts you into the spiritual rhythm of life, which provides a sense of oneness, belonging, peace, and joy.

Intuitive discernment also provides guidance for others based on one's intentions.

Springboards

- Keep yourself in a peace-filled inner state. This is the inner stage for knowing.
- At the same time, attend to your habitual eMAPs for daily living, including perceptions, thoughts, and feelings. Identify fear-based eMAPs. Place fear-based streams of thought in the background of your mind.
- Don't buy into a negative belief system.
- Notice different, subtle changes within. Discerning when your soul is talking requires noting atypical thoughts, emotions, and sensations that emanate from your core self. These thoughts and feelings are contrary to habitual, conditioned self-feelings and thoughts.
- Be comfortable with the atypical feelings, thoughts, and perceptions triggered by your soul.
- Be aware that existence manifests in, to, and through each of us.
- Write down revelations and insights.
- When an image presents as an answer to a problem to heal yourself beyond symptom control, ask, "Why did my core produce this image, and what does this particular image mean to me? What was my first thought? What insight is my wise core conveying?" Identify the emotional and mental issue supporting the physical problem.

Expanded Core Mindfulness

> Integrated, resisting delusion are those who long clearly for a foundation in themselves; they shall find all around them the materials to build. (Beatitude 4, interpreted from Aramaic by Neil Douglas-Klotz)

Within each of us, your core desires to weave together the human and spiritual fabric of one's life. Like intuitive discernment and objective observation, expanded core mindfulness is a tool that helps you to note how seamlessly everyday reality is interwoven. Having faith, trust, and full belief that your core self is able to move any matter on the earth for you, you witness external events occurring just for you. To track the events in your life, be fully present, moment to moment. Be mindful of your surroundings to notice atypical changes that reflect core external movement, and maintain a harmonious state of mind with complete love and acceptance of yourself. And, maintain a nondefensive attitude. Surrender and allow uncertainty and vulnerability as a way of inviting your core self into your life and know changes, which extend beyond synchronicities, can dramatically happen. These are the core ingredients of expanded core mindfulness. Remember the client *why me* who clearly recognized spiritual connection, declaring, "The Divine was talking to me using the voice of my mechanic" (page 46). This encounter culminated in her "getting the message." This is an example of being expanded core mindful.

I want to share a contact with a gentle, elderly, religious woman whose son died of a heroin overdose. I call her *I Am Angry at You, God*. The shock of drug usage to most families is overwhelming and difficult to handle. And having a child die of an overdose has the potential to truly devastate one's beliefs in one's god. At such times, it is not uncommon to turn away from all that you have known and trusted, such as your relationship with your god, and to be unable to find a reason for living. This client had struggled for years to help her son, and after his death, she desperately desired to return to her faith but felt angry at her god for allowing her son to die. But not to worry, for the universal God has "big shoulders" and can bear our rejection while carrying us through our grief. As her anger at God was becoming a habitual eMAP program, inner conflict erupted, so she entered therapy. She simply could not pray as she so fervently had in the past. In discussing her religious beliefs in therapy, she mentioned that she had a prayer card for St. Rita, her confirmation saint, and had been carrying it in her purse since her son's death. As St. Rita is the patron saint of impossibilities, I followed her expanded core mindfulness lead and asked *I Am Angry at You, God* to pray to this saint to intervene and help with her anger and concerns regarding her son. I also asked her to be expanded core mindful by staying alert to any changes in her world. And *I Am Angry at You, God* did so and also asked for a sign that her son was OK. Only a few weeks went by, and the prayer of *I Am Angry at You, God* was answered through a short but beautiful spiritual connection. In a short dream she received a vision in which St. Rita brought her son to her. In that dream moment, she saw that he was OK. Her open-heart vulnerability to St. Rita allowed spiritual awakening. She felt compassion for herself and all others struggling with addiction. She was able to forgive her son for his drug addiction and transitioning. And she forgave God and herself.

Your core manifests through any medium: people and other living creatures, television, or other media. For example, a client who had recently lost her mother, with whom she was very close, asked for a sign that her mother was happy and watching over her. That afternoon, as she was walking down the hallway at home, suddenly noticed a strong gingerbread scent in her home and recognized it as the scent of the cleaning solution used in her mother's hospital room. She did not own any such cleaner, nor did she employ a cleaning person who could have used the product. And she has not encountered the scent since that day. She knew her request was answered and her mom was OK. Smells are a powerful connection source. Friends, as well as strangers, will drop by to see you, although they may not know why they chose to do so. And they will have something to say or give you, and that something will be meaningful. Such happenings may range from a beloved, long-lost friend walking back into your life just when you most need support to something as simple as finding the perfect parking space or listening to a podcast or webinar that answers your intention request. Or perhaps you recognize that a difficult experience holds a lesson you need to learn. Paying attention and noticing these small blessings is using expanded core mindfulness. And being aware of these happenings is part of developing the maps on your miracle path.

You as well can ask of your core self for guidance and other requests. When doing so, ask for specific ways to receive, such as "Send me the right book," "Take me to the right place," or "Guide me to the right page and speak to me through my reading of this book." Use expanded core mindfulness to keep track of your intentions being answered through movement in the everyday reality of your life. Remember, the ego will work at forgetting until it transcends.

When your requests are shaped by unconditional love, don't be afraid to ask for spiritual happenings. Sincerely desire spiritual partnership, not primarily for personal or material gain but for spiritual sustenance and evolvement. This does not mean you should not ask for material things. But don't allow yourself to get addicted to materialism; that's ego movement. Then watch the material things on earth move for you. As external events answer your intentions and illuminate the spiritual pathway, expanded core mindfulness will help you recognize the signposts that indicate you are walking the right path.

Always keep in mind that we do not know the details and totality of spiritual life within and surrounding each of us. Sometimes, unexpected and undesired guidance may come your way. As you break free of conditioning bonds with expanded core mindfulness, moments will blossom with meaning. Your life-path horizon will broaden as you recognize the spiritual signposts that hold clues to the meaning and purpose of your life, life lessons, core messages, and blessings. Unexpected opportunities and grace-filled miracles will occur because you are one with your core who is one with God, who is the One. You are the energy of creation. And your core self is harnessing, directing, and enforcing the creation process at this moment as human self and "I am" core self are in alignment. Keep alert; stop, look, and listen. And remember you reside in a unified field of existence in which you are a primary member. The more you believe, the more movement on your behalf occurs. How can you not feel fearless and joyful?

Believe in your creative capacity within your intentions; quicken your path by thinking, feeling, and doing unconditional loving acts based within higher values of love, truth, and justice. And notice the external world movement just for you.

Expanded Core Mindfulness

Takeaways

When requested, your core self assists in designing your life, including moving external events on the earth.

Expanded core mindfulness is learning to track the flow of external movement of your core as it interacts within the external world to provide guideposts for spiritual awakening and blessings.

To track your life flow, be specific when you make requests, and keep alert for answers manifested through external events.

Springboard

- In the evenings, write down the events of your day. Note atypical happenings as well as answers to specific requests.

A Note

Intuitive core versus ego discernment and expanded core mindfulness often occur consecutively. The internal and external worlds flow together. For example, I previously spoke of my journey to having a therapy practice (Section-I am Intuitive). Besides having a psychiatrist offer me office space and a priest friend recommending clients for therapy, expanded core mindfulness examples, I also kept receiving internal core messages suggesting I start an "unwanted" private practice, which is intuitive discernment

Another example of these two manifesting tools working in agreement occurred when a client entered therapy because she was having difficulty with her son. He was refusing to move on with his life after high school by getting a job. She felt she was at the end of her patience rope with this child and now was thinking she should kick him out of her home so he would get busy creating his adult life. But she was internally feeling ambivalent about this decision due to her intuitive discernment practice. I call her *Don't Know What to Do*. Certainly, a way of being we each have felt. Notably, kicking her son out of her home was opposite to the present norm of having adult children live with their parents well into their children's midtwenties. But knowing I do not know what is best for another person, I stated I also don't know what to do but pray or set an intention for something to happen over the week that would give clarity as to whether to have her son move out or stay in her home for a period of time. I said I too would pray for an answer knowing "where two or more are gathered in my name there I AM."

The next week we reviewed the happenings of her week, an expanded core mindfulness practice. And *Don't Know What to Do* recalled an atypical happening she had forgotten. She was reading her Bible lesson for the week, which had to do with a fig tree and the owner wanting to cut it down because it bore no fruit. According to the biblical story, the owner's servant said, "Give it one more year and the servant will hoe it and enrich it with manure." The words had resonated for *Don't Know What to Do*, but she remained uncertain as to her dilemma regarding her son. I suggested to *Don't Know What to Do* that her answer as to what to do rested in the fig tree story because it *resonated* with her, intuitive core versus ego discernment. *Don't Know What to Do* continued to be present to the fig tree story images over the next week. She decided to specifically ask for a sign that the fig tree answer was supposed to be her answer. As we discussed her dilemma in therapy, she remembered that her son had, unusual for him, asked to taste a fig a month earlier, expanded core mindfulness at work. She felt this was a final confirming sign to allow him to live at home for another year and she would help him to "hoe and enrich his life."

SECTION 5

The Blessings

CHAPTER 11

Expect Miracles

> Miracles occur naturally as expressions of love. The real miracle is the love that inspires them. In this sense everything that comes from love is a miracle.
>
> —*A Course in Miracles*, Dr. Helen Schucman

A T THE PRESENT moment you are creating your life path based within one's beliefs. Yes, creating your life, including moving earth reality, determining the quality and character of your personal relationships is in your hands. Your thoughts, feelings, and actions vibrate within unified consciousness and manifest, with or without awareness. When you accept your true identity in proper alignment to your core, known through easily feeling contentment, love for self and others, reverence for all of life, you are in loving connection with consciousness. Consciousness loves you and follows your requests just as your hand moves as you will it. Through this awareness you release a flow of causative energy, resulting in blessings, graces, and miracles. You are one within the universe, which is one. As a product of spiritual oneness, you create and receive miracles. You are a full-fledged miracle being no longer creating your life according to the ego dictates.

We create within miracle territory. Miracle making is a surrendering process in which we allow our natural feelings of unconditional love to guide our life journey; desiring to love all is my higher will and is one in the same within higher consciousness. Yes, you have full belief, faith, and trust in your intuitive core self-connection, following intuitive hunches, noticing requests being answered, and being an "I am" consciously creating your own miracles.

Miracles are meant to remind each of us who we are: cocreators within God's unified, loving consciousness. When you are in the flow you set intentions and use your creator capacities for building a soul-based life, expressing spiritually based love in your thoughts, feelings, and actions; you activate miracles. I learned to do so when a patient begins therapy. Knowing that my client and I are spiritual presences, bonded to God's Spirit in divine consciousness, which assists in asking and receiving personal intentions, my client and I make specific requests. I ask the client to pray for an answer to his or her personal dilemma. Then I ask the client to believe, even if only for one month, in self as a loving, spiritual, core being. And I also ask the client to expectantly watch for an answer to the prayer request. I also remind the client that the ego will work at forgetting so notice personal thoughts and feelings that are different from usual internal chatter, intuitive discernment. I also strongly request from my core for an answer to my client's request, knowing the more persons pray and intend an event, the higher the likelihood of the event manifesting. When two trusting souls believe in core self's ability to provide what one needs in one's life, and it is a loving goal, a desired event often happens. In my experience, all types of perfectly timed events have happened-events my clients initially thought were impossible but nonetheless agreed to risk having hope and trust.

One of my first experiences of this process occurred working with a teenage patient during the 1990s, whom I refer to as I *Need a Heart* due to his serious congenital heart condition. He *required* heart surgery, which would have placed his family of six under dire financial strain. In fact, although both parents were employed full-time, the family could not afford the surgery, and at the time, universal health care was not available. The situation was causing overwhelming stress on the family. I was overcome with compassion. And as a therapist, I knew the stress could compromise the health of all family members. I asked the parents to pray for financial assistance. That evening, I entered into quiet meditation, connected with my inner core self, and put up my humbled and sincere prayer request that Christ attend to this family's needs. I immediately received a strong feeling that my sincere plea for help for this family was heard. And I fully believed that their need would be answered. As well, I knew that whatever the answer was, it would also resonate with respect to soul growth in the family. Yet I was shocked when during the very next therapy session, I *Need a Heart* told me that his father had won $1 million in the lottery. Chance or miracle? Coincidence or one's spiritual self within a unified, loving consciousness at work? This family was my first client miracle, a large one to make sure I was paying attention.

These human and spiritual journeys are no longer rare events. We are living on the cusp of a transformative time in which miracles are becoming more commonplace. For some people, personal transformation begins by asking, "What would Jesus do?" Others, from everyday people to celebrities, have been converted and transformed to the Kabbalah religion, recognizing their capacity for "becoming like God," as Rabbi Michael Berg reports. And yet others report miracles after having read "The Prayer of Jabez." Do you remember the news report of a murderer whose impending victim read *A Purpose-Driven Life* to him as a last request, which caused her would-be assailant to give up his murderous intent? Consider how people across the globe have fervently embraced the book *Conversations with God* by Neale Donald Walsch in which God makes these following statements, "I am with you always, I live in you, just listen to Me. And the authors of the Chicken Soup for Your Soul series, Jack Canfield, Mark Victor Hansen, and Kimberly Kirberger, report that miracles are occurring. People are following a spiritually driven loving path and talking to God these days and sensing and intuiting answers. God resides *within each of us,* which reaffirms our familiar childhood learnings that I am God's creation and I am a child of God. Because the spirit of God gives us life, we are living by the grace of God, and God grants us the capacity to create miracles within each of us.

These large miracles step completely outside of the ego's eMAP control parameters and we take notice. However, the powerful ego has us forget. And small miracles are likely sprinkled throughout your daily life, from getting the best parking space available to finding a short checkout line at the grocery store, to being protected from a downpour because you intuitively heard and heeded your soul's advice to take an umbrella, even though the forecast did not call for rain. Attend to these small miracles and express gratitude which increases your energy flow and feelings of self-love and being loved. When an event is positive, people often refer to the experience as "being in the vortex," being aware, or being in the flow as you witness core movement in every moment of your life, as your life miraculously unfolds.

Yet not all miracles are perceived as positive events. Often our true needs and desires are unknown. Perceived negative events may happen as a miraculous answer to your true needs. I recall a client who had difficulties with her boss. She was in conflict over how to feel when the boss was in a serious car accident in which her car was rammed by another. After spending months in the hospital with serious injuries, the boss returned to work and appeared to be a positively changed individual. My client asked me how anyone could feel grateful for such an accident. I asked my client if her boss was an individual who "rammed into" people. My client said, "Most definitely." Clearly, through the accident, the boss was experiencing the effects of her behavior toward others, and likely her innermost desire to break free of her conditioned personality and become a loving person was being answered. She was given an opportunity for spiritual awakening. As Deepak Chopra states in his *Book of Secrets*, "A car accident is neither right nor wrong-it is an opportunity to reclaim who you are, a co-creator."

Lovingly accept positive and negative events, and live without fear and within the holy perception of self as a spiritual being. Recognize you need not worry or stress yourself as you have surrendered your human will to the higher spiritual will of your eternal, loving, core self. However, a cautionary note is needed. As consciousness views you as its arms and legs it grants energized requests. Responsible choices, with careful consideration of the consequences from having a request answered, are my hopes for each of us. To aid miracle choosing, have a clear image of who you are and who you want to become. You are the hands and feet of consciousness creating the miracle.

Miracles

Takeaways

Miracles are daily experiences. However, we tend to not notice them because the ego blocks out spiritual happenings from memory.

When your will is set to believe in your core self as your true identity and accept your position as cocreators, you are in the vortex of core connection in which positive miraculous events are more likely to happen.

Springboards

- Love activates miracles. Love yourself. Talk to your higher self and to God, and believe miracles happen.
- Express gratitude, which is a natural outpouring of love for your higher self and God.
- Gratitude awakens each of us to blessings in life and the realization that you have never been alone, and always soul is working to awaken each of us to spiritual reality. Expressing gratitude keeps the communication door open to your higher self.

> Know yourself in the One Light where the miracle that is you is perfectly clear. (*A Course in Miracles,* Dr. Helen Schucman)

> Living in contentment is fertile soil for miracles to come forth. (Edgar Cayce)

> Spirit in man is a miracle-working power. (Eric Butterworth)

Notes

_____

_____

_____

_____

_____

_____

_____

Living as a Joy Being

> Our relationship to God changes from child to joint heir, from passive recipient to active participant, from creature to cocreator. We become able to respond to the deeper patterns of creation, through the integration of the human and divine within ourselves. (Barbara Marx Hubbard)

By choosing to reach the highest evolutionary pinnacle-to be loving companions to others on earth and cocreator within loving unified consciousness-you are a joy being, as your "I am" core self intends. You share your love with all others, forgive without difficulty, only wish the best for others, and take genuine pleasure in your accomplishments and others' accomplishments. Compassion mitigates your suffering and another's; you know the face of God exists in everyone and automatically treat others as you desire to be treated. Graced with inner peace, intuitive knowledge, and wisdom, along with experiencing God's profound love for you, you are gifted by God the creative power to create your miracle path; as you intend so you create. How could you not feel joy? In effect joy is being of one purpose, one mind, one thought, one emotion, one action to unconditionally love.

You Are a Joy Being
Meditation Number 11

Set aside twenty minutes. Take some deep breaths and release any tensions in the body. Allow yourself to relax, an inner smile. And as you do, acknowledge to yourself that I am in communion with and cherished by my own authentic "I am" core self, residing within a loving consciousness, and I recognize life is on my side. Repeat the following words or design your own affirmation to keep you on a miracle path:

> I trust the more I open to my inner core self, the more faith I will have in my core assisting in being the compass for my life, pointing to the path leading to joy. I can create a life of meaning and joy, the authentic life I desire. I know I walk a miracle path. I can let my core speak to me as I go through my day. I see the many ways nature shares its graces with me whether I walk along the shoreline, watch the falling snow, travel the highways, witness the meadows and mountains, view the stars at night, or feel the warmth of the sun. And I recognize that my hardships and discomforts push me further into a spiritual life as I evolve and grow.

When I trust that I am loved, I feel whole and complete. I attract loving people into my life.

I honor and accept my identity as a loving, spiritual being and recognize my unique capacities and skills. The more I express myself, open to the energies and opportunities provided me through spirit, allowing this energy to flow through me, I know I am in the flow of life, fuller, richer, whole, and complete. I am creation, intentional, spirit and soul filled, and unconditionally loving.

EPILOGUE

The following biblical quote (Joshua 1:8-9) has been instrumental throughout the course of writing this book: I intuitively heard, "Keep this Book of the Law always on your lips. Meditate on it day and night, so that you may observe carefully all that is written in it: then you will successfully attain your goal. I command you: be firm and steadfast! Do not be afraid; do not be discouraged, for the LORD, your God will be with you wherever you go." When I began to consider writing this book, this was the first biblical quote to which I was directed. Whenever I felt like giving up, or when life was busy and writing a book was time-consuming, I recalled this verse. And as I finished *Within Each of Us*, this verse still inspires me as I know each of us will experience times when the process of change is difficult and will need to follow Joshua's advice.

Working with the ideas and beliefs, springboards, guided imageries, spiritual practices, and meditations proposed, you have new tools in your life to help you negotiate and enjoy your life from a spiritual perspective. You have gained insight into who you truly are, recognizing your eternal nature, unbounded capacity to create, and how much you are profoundly loved. Loved so much by the creative force or forces governing the universe that a portion of this loving force resides within you and is you. My hope is you decide your true "I am" core self is your primary identity and that you rely on this portion of you to create your life.

Through core connection, you have freed yourself from conditioning limits, reorganized and shifted your thinking away from the ego's selfish focus to your spiritual core self's love-inspired perspective as the critical axis point for understanding the events in your life, including the perceived "bad" events. Indebtedness to human ego desires, such as the need for life to go one's way, and following harmful conditioned beliefs and emotions, eMAPs, which have blocked core connection have been identified and addressed. By labeling habits in terms of eMAPs, electronic mental, affective, and physical programs, you have stepped out of the prison of unhealthy conditioning and honor and rely on your true identity in thoughts, words, actions, emotions, and deeds. You will use your own thoughts and feelings to determine your actions based in a loving response. Recognizing suffering comes from lack of core self-connection, you value insight, intuition, and imagination, with inner courage, patience, and a humbled disposition.

You have uncovered that unconditional love for yourself and others is a sacred path which is known through one's individuated "I am" core self. With faith, trust, and belief you internalize the loving strengths—gifts within spirit and skills within your human self—to create your miracle life path. You have found your power to create your life, knowing firsthand the power of the intentions you set. These intentions manifest at warp speed when in communion with your core self rather than the human self alone.

You have attained higher wisdom, which lies within each of us as you have codesigned your spiritual-miracle path. External life is integrated with your inner life. Life has meaning and purpose as you now know yourself to be a divine being at your core here to create a unified world and to be unified within the force field of loving consciousness. Think about the synchronicities and miracles, large and small, scattered throughout your everyday life, like seashells tumbled ashore by the waves. No doubt you have observed that these blessings, which clarify the meaning and purpose of your human and spiritual life, now appear as common events. Yet you also realize they are not random happenings but are part of a greater life plan for you. That is, your personal place and position are intimately known, carefully held, and intricately woven into a unified consciousness divine tapestry. You express gratitude as a natural outpouring from witnessing the love God's universe has for you intuitively guiding your path and witnessed in the exterior world of events.

You have learned to partner with loving consciousness and your "I am" core self, to cocreate your life. You now consistently experience the inner peace and joy, with a depth of vision, which comes from living within your own spiritual presence. You are a joy being in communion with your "I am" core self, experiencing a deeply satisfying interior state. And your capacity to love extends to all others acknowledging that all souls are interconnected as one in the spiritual universe; care and respect are a natural expression.

Yes, the journey to self-discovery and spiritual growth is breathtaking and humbling. Trusting in an unseen, powerful spiritual force within you and surrounding you demands courage, as it takes you out of the comfort zone of everyday earthly reality-those things that you can touch, feel, hear, or otherwise physically discern. As well, all transformation, spiritual and physical, involves experiencing growing pains. But the movement you have experienced so far is not about reaching an end point; that is, maintaining self in a static state. Instead, it is about the need to continue transforming, in sync with the dynamic flow of life. We never stop learning and progressing on our human and divine journey. And so, setting the intention to continue to identify and change eMAPs blocking core connection as the unconscious release them, and to achieve the spiritual ideal of being a source of love in the world, while also helping others to be a source of love, are the continuing challenges I extend to you. Realize that your decision to do so will not prevent setbacks or unwanted happenings such as perceived negative events from occurring. But be patient and you will receive the deeper insight and intuition needed to process the lessons they contain. As you move forward on your spiritual path, always choose the love-based right way. Upon waking and before you retire, remind yourself of the infinitely powerful and precious gift from "I AM"-God-and your "I am" core self that you carry within. May it inspire you to be a source of peace and love in the world as you walk with your brothers and sisters, moment to moment, in perfect harmony.

APPENDIX 1

Glossary

Ascended consciousness. Awareness and connection with ascended loved ones or higher beings existing within a reality that is not earth's reality.

Atonement. Nothing stands in the way with your divine relationship with your core self and God.

Awakening. Being aware and having more conscious control over your life.

Awe. A feeling of oneness with all living things generated by an event. Feelings regarding one's personal destiny. May also uncover hidden meaning in your life events.

Christ consciousness. An energy form that promotes forms of love, such as inner peace, kindness, self-control, and gratitude, and guides all members of the human race to unite as a community of loving spiritual beings on the earth in thoughts, feelings, and actions.

Cocreator. Your role as a participant, within God's loving unified consciousness. Through intentions you create your life path.

Consciousness. At a personal level, it is awareness of existence. At a unified or cosmic level, it is all that exists.

Conditioned self. The conditioned concept of the person you have been taught to believe you are, as reflected in your thoughts, feelings, and actions. Your illusionary, false self, public face.

Creative forces. Loving energy within consciousness that guides human life.

Ego consciousness. Conditioned thoughts, feelings, and actions that create one's particular interpretation of reality, as determined by the ego.

Ego. The first-tier structure of the three-tier human brain, which is focused on safety, security, and self-enhancement.

eMAP. Represents the electronic like way mental, affective (emotional) and physical habits are conditioned to repeat by the lower ego mind.

Enlightened culture. A culture that supports personal autonomy, growth, and freedom and discourages the development of authoritarianism. Members feel mutual respect, and the basic needs of all members of the community are met.

Expanded consciousness. Awareness of yourself as a cocreator within consciousness.

Faith. Trust that the loving, creative-intelligence force that guides the universe loves you and also constitutes the loving divine core of your own being.

Firm authority. Maintaining control over your conditioned ego and its focus on narcissistic pursuits as you firmly pursue the path of spiritual awakening and soul progression. You achieve firm authority when you apply the human skills of courage, humility, patience, and loving acceptance to the spiritual base of faith, hope, and love.

God consciousness. The divine, loving, intelligent force of energy that guides all things toward unity or oneness.

Harmony. State of agreement in thoughts, feelings, and actions.

"I am." The real, authentic, loving, eternal, individuated you, your soul with spiritual energies for creating.

"I AM." The biblical name for God (Exodus 3:14: "I AM who I AM".

In the flow. Being aware of your own spiritual core designing an energized, love-focused life.

Intuition. A form of spontaneous knowing that provides helpful guidance in your life.

Joy being. Being in the flow of the eternal, spiritual stream of life as you lovingly desire interpersonal oneness with others, who will help you, just as you will help them, to build a meaningful life. Occurs when mind, body, heart, and soul are integrated as one.

Loving consciousness. A state of consciousness in which your thoughts, feelings, and actions reflect unconditional care and love toward self and others.

Miracles. Happenings that are intended to help each of us increase awareness of self as a loved, powerful cocreator within consciousness.

Personal integration. Consciously and unconsciously differentiated thoughts and emotions linked together to form a coherent, stable, and yet adaptable inner state that supports fundamental well-being. This internal state of unity and harmony in thoughts, feelings, and physical self is aligned with the "I am" core self.

Presence. Being profoundly aware of reality while maintaining a calm and clear mental state in which you are open-minded and flexible and nonjudgmentally accept all happenings, just as you freely allow people and things to move away from your attention.

Safety. Feeling physically safe, with sufficient food, shelter, and close personal connections.

Security. Feeling emotionally centered and loved, knowing you are not alone in the physical or spiritual world.

Soul. A spiritualized, individuated energy force that guides and enriches your human life, if you so choose, as the human self progresses in spiritual awakening.

Spirit. The energizing force of creation within consciousness, which exists within self. It sustains your life, and it enables you to move and transform the material world based on your conscious intentions.

Spiritual awakening. Achieving a higher level of understanding of your thoughts, feelings, actions, and life experiences, which includes awareness of self as a powerfully creative intentional being and builder of consciousness.

Spiritual being. Every human has a soul energized with spirit.

Spiritual consciousness. Awareness of your authentic, divine, loving, and eternal nature and position as a creator within unified consciousness.

Spiritual life. Conscious of soul and spirit within you, choosing love as the foundation upon which to build one's life.

Transcendence. Reaching beyond conceptual limits in thoughts, feelings of love, and actions.

Transformation. Moving toward personal integration through core self-identity.

Unconditional loving. Recognizing that all life constitutes a unified whole, you feel and express love for self and others, without imposing conditions to be met, always relating empathetically and nondefensively. Unconditional love activates inner peace; intuitive guidance and wisdom; and harmony among mind, body, heart, and soul.

Unhealthy conditioning limits. Ways of thinking feeling and acting that follow the ego's narcissistic goals of personal security, safety, and self enhancement, which emphasize the overarching importance of "I," "me," and "mine."

Unified, loving consciousness. Awareness that all creatures and all things are interconnected and represent one. This is the author's name for God.

Wisdom. Having access to the divine intelligence, commonly known as God, which governs the universe. Or access to creation.

APPENDIX 2

Quotes

Mahatma Gandhi

"The future depends on what we do in the present."

"Our greatest ability is not to change the world, but to change ourselves."

"Nobody can hurt me without my permission."

Buddha

"Relationships are based on four principles, respect, understanding, acceptance and appreciation."

"It's easy to stand with the crowd, it takes courage to stand alone."

"Carefully watch your thoughts, for they become your words. Manage and watch your words, for they become your actions. Consider and judge your actions, for they have become your habits."

"Acknowledge and watch your habits, for they shall become your values. Understand and embrace your values, for they become your destiny."

Albert Einstein

"Strive not to be a success, but rather to be of value."

Socrates

"An unexamined life is not worth living."

Edgar Cayce

"Life is the expression in a mental and material world, is only a mental and material manifestation of your soul itself."

"To live love is to be love."

Thich Nhat Hanh

"We can smile and relax. Everything we want is right here in the present moment.

Daniel Siegel

"Kindness and compassion are to the brain what the breath is to life."

"Compassion enables us to offer kindness under stress, forgiveness with mistakes, tenderness with vulnerability, and perspective when confused."

Paul McCartney

"And in the end the love you take is equal to the love you make."

Eric Butterworth

"Satan is simply a force of human consciousness."

Erich Fromm

Without Love, humanity could not exist for a day.

BIBLIOGRAPHY

Allen, James. *As A Man Thinketh*, 1971, Hallmark Cards Inc., Kansas City, Missouri.

Ambrose, Kala. *The Awakened Aura*, 2020, Llewellyn Publications, Woodbury, Minnesota.

Ashlag, Yehuda, Rabbi. *Ten Luminous Emanations*, 1969, Kabbalah Centre Books.

Berg, Michael. *Becoming Like God*, 2004, Kabbalah Centre International, New York, New York.

Berg, Michael. *The Way*, 2001, John Wiley & Sons Inc., Hoboken, New Jersey.

Bolen, Jean Shinoda Bolen, MD. *The Tao of Psychology*, 1982, Harper and Row Publishers, New York, New York.

Brennan, Barbara. *Seeds of the Spirit*, 1998, Barbara Brennan Inc.

Burns, David D. *The Feeling Good Handbook*, First Plume Printing, 1990.

Butterworth, Eric. *Discover the Power Within You*, 1992, Harper Collins Publishers, San Francisco, California.

Cayce, Edgar. *Soul and Spirit,* 2006, ARE Press, Virginia Beach, Virginia.

Coelho, Paulo. *The Alchemist.*

Chopra, Deepak. *Ageless Body, Timeless Mind.* Crown Publishing Group, 1993, New York, New York.

Chopra, Deepak. *Book of Secrets,* Crown Publishing Group, 2004, New York, New York.

Chopra, Deepak. *How to Know God,* 2000, Harmony Books, New York, New York.

Chopra, Deepak. *Metahuman,* 2019, Harmony Books, New York, New York.

Dale, Ralph A. *Tao Te Ching,* 2002, Sounds True, Boulder, Colorado.

Douglas-Klotz, Neil. *Healing Breath, Body-Based Meditations on the Aramaic Beatitudes,* Sounds True, Boulder Colorado.

Frankl, Victor. *Man's Search for Meaning,* 1984, Beacon Press, Boston.

Green, S. J., Thomas H. *Opening to God,* 1987, Ave Maria Press, Notre Dame, Indiana.

Haisch, Bernard. *The God Theory,* 2006, Weiser Books, San Francisco, California.

Hay, Louise. *You Can Change Your Life,* 1984, Hay House.

Hillman, James. *The Soul's Code,* 1996, Penguin Random House LLC., New York, New York.

Hubbard, Barbara Marx. *Emergence, the Shift from Ego to Essence,* 2001, Hampton Roads Publishing Company Inc. Charlottesville, Virginia.

Huxley, Aldous. *Bhagavad-Gita,* 1944, Barnes & Noble Books, New York, New York.

James, William. *The Varieties of Religious Experience,* 1902, Longmass, Green and Co, London.

Jung, C. G. *Memories, Dreams Reflections,* 1973, Pantheon Books, New York, New York.

Kaufman, Scott Barry, PhD. *Transcend,* 2020, Penguin Random House, New York, New York.

Luoma, J., Hayes, S., Walser, R. *Learning ACT,* 2017, Context Press, Oakland, California.

Moorjani, Anita. *Dying to Be Me,* 2012, Hay House.

Moore, Thomas. *Dark Nights of the Soul,* 2004, Gotham Books, New York, New York.

Moore, Thomas. *The Soul's Religion,* 2002, Harper Collins Publishers, New York, New York.

Moore, Thomas. *Care of the Soul,* 1992, Harper Collins Publishers, New York, New York.

Myss, Caroline. *Sacred Contracts,* 2001, Harmony Books, New York, New York.

Newton, Michael, PhD. *Journey of Souls,* 2016, Llewellyn, Woodbury, Minnesota.

Prabhavananda, Swami, and Isherwood, Christopher. *Bhagavad-Gita,* Barnes & Noble Books, Hollywood, California.

Redfield, James. *The Celestine Prophecy,* 1993, Satori Publishing, Hoover, Alabama.

Rinpoche, Sogyal. *The Tibetan Book of Living and Dying*, 1994, Harper, San Francisco, California.

Scaer, Robert C., MD. *The Body Bears the Burden*, 2001, The Haworth Medical Press Inc., New York, New York.

Schuman Helen and Thetford, William. *A Course in Miracles*, 1985, The Foundation for Inner peace, Glen Ellen, California.

Thurston, Mark, PhD. *The Great Teachings of Edgar Cayce*, 1996, ARE Press, Virginia Beach, Virginia.

Tolle, Eckhart. *A New Earth*, 2005, Penguin Group, New York, New York.

Trine, Ralph Waldo. *The Higher Powers of Mind and Spirit*, 1917. Dodge Publishing Company, New York, New York.

Wilber, Ken. *Integral Spirituality*, 2007, Integral Books, Boston, Maine.

Wilhelm, Richard. *The Secret of the Golden Flower*, 1962, Harcourt, Brace Janovich, Publishers, Orlando, Florida.

Printed in the United States
by Baker & Taylor Publisher Services